Day by Day with the Early Church Fathers

Compiled and Edited by
Christopher D. Hudson, J. Alan Sharrer,
and Lindsay Vanker

Hendrickson Publishers, Peabody MA

Day by Day with the Early Church Fathers
Copyright © 1999 by Hendrickson Publishers, Inc.
P.O. Box 3473
Peabody, Massachusetts, 01961-3473

Printed in the United States of America

ISBN 1-56563-396-2

First printing—June 1999

All Scripture references in this book are taken from the *Holy Bible: King James Version*.

Cover design by Richmond & Williams, Nashville, Tennessee
Interior design by Design Corps, Batavia, Illinois
Developed and produced exclusively for Hendrickson Publishers by The Livingstone Corporation, Carol Stream, Illinois
Compiled and edited by Christopher D. Hudson, J. Alan Sharrer, and Lindsay Vanker

First hardcover edition Christian Book Club: 1999

Library of Congress Cataloging-in-Publication Data

Day by Day with the early church fathers / J. Alan Sharrer, editor;
    Christopher D. Hudson, editor; Lindsay Vanker, editor
        ISBN 1-56563-396-2 (cloth)
            1. Devotional calendars.   I. Sharrer, J. Alan. II. Hudson,
    Christopher D. III. Vanker, Lindsay
    BV4810.D345   1999
    242' .2-dc21   99-29485
                                                     CIP

Introduction

"You will be My witnesses . . ." (Acts 1:8). With those words, Jesus declared that the way of salvation would be known to people throughout the world.

The New Testament records the beginnings of Christianity, from Peter's speech at Pentecost to John's vision on Patmos. After the apostles went to be with the Lord in heaven, a group of individuals proclaimed and protected the Christian faith from the constant winds of heresy. They are commonly known as the early church fathers.

Each church father faced a unique challenge in his respective ministry. Some were made to assume positions of church authority against their will. Others were assailed by leaders of heretical sects. All faced the constant danger of persecutions and death for confessing their faith in Jesus. But through their guidance, the church extended its roots into Europe, Asia Minor, and Northern Africa.

For centuries, Christians have been impacted and challenged by the teachings of the early church fathers. Names such as Martin Luther, John Calvin, and John Wesley benefited from the words of Augustine, Chrysostom, and other heroes of the church.

Now it's your turn.

The devotional readings in this book have been carefully selected from the 38-volume series *The Early Church Fathers*, first published in 1885. Each volume in the series was carefully studied in an attempt to gather selections which were both varied and powerful. After the selection process was finished, each devotion was edited in a procedure that updated the language yet preserved the original meaning the church father intended.

Since many church fathers would start on a topic and finish after introducing another topic, ellipses (. . .) have been used for purposes of clarity. In addition, the scripture selections in each devotion may not match many of today's translations. This is due to each church father's own translation of the Greek or Hebrew manuscripts.

In the back of the book, biographies of each of the thirty-nine church fathers are featured, along with the dates where their selections are found.

It is our prayer that as you read what the fathers have to say, God would minister to you and challenge you to become more like His Son Jesus.

J. Alan Sharrer, Christopher D. Hudson, and Lindsay Vanker
July 1999

Preface

Read this treatise carefully, and if you understand it, praise God. If you can't understand it, pray for understanding, for God will give you understanding. Remember what the Scriptures say: "If any of you lack wisdom, let him ask of God, who giveth to all men liberally, and upbraideth not; and it shall be given to him." Wisdom itself comes down from above, as the Apostle James tells us.

There is, however, another wisdom which you must drive away. Pray that it will leave you entirely. James expressed his hatred for this kind of wisdom when he said, "But if ye have bitter envying and strife in your hearts, . . . this is not the wisdom which descendeth from above, but is earthly, sensual, devilish. For wherever there is envying and strife, there is also confusion and every evil work. But the wisdom which is from above is first pure, then peaceable, gentle, and easy to be entreated, full of mercy and good works, without partiality, and without hypocrisy." What a great blessing, then, that if we pray for this wisdom we will receive it from the Lord! As a result, you can understand what grace is, for if this wisdom was from ourselves, it wouldn't be from above and we wouldn't need to ask it from the God who created us.

Augustine

Tears and Joy
Chrysostom

How does Paul say, "Rejoice in the Lord always"? The joy he is speaking of springs from tears of mourning. For just as worldly joy comes with sorrow, godly tears produce never-ending, unfading joy. The harlot, who obtained more honor than virgins, experienced joy when seized by this fire. Thoroughly warmed by repentance, she was moved by her longing desire for Christ. She loosened her hair, drenched His holy feet with her tears, wiped them with her tresses, and poured out all the ointment. But these were only outward expressions. Those emotions in her mind were much more fervent—things only God could see. Therefore, everyone who hears of this woman rejoices with her, delights in her good works, and acquits her of every sin. If we, who are evil, judge her this way, imagine what sentence she obtained from God, who loves mankind. Consider how much, even before she received God's gifts, she was blessed by her repentance. . . . For I seek those tears shed, not for display, but in repentance; I want those that trickle down secretly and in closets, out of sight, softly and noiselessly. I desire those that rise from depth of mind, those shed in anguish and sorrow, those which are for God alone.

Blessed are they that mourn: for they shall be comforted.
—*Matthew 5:4*

" I seek those tears shed, not for display, but in repentance."

Complete Work
Gregory of Nyssa

For other foundation can no man lay than that is laid, which is Jesus Christ. Now if any man build upon this foundation gold, silver, precious stones, wood, hay, stubble; Every man's work shall be made manifest: for the day shall declare it, because it shall be revealed by fire; and the fire shall try every man's work of what sort it is.

—1 Corinthians 3:11-13

Soldiers don't arm themselves partially, leaving the rest of their bodies unprotected. For if they received their death wounds in the unprotected area, what would be the point of their partial armor? Again, who would consider some feature flawless when in an accident it lost something essential to beauty? The disfigurement of the mutilated part destroys the grace of the untouched part. The gospel implies that those who try to build a tower, but spend all their time on the foundation and never finish, are ridiculous. From the Parable of the Tower, we also learn to work hard and finish every lofty goal, to complete the work of God through the varied structures of His commandments. Of course, one stone doesn't make an entire tower any more than obeying one commandment lifts the soul to the required height of perfection. By all means, the foundation must be laid first. But, as the Apostle Paul says, the structure of gold and precious gems must be built over it. For the psalmist cries, "I have loved Thy commandment above gold and many a precious stone."

> "One stone doesn't make an entire tower any more than obeying one commandment lifts the soul to the required height of perfection."

Denying Self
Origen

Those who have not denied themselves cannot follow Jesus. For choosing to follow Jesus and to actually follow Him springs from no ordinary courage. Those who deny themselves wipe out their former, wicked lives. For example, those who once were immoral deny their immoral selves and become self-controlled forever. . . . Those who have become righteous don't confess themselves but Christ. Those who find wisdom, because they possess wisdom, also confess Christ. And those who, "with the heart believe unto righteousness, and with the mouth make confession unto salvation," and testify for Christ's works by confessing them to others, will be confessed by Christ before His Father in heaven. . . . As a result, let every thought, every purpose, every word, and every action become a denial of ourselves and a testimony about Christ and in Christ. I am persuaded that the perfect person's every action is a testimony to Christ Jesus and that abstinence from every sin is a denial of self, leading to Christ. Those people are crucified with Christ. They take up their own crosses to follow Him who, for our sake, bears His own cross.

Yea doubtless, and I count all things but loss for the excellency of the knowledge of Christ Jesus my Lord: for whom I have suffered the loss of all things, and do count them but dung, that I may win Christ.
—*Philippians 3:8*

> "The perfect person's every action is a testimony to Christ Jesus and that abstinence from every sin is a denial of self, leading to Christ."

Memorials
Theodoret

Take, my brethren, the prophets, who have spoken in the name of the Lord, for an example of suffering affliction, and of patience.
—*James 5:10*

Even if a prize wasn't offered to those who fight for true religion, Truth alone would persuade her lovers to welcome any danger for her. The divine Apostle Paul attests to this. He says . . . "For I am persuaded, that neither death, nor life, nor angels, nor principalities, nor powers, nor things present, nor things to come, nor height, nor depth, nor any other creature, shall be able to separate us from the love of God, which is in Christ Jesus our Lord." My friend, see the flame of this affection; see the torch of love.

Paul doesn't covet what is His. I only long for Him, he says. And this love of mine is an unquenchable love. I would gladly pass up every present and future happiness, yes, suffer and endure all kinds of pain again in order to keep this flame with me in all its force. Paul exemplified this in action and in word. For he left memorials of his sufferings behind him. When I remember him and the rest of the patriarchs, prophets, apostles, martyrs, and priests, I can't help but delight in what we commonly consider miserable. I am ashamed when I remember how those who never learned the lessons we have learned, but followed human nature alone, have won notable places in the race of virtue.

> "Even if a prize wasn't offered to those who fight for true religion, Truth alone would persuade her lovers to welcome any danger for her."

The Good Shepherd

Clement of Alexandria

Feed us, Your children, as sheep. Master, fill us with righteousness from Your own pasture. Instructor, give us food on Your holy mountain, the church, which towers in the air, is above the clouds, and touches heaven. "And I will be," He says, "their Shepherd," and will be as near to them as clothes to their skin. He wants to save my flesh by enveloping it in the robe of immortality, and He has anointed my body. "They shall call Me," He says, "and I will say, Here am I." You heard sooner than I expected, Master. "And if they pass over, they shall not slip," says the Lord. For we who are passing over to eternal life will not fall into corruption because He will sustain us. For so He has said and so He has willed. Our Instructor is righteously good. "I came not," He says, "to be ministered unto, but to minister." Therefore, He is introduced in the Gospel as "wearied," because He toiled for us and promised "to give His life as a ransom for many." For Christ alone is the Good Shepherd. He is generous and gives us the greatest of all gifts, His own life. He is extremely good and loving to men, while, when He might have been Lord, He wished to become a brother to humanity. He was so good that He died for us.

He shall feed his flock like a shepherd: he shall gather the lambs with his arm, and carry them in his bosom, and shall gently lead those that are with young.
—*Isaiah 40:11*

End Well

Basil

Not even David was blameless. For his thoughts were diverted and he sinned against Uriah's wife. Another example is surely enough to keep one who is living a godly life safe. This example is Judas's fall from better to worse. After being Christ's disciple for so long, he sold his Master for his own profit but received punishment instead. Learn from this, beloved, that the one who begins well isn't perfect. It is the one who ends well whom God approves of. So then, don't allow your eyes to sleep or your eyelids to slumber so that you can be saved like "a roe from the net and a bird from the snare." For you are passing through the midst of traps. You are walking on top of a high wall where a fall is much more dangerous. Therefore, don't try to be extremely disciplined right away. Above everything beware of your own confidence, lest you fall from a height of discipline because of lack of training. It is better to move ahead a little at a time. So then, withdraw from the pleasures of life little by little. Gradually destroy all your evil habits, lest you bring on yourself a mass of temptations by stirring up all of your passions at once. When you have mastered one passion, then begin waging war against another. And before long you will get the better of them all.

> "Beware of your own confidence, lest you fall from a height of discipline because of lack of training. It is better to move ahead a little at a time."

God Knows Us
Augustine

You, Lord, are the one who judges me. For, although no "man knoweth the things of a man, save the spirit of man which is in him," there is something in a person that "the spirit of man which is in him" doesn't know about itself. But You, Lord, who made us, know us completely. Although I despise who I am in Your sight and consider myself but "dust and ashes," I undeniably know something about You that I don't know about myself. To be sure, "now we see through a glass darkly" and not yet "face to face." So, as long as I am "absent" from You, I am more "present" with my body than with You. I know that You can't sin, but I don't know what temptations I can resist and which ones I can't. But there is hope because You are faithful. You won't allow us to be tempted beyond what we are able to endure, but will always make a way to escape the temptation so that we can bear it. Therefore, I will confess what I know about myself. I will also confess what I don't know about myself. What I do know about myself, I know by Your enlightenment. And what I don't about myself, I won't know until the time when You will see my "darkness as the noonday."

For thou wilt light my candle: the Lord my God will enlighten my darkness.
—*Psalm 18:28*

"I don't know what temptations I can resist, and which ones I can't. But there is hope because You are faithful."

Lasting Glory
Chrysostom

For, behold, the day cometh, that shall burn as an oven; and all the proud, yea, and all that do wickedly, shall be stubble: and the day that cometh shall burn them up, saith the Lord of hosts, that it shall leave them neither root nor branch.
—Malachi 4:1

Run from pride, for it is a passion more treacherous than any other. Covetousness and love for wealth spring from it as well as hatred, wars, and fights. For those who want more than they have will never be able to stop. Their desires come from nothing other than their love of displaying their accomplishments. . . . If we cut off pride (the head of all evil), we would kill all the other members of wickedness with it. Then nothing could keep us from living on earth as though it were heaven. Pride doesn't just thrust its captives into wickedness, but even co-exists with their righteousness. When it can't get rid of all their virtues, it severely damages their ability to exercise them. It forces us to work hard and deprives us of the fruit. . . .

Therefore, if we want to earn glory, we must flee from human glory and only desire glory from God. Then we will obtain and enjoy both through the grace and loving-kindness of our Lord Jesus Christ.

> "Run from pride, for it is a passion more treacherous than any other."

A Pure Heart
Hermas

Be humble and innocent, and you will be like the children who don't know the wickedness that ruins men's lives. First, then, speak evil of no one, nor listen with pleasure to anyone who speaks evil of another. But if you listen and believe the slander which you hear, you will participate in the sin of him who speaks evil. For believing it, you will also have something to say against your brother. Therefore, you will be guilty of the sin of him who slanders. Slander is evil and an unsteady demon. It never abides in peace, but always remains in conflict. Keep yourself from it, and you will always be at peace with everyone. Put on a holiness that will not offend with wickedness, but whose actions are all steady and joyful. Practice goodness; and from your profit, . . . give to all, for God wants His gifts to be shared among everyone. . . . He, then, who gives is guiltless. For as he received from the Lord, so has he innocently completed his service by not debating to whom he should give and to whom he should not give. This service, then, if completed in humility, is glorious to God. He, therefore, who ministers with humility, will live to God. Therefore keep these commandments as I have given them to you so that your repentance and the repentance of your house may be found innocent and your heart may be pure and stainless.

But to do good and to communicate forget not: for with such sacrifices God is well pleased.
—Hebrews 13:16

True Humility
Chrysostom

There is a generation that are pure in their own eyes, and yet is not washed from their filthiness.
—*Proverbs 30:12*

In whatever you do for a fellow-servant, remember that your Master has done it to your servants. Listen and shudder! Never be pleased by your humility! . . . Perhaps you laugh at that statement, as if humility could puff you up. But don't be surprised if it puffs you up when it isn't genuine. How and in what way could it do this? When it is practiced to gain human favor and not God's favor. When it is practiced so that we could be praised and be considered great. For this is of the devil. Those who boast because they aren't boastful please themselves by their humility and high regard. . . . Have you done any act out of humility? Don't be proud of it, otherwise all its merit is lost. The Pharisee was like this. He was puffed up because he gave his tithes to the poor, and, as a result, he lost the honor of the deed. But not so

> "Have you done any act out of humility? Don't be proud of it, otherwise all its merit is lost."

with the tax collector. Nor with Paul who said, "I know nothing by myself, yet am I not hereby justified." See how he doesn't exalt himself, but in every way lowers and humbles himself, even when he had arrived at the summit. . . . When you think about admiring yourself because you are humble, consider your Master. Remember what He descended into and you won't admire or praise yourself anymore.

The Transformation

Lactantius

The power of divine wisdom is so great that, when infused into one's heart, it expels foolishness (the mother of all fault) by one impulse—once and for all. This wisdom doesn't need payment, books, or nightly studies to come about. But the results are accomplished freely, easily, and quickly, if only ears are open and the heart thirsts for wisdom. Don't be afraid: we don't sell water or offer the sun as a reward. The fountain of God, most abundant and full, is open to everyone. This heavenly light rises for everyone who has eyes. Did the philosophers bring about these things, or can they accomplish these results if they want? For although they spend their lives studying philosophy, they can neither improve any person nor improve themselves. . . . Their wisdom at its best doesn't eradicate, but actually hides faults. However, a few of God's principles will change people so completely and make them new by having them put off their old selves so that you wouldn't recognize them as the same.

And have put on the new man, which is renewed in knowledge after the image of him that created him.
—*Colossians 3:10*

> "The power of divine wisdom is so great that, when infused into one's heart, it expels foolishness by one impulse—once and for all."

Changed Lives
Justin Martyr

Let the wicked forsake his way, and the unrighteous man his thoughts: and let him return unto the Lord, and he will have mercy upon him; and to our God, for he will abundantly pardon.

—Isaiah 55:7

We forewarn you to be on your guard, lest evil spirits deceive you and distract you from reading and understanding what we say. For they strive to hold you as their slaves and servants. And sometimes by appearances in dreams and sometimes by magical deceptions, they subdue all those who fail to make strong opposing efforts for their own salvation. Since we are persuaded by the Word, we stand aloof from the demons and follow the only self-existing God through His Son. We who formerly delighted in sexual immorality now embrace chastity alone. We who formerly used magical arts dedicate ourselves to the good and self-existing God. We who valued above all things the acquisition of wealth and possessions now bring what we have into a common stock and share with everyone in need. We who hated and destroyed one another and on account of their different manners would not live with men of a different tribe now, since the coming of Christ, live with them intimately. Now we pray for our enemies and try to persuade those who hate us unjustly to comply with Christ's good principles and commands to the end that they may come to share with us the same joyful hope of a reward from God, the ruler of all.

Tested by Fire
Chrysostom

Refiners throw pieces of gold into the furnace to be tested and purified by the fire. In the same way, God allows human souls to be tested by troubles until they become pure, transparent, and have profited greatly from the process. Therefore, this is the greatest advantage we have. So then, we shouldn't be disturbed or discouraged when trials happen to us. For if refiners know how long to leave a piece of gold in the furnace, and when to draw it out, if they don't allow it to remain in the fire until it is burnt up and destroyed, how much better does God understand this process! When He sees that we have become purer, He frees us from our trials so that we won't be crushed and defeated by them. Therefore, we shouldn't retreat or lose heart when unexpected things happen to us. Instead, we should submit to the One who knows best and who will test our hearts by fire as long as He likes. He does this for a reason and for the good of those who are tried.

And I will bring the third part through the fire, and will refine them as silver is refined, and will try them as gold is tried: they shall call on my name, and I will hear them: I will say, It is my people: and they shall say, The Lord is my God.
—Zechariah 13:9

"We shouldn't retreat or lose heart when unexpected things happen to us. Instead, we should submit to the One who knows best and who will test our hearts by fire as long as He likes."

Hidden Truth

Jerome

Open thou mine eyes, that I may behold wondrous things out of thy law.

—Psalm 119:18

In Revelation, a book is shown that is sealed with seven seals. If you gave it to someone learned and said, "Read this," he would answer, "I can't because it is sealed." There are many today who consider themselves learned, yet the Scriptures are a sealed book to them. They can't open it without the help of Him who has the key of David. "He that openeth and no man shutteth; and shutteth and no man openeth." In the Acts of the Apostles there was a holy eunuch (or, as Scripture calls him, a "man"). When he was reading Isaiah, Philip asked him, "Understandest thou what thou readest?" He answered, "How can I except some man should guide me?" . . . Then Philip came and showed him Jesus who was concealed in the letters. What an excellent teacher! That same hour, the eunuch believed and was baptized. He became one of the faithful and a saint. He wasn't a student any longer but a master. And he found more in the church's writings there in the wilderness than he had ever found in the gilded temple of the synagogue. . . . It is useless to try to teach what you don't know, and—if I may speak with some warmth—is worse still to be ignorant of your ignorance.

> "It is useless to try to teach what you don't know, and is worse still to be ignorant of your ignorance."

Sharing in Suffering

Theodoret

The greatest comfort for those who suffer from false accusations is given by the words of Scripture. When sufferers are wounded by the lying words of an unbridled tongue, and feel the sharp stings of distress, they can remember the story of Joseph. For Joseph was an example of righteousness while suffering under a slanderous charge. He was imprisoned for invading another man's bed and spent a long time in a dungeon. When they look at Joseph's model of purity, their pain is eased by the remedy the story provides. They find the same thing when they look at David, who Saul hunted like a tyrant. When David caught his enemy and let him go unharmed, he received comfort in his distress. Then there is the story of the Lord Christ Himself, Maker of the ages, Creator of all things, very God, and Son of the very God. Yet He was called a gluttonous man and a drunkard by the wicked Jews. Christ's suffering is not only comforting but provides great joy to those who suffer. For they are counted worthy of sharing the sufferings of the Lord.

Blessed are ye, when men shall revile you, and persecute you, and shall say all manner of evil against you falsely, for my sake. Rejoice, and be exceeding glad: for great is your reward in heaven: for so persecuted they the prophets which were before you.
—*Matthew 5:11-12*

> "The greatest comfort for those who suffer from false accusations is given by the words of Scripture."

15

God Gives All

Gregory Nazianzen

So then it is not of him that willeth, nor of him that runneth, but of God that sheweth mercy.

—*Romans 9:16*

I agree that people have certain capabilities—one person has more, another less. But these capabilities alone can't perfect them. . . . Some people are proud of their successes. They attribute everything to themselves and nothing to the One who made them, gave them wisdom, and supplied them with good things. Such people need to learn that even in wishing well to someone, they need God's help. Even choosing what is right is a gift of God's mercy. For it is necessary both that we should master ourselves and that God should save us. This is why He doesn't talk about people who only will or run but about those who also depend on God. That demonstrates mercy. There is a good reason why everything is attributed to God. For no matter how much you run, or how much you wrestle, you need someone to give the reward. If the Lord didn't build the house, those who built it labored in vain. If the Lord doesn't watch over the city, those who watch over it wait in vain. I know, Solomon says, that the race isn't to the swift, the battle to the strong, the victory to the fighters, or the harbors to the good sailors. But it is God who brings about victory. He brings the ship safely in the harbor.

> "It is necessary that we both master ourselves and that God saves us."

Pure Souls
Augustine

No one can see the "face," that is, the appearance of God's wisdom, and live. For all who strive to love God with all their heart, soul, and mind longs to study this revelation. Through its study, those who love their neighbors encourage them as much as they can. All the Law and the prophets hang on these two commandments. . . . Therefore this "appearance" wisks away every rational soul with the desire for it, and makes the soul even more pure and eager for it. For souls become purer the more they rise to spiritual things. They rise more to spiritual things the more they die to fleshly things. So, while we are absent from the Lord and walk by faith instead of sight, we should see the "back parts" or flesh of Christ. By that very faith, we stand on the solid foundation and rock of faith and we observe it from a safe watch tower. . . . For we come to love to see the face of Christ even more as we recognize how much Christ first loved us in His flesh.

As newborn babes, desire the sincere milk of the word, that ye may grow thereby.
—1 Peter 2:2

"Souls rise more to spiritual things the more they die to fleshly things."

Heavenly Treasure

Clement of Alexandria

For which cause we faint not; but though our outward man perish, yet the inward man is renewed day by day.

—2 Corinthians 4:16

There are some who, like worms wallowing in marshes and mud, feed on foolish and useless pleasures. People are like pigs. For pigs, it is said, like mud better than pure water. Let us not, then, be enslaved or become like pigs. Instead, as true children of the light, let us raise our eyes and look at light, lest the Lord discover us to be superficial. Therefore, let us repent and move from ignorance to knowledge, from foolishness to wisdom, from self-indulgence to self-restraint, from unrighteousness to righteousness, from godlessness to God. By striving toward God, one shows noble daring. The enjoyment of many good things is within the reach of those who love righteousness and who pursue eternal life, especially those things which God alludes to in Isaiah. He says, "There is an inheritance for those who serve the Lord." Noble and desirable is this inheritance, not gold, not silver, not clothing, that the moths destroy, nor things of earth that robbers attack because they are dazzled by worldly wealth. Instead, it is the treasure of salvation which we must hurry to by becoming lovers of the Word. Then praiseworthy works will descend to us and fly with us on the wing of truth. This is the inheritance God grants us with His eternal covenant, conveying the everlasting gift of grace. Consequently, our loving Father— the true Father—never stops urging, admonishing, training, or loving us.

Revelation of God

Hilary of Poitiers

Our nature can't contemplate heavenly things by its own strength. We must learn from God what we should think of Him. We have no source of knowledge but God Himself. You might be as well trained in secular philosophy as possible, and you may have lived a life of righteousness. But, although all of this will add to your mental satisfaction, it won't help you know God. Moses was adopted as the queen's son. He was instructed in all the Egyptians' wisdom. Moreover, out of loyalty to his race, Moses avenged the Hebrew by slaying the Egyptian who wronged him. Yet he didn't know the God who blessed his fathers. For when he left Egypt afraid of his deed being discovered, he lived as a shepherd in the land of Midian. There he saw a fire in the bush, but the bush wasn't consumed. Then he heard the voice of God, asked His name, and learned His nature. Despite all this he couldn't have known anything except through God Himself. We, in the same way, must confine whatever we say about God to the words He has spoken to us about Himself.

He revealeth the deep and secret things: he knoweth what is in the darkness, and the light dwelleth with him.

—Daniel 2:22

> "We have no source of knowledge but God Himself."

19

Clear Vision
Clement of Alexandria

Now faith is the substance of things hoped for, the evidence of things not seen.

—Hebrews 11:1

Faith lacks nothing. It is perfect and complete in itself. If it lacks anything, it is not completely perfect. But faith isn't disabled in any respect. After we leave this world, it doesn't make we who have believed wait. Instead, we receive the pledge of future good without distinction. . . . Where faith is, there is the promise. And the completion of the promise is rest. In addition, through illumination we receive knowledge, and the end of knowledge is rest. . . . So, then, just as inexperience ends by experience and bewilderment by finding a clear way out, so darkness must disappear by illumination. The darkness is ignorance. Through it we fall into sins, completely blind to the truth. Knowledge, then, is the illumination we receive that makes ignorance disappear. It gives us clear vision. . . . Bonds of ignorance are quickly loosened by human faith and divine grace, and our sins are taken away by the medicine of the Word. We are washed from all of our sins and are no longer entangled in evil. Our character isn't the same as before our washing. Since knowledge springs up with illumination the moment we hear, we who were untaught become disciples. For instruction leads to faith, and faith with baptism is taught by the Holy Spirit. That faith is the one universal salvation of humanity.

> "Faith lacks nothing. It is perfect and complete in itself."

Rich Fools
Cyprian

Jesus teaches us not only that riches are to be despised, but that also they are full of danger. They are the root of seducing evils and deceive the blind human mind by hidden deception. God rebukes rich fools who think only of their earthly wealth and boast in the abundance of their overflowing harvests. He says, "Thou fool, this night thy soul shall be required of thee; then whose shall those things be which thou hast provided?" The fool was rejoicing in his supplies when he would die that very night; one whose life was already failing was thinking about the abundance of his food. However, the Lord tells us that those who sell all their possessions and distribute them for the poor become perfect and complete. In so doing, they lay up treasures for themselves in heaven. He says that those who follow Him . . . and aren't entangled by worldly possessions . . . accompany their possessions which they send to God. For such a reward, let us all prepare ourselves, learn to pray, and discern from our prayers what we should become, . . . for He promises that all things will be added to those who seek God's kingdom and righteousness.

But they that will be rich fall into temptation and a snare, and into many foolish and hurtful lusts, which drown men in destruction and perdition.
—1 Timothy 6:9

Forgiving Enemies

Ambrose

Then said Jesus, Father, forgive them; for they know not what they do. And they parted his raiment, and cast lots.
—Luke 23:34

We must remember the value of right belief. It is profitable for me to know that Christ bore my diseases and submitted Himself to my lusts for my sake. He became sin and a curse for me—for everyone, that is. He was humbled and became a servant for me. He is the Lamb, the Vine, the Rock, the Servant, and the Son of a handmaid for me. He doesn't know the Day of Judgment, but, for my sake, is ignorant of the day and hour. . . . What a glorious remedy—to have comfort in Christ! For He bore these things with enormous patience for our sakes—so we definitely can't bear them just for the glory of His name with common patience! Who wouldn't learn to forgive their enemies when they see that, even on the cross, Christ prayed for those who persecuted Him? Don't you see that the weaknesses of Christ's are your strength? So why do you ask Him about remedies for us? His tears wash us and His weeping cleanses us. . . . But if you begin to doubt, you will despair. For the greater the insult, the greater gratitude is due.

> "What a glorious remedy—to have comfort in Christ!"

Bear Witness
Chrysostom

Everyone looks at what we do and not what we say. Scripture says, "Thou shalt be a witness unto all men," not just to friendly people, but also to unbelievers. For witnesses aren't meant to persuade those who already know, but those who don't know. Let us be trustworthy witnesses. How can we be trustworthy? By the life we lead. The Jews assaulted Christ and our passions assault us. They tell us to reject our testimony. But we must not obey them. We are witnesses from God. But He has sent us to testify of Him. Let us testify and persuade those who need to decide who He is. If we don't testify, then we also have to answer for their mistake. If people wouldn't accept an exceedingly wicked witness in an earthly court, much less would they accept one here when considering such great issues. We say that we have heard Christ and that we believe the things He has promised. Then, they say, show it by your works. For your life testifies of the opposite—that you don't believe. . . . We and not just the martyrs will be witnesses for Christ. They are called martyrs because they endured everything to speak the truth when told to reject the faith. So, we must not be overcome when our passions tell us we are to reject Him.

For as the body without the spirit is dead, so faith without works is dead also.

—James 2:26

> "We say that we have heard Christ and that we believe the things He has promised. Then, they say, show it by your works."

Friendship
Origen

And without contro-
versy great is the
mystery of godliness:
God was manifest in
the flesh, justified in
the Spirit, seen of
angels, preached unto
the Gentiles, believed
on in the world,
received up into glory.
—*1 Timothy 3:16*

The God of all things and of His holy angels was made known beforehand through the prophets. . . . As a result, all the Jewish people hung in expectation of His coming. After Jesus' arrival, however, they fell into a keen dispute with each other. A large number acknowledged Christ and believed Him to be the object of prophecy, while others didn't believe in Him. . . . Instead, they dared to inflict upon Jesus cruelties His disciples truthfully and candidly recorded. But both Jesus and His disciples desired that His followers wouldn't believe merely in His Godhead and miracles (as if He hadn't also taken on human nature and assumed the human flesh which "lusteth against the Spirit"), but that they would also see that He had descended into human nature and into the midst of human miseries. He assumed a human soul and body. From Him there began the union of the divine with the human nature, in order that the human, by communion with the divine, might rise to be divine. . . . Everyone who lives according to Jesus' teaching rises to a friendship with God and communion with Him.

Evaluate Daily
Athanasius

"Let not the sun go down upon your wrath." Antony believed this verse applied not only to wrath but to all the commandments. The sun shouldn't go down on any of our sins. For it is important that neither the sun nor the moon can condemn our evil acts or thoughts. In order to be pure, it is good to hear the apostle Paul and keep his words. For he says, "Try your own selves and prove your own selves." Therefore, every day we should consider what we have done that day and night. If we have sinned, we must stop. But if we haven't, we must not be proud. Instead, we must live in goodness without being negligent. We must not condemn our neighbors or justify ourselves "until the Lord come who searcheth out hidden things." For we often ignorantly do things. The Lord, however, sees everything. Therefore, leaving judgment to Him, we must have sympathy for one another. We must bear each other's burdens. But we must also examine ourselves quickly to improve the areas in which we are lacking.

Let us search and try our ways, and turn again to the Lord.
—*Lamentations 3:40*

> "Every day we should consider what we have done that day and night. If we have sinned, we must stop. But if we haven't, we must not be proud."

Money and Salvation
Clement of Alexandria

Behold, I stand at the door, and knock: if any man hear my voice, and open the door, I will come in to him, and will sup with him, and he with me.
—Revelation 3:20

Among those with worldly wealth, one man did not submit his name for the contest because he was not confident of his ability to win and receive the prize. Another, inspired by the hope of victory, but who did not work, diet, and exercise appropriately, remained unrewarded and frustrated. Therefore, don't let the wealthy consider themselves excluded from the Savior's lists at the outset, provided they are believers and contemplate the greatness of God's generosity. Don't let them expect to gain the crowns of eternal life without struggle and effort, training or challenge. Instead, let them put themselves under the Word as their trainer and Christ as the official of the contest. For their prescribed food and drink, let them have the New Testament of the Lord; for exercises, the commandments; and for elegance and adornment, the beauty of love, faith, hope, knowledge of the truth, gentleness, humility, compassion, and dignity. Then, when the last trumpet signals the race and departure from the stadium of life, they may, with good consciences, present themselves victorious to the Judge who gives the rewards. They will be worthy of their heavenly Fatherland, to which they will return with crowns and the praise of angels.

Unceasing Requests
Augustine

He who knows what we need before we ask Him has urged us to pray by saying: "Men ought always to pray and not to faint." The Lord told the story of a widow who wanted justice done to her enemy. By her unceasing requests, she persuaded an evil judge to listen to her. The judge wasn't moved because of justice or mercy, but because he was overcome by her wearisome pleas. The story encourages us that the Lord God, who is merciful and just, pays attention to our continual prayers more than when this widow won over the indifferent, unjust, and wicked judge by her unceasing requests. . . . The Lord gives a similar lesson in the parable of the man who had nothing to give to a traveling friend. He tried to borrow three loaves . . . from another friend who was already asleep. By his very urgent and insistent requests, he succeeded in waking the friend, who gave him as many loaves as he needed. But this friend was motivated by his wish to avoid further annoyances, not by generosity. Through this story, the Lord taught that those who are asleep are compelled to give to the person who disturbs them, but those who never sleep will give with much more kindness. In fact, He even rouses us from sleep so that we can ask from Him.

And it shall come to pass, that before they call, I will answer; and while they are yet speaking, I will hear.
—*Isaiah 65:24*

> "The Lord God, who is merciful and just, pays attention to our continual prayers."

Understanding God
Origen

And thine age shall be clearer than the noonday; thou shalt shine forth, thou shalt be as the morning.

—Job 11:17

No matter what knowledge of God we can gain by observing or reflecting on Him, He is far better than how we perceive Him. Say we wanted to acquaint someone who couldn't bear a spark of light or the flame of a very small lamp with the brightness and splendor of the sun. Wouldn't it be necessary to tell him that the sun's splendor was unspeakably and incalculably more glorious than all the light he had already seen? In the same way, our knowledge of God is restrained by flesh and blood. Due to our participation in material things, our minds are dull in their attempts to understand spiritual things, although our understanding hardly compares to a spark or lamp. However, among all intelligent, spiritual beings, God is superior to all others—so unspeakably and incalculably superior. Even the purest and brightest human understanding can't comprehend His nature.

"Even the purest and brightest human understanding can't comprehend His nature."

28

Like God
Chrysostom

How is it possible to be a child of God? By being free from all passions and showing gentleness to those who offend and wrong us. . . . There is nothing that brings us as near to God and makes us so much like Him as doing these good things. Therefore, when Paul says, "Be ye followers of God," he means that they become followers by doing these things. For we need to do all good deeds, but above all we must love others and show gentleness. Since we sin many times each day, we need much of His love ourselves. Therefore, we also need to show much mercy. Much and little aren't measured by the quantity of things given, but by the givers' means. . . . And if you don't have anything but have a compassionate soul, this will prepare a reward for you. . . . So then, let us then be inclined to show mercy and all other blessings will follow. For those who have a spirit of love and mercy will give money away if they have it. If they see anyone in distress, they will weep. If they encounter people who have been wronged, they will stand up for them. If they see others treated maliciously, they will reach out their hand to them. For those that have a treasure house of blessings, a loving and merciful soul will make it overflow to meet all of their neighbors' needs. Such people will enjoy all the rewards God has prepared.

Be ye therefore merciful, as your Father also is merciful.
—*Luke 6:36*

> "Let us be inclined to show mercy and all other blessings will follow."

29

Christ's Temple

Jerome

If there be among you a poor man of one of thy brethren within any of thy gates in thy land which the Lord thy God giveth thee, thou shalt not harden thine heart, nor shut thine hand from thy poor brother.

—Deuteronomy 15:7

The true temple of Christ is the believer's soul. Decorate it, dress it, offer gifts to it, welcome Christ in it. For what use are walls that blaze with jewels when Christ, in His poor people, is in danger of starving to death? Your possessions aren't yours anymore, but they have been entrusted to your stewardship. Remember Ananias and Sapphira—because they were afraid of the future, they kept what they owned. Be careful not to rashly waste what is Christ's. That is, don't foolishly give the poor's property to those who aren't poor. Otherwise, as a wise man once told us, charity would actually destroy charity. . . . For to be a Christian and not merely seem like one is the greatest thing. But, somehow or other, those who please the world most please Christ the least. . . . I am warning you as a friend warns a friend before you embark on your new lifestyle. I would rather fail by my ability than by my will in serving you. For I want you to keep your footing where I have fallen.

Precious Talents
Ambrose

I long to say truthfully of you, "Lord, Thou gavest me five talents, behold I have gained five other talents." Then, I could show the precious talents of your righteousness! "For we have a treasure in earthen vessels." These are the talents which the Lord begs us to trade with spiritually: the two coins of the New and the Old Testament that the Samaritan left for the robbed man to get his wounds healed. . . . Therefore, we must not keep the Lord's money buried and hidden in the flesh. Don't hide your one talent in a napkin, but like a good business person, always work with your mind, body, and a steady, ready will to distribute it. Then the Word will be near you, in your mouth and heart. The Word of the Lord is the precious talent that redeems you. Such money must often be seen on people's tables so that, by constantly trading the good coins, they can go into every land and purchase eternal life. "This is eternal life," which You, Almighty Father, give freely: that we may know "Thee the only true God, and Jesus Christ whom Thou hast sent."

For Ezra had prepared his heart to seek the law of the Lord, and to do it, and to teach in Israel statutes and judgments.

—Ezra 7:10

> "Don't hide your one talent in a napkin, but like a good business person, always work with your mind, body, and a steady, ready will to distribute it."

Loving Others
Cyprian

By this shall all men know that ye are my disciples, if ye have love one to another.

—John 13:35

We should remember what name Christ calls His people, by what title He gives to His flock. He calls them sheep, that their Christian innocence might be like that of sheep. He calls them lambs, that their simplicity of mind might imitate the simple nature of lambs. Why does the wolf lurk under the appearance of sheep? Why does he who falsely claims to be a Christian dishonor the flock of Christ? To put on the name of Christ and not to walk in the way of Christ is a mockery of the Divine name and a desertion of the way of salvation. Christ teaches that one who keeps His commandments will receive life, and one who hears and does His words is wise. Moreover, he who both does and teaches that which has been well and usefully preached will be advantageous to the preacher. One is called the greatest in the kingdom of heaven if what he says he does. But what did the Lord most often instill into His disciples? What more among His saving commands and heavenly principles did He charge to guard and observe than to love one another with the love He had for the disciples? And how can people keep the peace or the love of the Lord when they can't be peaceable or loving because they are jealous?

Worship Due

Ambrose

We read and believe many things in light of the Incarnation. But even in our human feelings, we can observe God's greatness. For example, Jesus is wearied by His journey so that He can refresh the weary. He desires a drink when He is about to give spiritual water to the thirsty. He was hungry when He was about to supply the food of salvation to the hungry. He dies to live again. He is buried to rise again. He hangs on the dreadful cross to strengthen those in dread. He veils the heaven with thick darkness so that He can give light. He makes the earth shake so that He may make it strong. He rouses the sea so that He can calm it. He opens the tombs of the dead so that He can show that they are the homes of the living. He is born of a virgin so that people can believe He is born of God. He pretends not to know so that He can make the ignorant know. As a Jew He is said to worship so that the Son may be worshiped as the true God.

But made himself of no reputation, and took upon him the form of a servant, and was made in the likeness of men: And being found in fashion as a man, he humbled himself, and became obedient unto death, even the death of the cross.

—Philippians 2:7-8

> "Even in our human feelings we can observe God's greatness."

Trampling Death

Athanasius

But is now made manifest by the appearing of our Saviour Jesus Christ, who hath abolished death, and hath brought life and immortality to light through the gospel.

—2 Timothy 1:10

Death is destroyed. The cross has triumphed over it. It no longer has any power but is truly dead. This is why all of Christ's disciples despise death and no longer fear it. They take the offensive against it. And by the sign of the cross and by faith in Christ they trample it down as dead. Before the Savior came, death was terrible to the saints. Everyone wept for the dead as though they perished. But now that the Savior has risen, death isn't terrible anymore. For everyone who believes in Christ tramples over death. They would rather die than deny their faith in Christ. For they know that when they die they aren't destroyed, but actually begin to live. Through the Resurrection they become incorruptible. For the devil, who once maliciously rejoiced in death, is the only one truly dead now that we are relieved of death's pains. As proof of this, people are cowards and terrified of death before they believe Christ. But when they have turned to Christ's faith and teaching, they despise death so much that they even eagerly rush up to it. They testify of Christ's victorious Resurrection.

> "Now that the Savior has risen, death isn't terrible anymore. For everyone who believes in Christ tramples over death."

Building Up the Church

Origen

We pray that words may be given to us, as it is written in the book of Jeremiah, "The Lord said to the prophet: 'Behold, I have put My words in thy mouth as fire. See, I have set thee this day over the nations, and over the kingdoms, to root out and to pull down, and to destroy, and to throw down, and to build and to plant.' " For we need words now that will root out of every wounded soul the disgraces spoken against the truth. . . . We also need thoughts that will pull down all edifices based on false opinions. . . . And we require a wisdom that will throw down all high things that rise against the knowledge of God. Just as we must not stop rooting out and pulling down the hindrances that have just been mentioned, we must, in place of what has been rooted out, plant the plants of God's field. In place of what has been pulled down, we must raise the building of God and the temple of His glory. For that reason, we must also pray to the Lord who gave the gifts named in the book of Jeremiah. Pray that He may grant us words for building up the temple of Christ, for planting the spiritual law, and for teaching others to do the same.

Preach the word; be instant in season, out of season; reprove, rebuke, exhort with all longsuffering and doctrine.

—2 Timothy 4:2

35

Desired Glory
Augustine

He that followeth after righteousness and mercy findeth life, righteousness, and honour.
—*Proverbs 21:21*

Let the desire for glory be surpassed by the love of righteousness. When our love of glory exceeds the fear or love of God in our heart, it becomes an evil that is hostile to faith. The Lord said, "How can ye believe, who look for glory from one another, and do not seek the glory which is from God alone?" . . . The holy apostles proclaimed the name of Christ where it was only discredited and neglected. . . . Even amidst curses, accusations, persecutions, and cruel treatment, they weren't deterred from preaching human salvation by the noise of human anger. As they spoke about and did godly things and lived godly lives, they conquered hard hearts and introduced them to the peace of righteousness. Then great glory followed them in the church of Christ. They didn't rest in that reward as the goal of their holiness. They referred the glory to God. For by His grace they were what they were. Therefore, they sought to kindle minds to love God. By Him these people could be made to be what the apostles were.

> "Let the desire for glory be surpassed by the love of righteousness."

Christ's Cross
Rufinus

The cross of Christ made those who abused their authority subject to their former subjects. The cross teaches us, first of all, to resist sin to the point of death and to die willingly for the sake of religion. It also sets an example of obedience for us, and in the same way it punishes the stubbornness of those who once ruled us. Listen to how the Apostle Paul taught us obedience by the cross of Christ: "Let this mind be in you, which was in Christ Jesus who, being in the form of God, thought it not robbery to be equal with God, but made Himself of no reputation, taking upon Him the form of a servant, being made in the likeness of men; and, being found in fashion as a man, He became obedient unto death, even the death of the cross." So, then, as a skilled master teaches both by example and command, so Christ taught us obedience, even to the point of death, by dying to Himself in obedience.

And that he died for all, that they which live should not henceforth live unto themselves, but unto him which died for them, and rose again.

—2 Corinthians 5:15

"The cross teaches us to resist sin to the point of death and to die willingly for the sake of religion. It also sets an example of obedience for us."

Do Good
Clement of Rome

But glory, honour, and peace, to every man that worketh good.
—Romans 2:10a

The good servant receives the bread of his labor with confidence. The lazy servant can't look his employer in the face. It is essential, therefore, that we be quick to practice good works, for of Him are all things. He warns us, "Behold, the Lord cometh, and His reward is before His face, to render to every man according to his work." He urges us, therefore, to attend to our work with a whole heart so that we won't be lazy in any good work. Let our boasting and our confidence be in Him. Let us submit ourselves to His will. Let us consider the whole multitude of His angels, how they always stand ready to serve His will. For the Scripture says, "Ten thousand times ten thousand stood around Him, and thousands of thousands ministered unto Him, and cried, 'Holy, holy, holy, is the Lord of Sabaoth; the whole creation is full of His glory.'" Let us, therefore, gather together in harmony and cry to Him earnestly as with one mouth, so that we can share in His great and glorious promises. For the Scripture says, "Eye hath not seen, nor ear heard, neither have entered into the heart of man, the things which He hath prepared for them that wait for Him."

Every Deed
Origen

Every good deed we do to our neighbors is entered in the Gospel, which is written on heavenly tablets and read by all who are worthy of the knowledge of the whole of things. But on the other hand, there is a part of the Gospel which condemns those who do the same evil deeds done to Jesus. The Gospel includes the treachery of Judas and the shouts of the wicked crowd when it said, "Away with such a one from the earth," "Crucify Him, crucify Him," the mockings of those who crowned Him with thorns, and everything of that kind. There are those who still have thorns with which they crown and dishonor Jesus namely, those people who are choked by the cares, riches, and pleasures of life. Though they have received the Word of God, they don't carry it out. Therefore, we must beware, lest we crown Jesus with thorns of our own. In that case those who are learning about Jesus—who is in all and present with all who are rational and holy—would be reading about us in that light, and about how Jesus is anointed with oil and dined and praised, or on the other hand dishonored and mocked and beaten. All this helps show that both our good actions and the sins of those who stumble have their place in the Gospel, either to everlasting life or to guilt and everlasting shame.

And I saw the dead, small and great, stand before God; and the books were opened: and another book was opened, which is the book of life: and the dead were judged out of those things which were written in the books, according to their works.
—Revelation 20:12

> "We must beware, lest we crown Jesus with thorns of our own."

To Reveal God
Augustine

Let your light so shine before men, that they may see your good works, and glorify your Father which is in heaven.

—*Matthew 5:16*

Whoever wants others to see their good works so that God, who gave them their good works, may be glorified, their light truly shines before others. . . . These people don't do good to be seen, but so that God may be revealed through them. . . . The Apostle Paul said, "Please all men in all things, as I also please all men in all things." But he didn't stop there, as if pleasing others was his goal. Otherwise he would have said wrongly, "If I yet pleased men, I should not be the servant of Christ." Instead, he immediately added why he pleased others. "Not seeking mine own profit, but the profit of many, that they may be saved." So then, he didn't please others for his own profit or fear of not serving Christ, but at the same time he did please others for their salvation's sake so that he would be a faithful servant of Christ. For him it was enough for God to know His conscience and for others to have something to imitate in him.

> "These people don't do good to be seen, but so that God may be revealed through them."

Coming Storms
Gregory I

Those who navigate a ship must watch all the more carefully the farther they move from shore. Then they can see signs of coming storms. When small storms come, the ship can ride over them in a straight path. If storms swell up violently, navigators must avoid them by steering sideways. They often watch alone when everyone else not in charge of the ship is resting. . . . But if the power of the Holy Spirit breathes on an afflicted mind, what was done physically for the Israelites takes place spiritually in us. For it is written, "But the children of Israel walked upon dry land in the midst of the sea." And the prophet of the Lord promises, "When thou passest through the waters, I will be with thee, and the rivers shall not overflow thee." The rivers flood on those whose minds are shaken up by the world's activity. But those whose minds are persistent by the Holy Spirit's grace pass through the water and aren't flooded by rivers. This is because such people move along in the midst of crowds but don't sink the head of their minds beneath the activity of the world.

He keepeth the paths of judgment, and preserveth the way of his saints.

—*Proverbs 2:8*

More Than Master

Ambrose

And when he was gone forth into the way, there came one running, and kneeled to him, and asked him, Good Master, what shall I do that I may inherit eternal life? And Jesus said unto him, Why callest thou me good? there is none good but one, that is, God.

—Mark 10:17-18

What youth don't believe, Christ helps them understand so that they can believe God's Son is not a good master, but the good God. For if whoever glorifies the "One God" also fully glorifies the Son of God, how can the Only-begotten Son not have God's goodness when only God is good? . . . So then, with divinely inspired comprehension our Lord didn't say, "There is none good but the Father alone," but "There is none good but God alone." For the proper name for one who produces children is "Father." But God's unity by no means excludes the Godhead of each of the three Persons. Therefore, it is His nature that is worshiped. Goodness is from God's nature and the Son of God exists in the nature of God. Therefore, goodness doesn't express just one Person, but the complete unity of the Godhead. The Lord, then, doesn't deny His goodness, but rebukes the disciple who doubts His deity. When the scribe said, "Good Master," the Lord answered, "Why callest thou Me good?" He is saying there, "It isn't enough to call someone good who you don't believe is God. I don't want such people to be My disciples—people who consider My manhood and see Me as a good master, rather than look to My Deity and believe that I am the good God."

Secret Sin
Tertullian

Most people think idolatry is only burning incense, sacrificing a victim, committing to sacred ceremonies or priesthoods. Similarly, some find adultery only in kisses, embraces, and actual fleshly contact, or murder only in the shedding of blood and the actual taking of life. But the Lord looks at these crimes in much broader terms. He says adultery exists even in lust, "if one shall have cast an eye lustfully on" and stirred his soul with immodest excitement. He sees murder even in a curse or reproach, in every impulse of anger, and in the neglect of kindness toward a neighbor. As John teaches, he who hates his neighbor is a murderer. If we were judged only by the faults even wicked nations consider punishable, then both the devil's schemes and the Lord's discipline by which He strengthens us against the devil would have little significance. For how, unless we have stood firm through an abundance of unrighteousness, will our "righteousness abound above that of the scribes and Pharisees," as the Lord commanded? So if the head of unrighteousness is idolatry, we must strengthen ourselves ahead of time against both secret and evident manifestations of sin.

The LORD hates . . .
A heart that deviseth
wicked imaginations,
feet that be swift in
running to mischief.
—*Proverbs 6:16a,18*

> "We must strengthen ourselves ahead of time against secret and evident manifestations of sin."

Waiting For Us
Cyprian

For our conversation is in heaven; from whence also we look for the Saviour, the Lord Jesus Christ.
—Philippians 3:20

Always remember that we have renounced the world and are living here as guests and strangers in the meantime. Anticipate the day assigned to each of us for our homecoming. This day will snatch us up, set us free from the snares of the world, and return us to Paradise and the kingdom. Who, in foreign lands, wouldn't hurry to return to their own country? Who, when rushing to return to his friends, wouldn't eagerly want the winds at his back so that he could embrace those dear to him sooner? We consider paradise as our country. We already consider the patriarchs as our parents. Why don't we hurry and run, so that we can see our country and greet our parents? A great number of our dear ones are waiting for us there. A dense crowd of parents, brothers, and children is longing for us, already assured of their own safety and eager for our salvation. . . . Beloved, let us hurry to these people eagerly. Let us long to be with them and to come to Christ quickly. May God see our eager desire. May the Lord Jesus Christ look at the purpose of our mind and faith. He will give the larger rewards of His glory to those with a greater desire for Him!

> "Anticipate the day assigned to each of us for our homecoming."

Made Holy
Augustine

We must be persuaded how much God loved us so that we don't shrink from Him in despair. And we need to be shown also what kind of people we are whom He loved so that we also don't withdraw from Him out of pride. But He dealt with us so that we could profit from His strength, and, in the weakness of humility, our holiness could be perfected. One of the Psalms implies this. It says, "Thou, O God, didst send a spontaneous rain, whereby Thou didst make Thine inheritance perfect, when it was weary." The "spontaneous rain" is grace given freely and not according to merit. He didn't give it because we were worthy, but because He willed. Knowing this, we shouldn't trust in ourselves. That is what is meant by being made "weak." However, He perfects us and says to the Apostle Paul, "My grace is sufficient for thee, for my strength is made perfect in weakness." We, then, must be persuaded how much God loved us and what type of people we were whom He loved. The former is important, lest we despair; the latter, lest we become proud.

Thou therefore, my son, be strong in the grace that is in Christ Jesus.
—2 Timothy 2:1

> "We must be persuaded how much God loved us and what type of people we were whom He loved."

Bold Speech
Chrysostom

Sound speech, that cannot be condemned; that he that is of the contrary part may be ashamed, having no evil thing to say of you.
—Titus 2:8

It is always time to speak boldly. For the psalmist said, "I spake in Thy testimonies before kings, and was not ashamed." If we happen to be around heathens, we should shut them up without harshness or anger. If we do it in anger, we do it with passion and the boldness of those who are confident of their case. But if we speak with gentleness, this is boldness. Boldness is a success and anger is a failure. And success and failure can't possibly go together. Therefore, if we want to have boldness, we must clear away our anger so that no one can attribute our words to it. No matter how sound your words may be, no matter how boldly you speak, how fairly you correct, or what not, you ruin everything when you speak with anger. Look at Stephen and how free his words to his persecutors were from passion. He didn't abuse them but reminded them of the prophets' words. In order to show you that it wasn't done in anger, he prayed as he suffered evil from their hands, "Lay not to their charge this sin." He was far from speaking these words in anger. No, he spoke out of grief and sorrow for their sakes. Certainly, the Bible talks about his appearance, that "they saw his face as it had been the face of an angel," so that they might believe his words.

> "If we want to have boldness, we must clear away our anger so that no one can attribute our words to it."

Divided Loyalty
Cyprian

One who delights in the world, who is enticed by flattering and deceiving earthly pleasures wants to remain in the world a long time. . . . Since the world hates Christians, why do you love that which hates you? And why don't you follow Christ instead, who both redeemed you and loves you? John, in his epistle, cries and urges us not to follow fleshly desires and love the world. "Love not the world," he says, "neither the things which are in the world. If any man love the world, the love of the Father is not in him. For all that is in the world is the lust of the flesh, and the lust of the eyes, and the pride of life, which is not of the Father, but of the lust of the world. And the world shall pass away, and the lust thereof; but he who doeth the will of God abideth for ever, even as God abideth for ever." Instead, beloved, let us be prepared for the will of God with a sound mind, a firm faith, and strong virtue. Laying aside the fear of death, let us think on the eternal life to come. Through this knowledge, let us demonstrate that we are what we believe. . . . Then we won't delay or resist the Lord on the day He calls us to Himself.

For what is a man profited, if he shall gain the whole world, and lose his own soul? or what shall a man give in exchange for his soul?
—Matthew 16:26

> "𝕷et us be prepared for the will of 𝕲od with a sound mind, a firm faith, and strong virtue."

Be Still
Cyril of Jerusalem

Be still, and know that I am God: I will be exalted among the nations, I will be exalted in the earth.
—Psalm 46:10

The time for confession is now. Confess what you have done in word or action, by night or by day. Confess while it is the acceptable time, and receive heavenly treasure in the day of salvation. . . . Blot out every earthly care from your mind, for you are running for your soul. You are completely forsaking the things of the world. But the things you are forsaking are little, while what the Lord is giving is great. Forsake present things, and trust in the things to come.

Have you run in circles and busied yourself in vain with worldly things? . . . "Be still, and know that I am God," Scripture said. Excuse yourself from saying many useless words. Don't backbite or willingly listen to backbiters. Rather, promptly run to prayer. In exercising self-denial, show that your heart is strong. Cleanse your vessel so that you can receive grace more abundantly. For although remission of sins is equally given to everyone, communion with the Holy Ghost is given in proportion to each person's faith. If you have worked little, you receive little. But if you have worked hard, the reward is great.

Spiritual Exercise
Basil

Preparing the heart means unlearning evil prejudices. It is dusting off the tablet before attempting to write on it. Now solitude is most useful for this purpose. It quiets our passions and makes room for holiness to cut them out of the soul. . . . So then, set aside a place for yourself, separate from contact with other people so that your spiritual exercises won't be interrupted. Pure, devoted exercises nourish the soul with godly thoughts. What can be better than imitating angel choruses on earth, or beginning the day with prayer and honoring our Maker with hymns and songs, or, as the day brightens, praying throughout our duties and seasoning our work with hymns, as with salt? Soothing hymns compose the mind, bringing it into a calm, cheerful state. So then, as I have said, quiet is the first step in our sanctification. It is the tongue that has been purified of the world's gossip. It is the eyes that are unexcited by beautiful color or lovely shape. It is the ear that doesn't relax the tone or mind by sensual songs, nor talk flippantly and joke about people. In this way, the mind is saved from external sensations. It falls back on itself and not on worldly senses. As a result, the mind rises up to contemplating God.

For bodily exercise profiteth little: but godliness is profitable unto all things, having promise of the life that now is, and of that which is to come.
—1 Timothy 4:8

> "Set aside a place for yourself so that your spiritual exercises won't be interrupted. Pure, devoted exercises nourish the soul with godly thoughts."

Against Our Will

Chrysostom

And we know that all things work together for good to them that love God, to them who are the called according to his purpose.

—Romans 8:28

Paul says to let this be your work: to give thanks in your prayers for the seen and the unseen benefits and for God's goodness to the willing and the unwilling. . . . I know a certain holy man who prayed this way: "We thank You for all the goodness You have shown us from the first day until now even when we are so unworthy. We thank You for what we know You have done and what we don't know, for gifts seen and unseen, for gifts of word and action, whether we have received them willingly or not—for all these things that have been given to us, the unworthy. We give thanks for tribulations and refreshments, for hell, for punishment, and the kingdom of heaven. We beg of You to keep our souls holy, and our consciences pure, worthy of Your lovingkindness. . . . You who gave the Only-begotten for us and sent Your Holy Spirit to wipe out our sins, if we have willfully or unwillingly disobeyed You, forgive us. Don't attribute our sins to us. Remember everyone who called on Your name in truth. Remember everyone who wishes us well, or the contrary, for we are all human." . . . He prayed this because God gives us many benefits even against our will and maybe even without our knowing it. When we pray for one thing and He does the reverse, it is plain that He is doing good even when we don't know it.

Honest Praise
Augustine

Reading about the great trials Job endured makes one shudder, cringe, and quake. Yet, in the end, what did he receive? Double what he had lost. However, don't let one who has an eye for temporal rewards suffer patiently, and say to himself, . . . "Let me bear evils, and God will repay me as He repaid Job." Such attitudes aren't really patience but greed. For if Job didn't suffer with patience and endurance in order to bravely testify of the Lord's providence, why did He suffer? . . . Beloved, don't let those who bear such tribulations look for a reward. If they suffer any losses, don't let them say, perhaps, "The Lord gave, the Lord hath taken away; as it pleased the Lord, so is it done: blessed be the name of the Lord," when all they want is to receive twice as much again. Let your patience praise God, not greed. For if you try to receive double your losses by praising God, you praise Him out of covetousness, not from love.

But he said unto her, Thou speakest as one of the foolish women speaketh. What? shall we receive good at the hand of God, and shall we not receive evil? In all this did not Job sin with his lips.
—*Job 2:10*

"If you try to receive double your losses by praising God, you praise Him out of covetousness, not from love."

Temple of God
Lactantius

Let your conversation be without covetousness; and be content with such things as ye have: for he hath said, I will never leave thee, nor forsake thee.

—Hebrews 13:5

We should bring sacrifices to God through our words since God said He is the Word. Therefore the supreme act of worshiping God is praise toward Him from the mouth of a righteous person. However, to be accepted by God, there must be humility, fear, and devotion to the greatest degree. If people place confidence in their own integrity and innocence, they will be charged with pride and arrogance and lose the reward of their morality. But in order to obtain God's favor and be freed from every stain, always beg for God's mercy. Pray for nothing other than pardon for your sins, even if you don't have any. If you want anything else, there is no need to express it in words to the One who knows what we wish. If anything good happens to you, give thanks. If any evil, make amends and confess that the evil has happened to you because of your own faults. Even in evils give thanks and make amends in good times, so that you can be the same at all times. Be firm, unchangeable, and unshaken. Don't suppose that these things are to be done only in the temple, but at home, and even in your bed. In short, always have God with you and devote your heart to Him since you are a temple of God.

> "The supreme act of worshiping God is praise toward Him from the mouth of a righteous person."

The Mighty Weapon
Chrysostom

Prayer is a mighty weapon if it is done in the right mindset. Prayer is so strong that continual pleas have overcome shamelessness, injustice, and savage cruelty. . . . It has also overcome laziness and things that friendship could not bring about. For, "although he will not give him because he is his friend, yet because of his appeals he will rise and give to him." In addition, continual requests made an unworthy woman worthy. "It is not meet," Jesus said, "to take the children's bread and to cast it to the dogs." But the woman said, "Yea! Lord! For even the dogs eat the crumbs from their master's table."

Let us pray diligently. Prayer is a mighty weapon if used with earnestness and sincerity, without drawing attention to ourselves. It has turned back wars and benefited an entire undeserving nation. . . . So then, if we pray with humility, beating our chests like the tax gatherer and saying what he did, "Be merciful to me a sinner," we will obtain everything we ask for . . . We need much repentance, beloved, much prayer, much endurance, and much perseverance to gain the good things that have been promised to us.

And all things, whatsoever ye shall ask in prayer, believing, ye shall receive.

—*Matthew 21:22*

"Prayer is a mighty weapon if used with earnestness and sincerity, without drawing attention to ourselves."

Maintain Faith
Irenaeus

And ye shall be hated of all men for my name's sake: but he that endureth to the end shall be saved.
—Matthew 10:22

Why did Christ urge His disciples to take up the cross and follow Him? . . . With respect to the suffering He would experience and His disciples would endure, He suggests, "For whosoever will save his life, shall lose it; and whosoever will lose his life, shall find it." And because His disciples must suffer for His sake, Christ said to them, "Behold, I send you prophets and wise men and scribes; and some of them ye shall kill and crucify." . . . Therefore He knew both those who would suffer persecution and those who would be whipped and killed because of Him. He didn't speak about any other cross but of the suffering He would experience. . . . As a result, He gave them this encouragement: "Fear not them which kill the body, but are not able to kill the soul; but rather fear Him who is able to send both soul and body into hell." He urged them to hold tightly to their professions of faith in Him. For He promised to confess before His Father those who confess His name before men. But He announced that He would deny those who deny Him and would be ashamed of those who were ashamed to confess allegiance to Him.

Soul Music

Chrysostom

Let us allow Christ to speak through us. He desires it more than we do. For He made this instrument and wouldn't want it to be useless and idle. He always wants to keep it in His hands. Why, then, don't you make it useful for the Maker's hand? Why do you allow your soul to be unstrung, relaxed through luxury, and allow the whole harp to be useless to Him? You should keep all its parts completely stretched, well strung, and reinforced with spiritual salt. For if Christ sees your soul tuned this way, He will make His music through it. When this has taken place, you will see angels leaping for joy (archangels and the cherubim too).

So then, let us become worthy of His spotless hands. Let us invite Him to strike our hearts. Rather, He doesn't need inviting. If you make it worthy of His touch, He will be the first to run to you. Considering that He runs to those who haven't become their best yet, when He sees one completely equipped, what won't He do? If Christ makes music and the Spirit rests on us, we will be better than heaven. Although we won't have the sun and the moon adorning our body, the Lord of the sun, moon, and angels will be dwelling and walking in us.

If a man therefore purge himself from these, he shall be a vessel unto honour, sanctified, and meet for the master's use, and prepared unto every good work.
—2 Timothy 2:21

"You should keep all your soul's parts completely stretched, well strung, and reinforced with spiritual salt."

Earthly Lusts
John Cassian

And Jesus said unto him, No man, having put his hand to the plough, and looking back, is fit for the kingdom of God.
—Luke 9:62

Be careful that you don't pick up again anything you once renounced and forsook. Beware that you don't turn away from the field of evangelical work, contrary to the Lord's command, and find yourself clothed in the coat you once stripped off. Don't sink back to the world's low, earthly lusts and desires. Don't defy Christ's word, come down from the roof of perfection, and dare to take up anything you have renounced and forsaken. Beware that you don't remember your relationships or former affections, that you aren't called back to the cares and anxieties of this world. As our Lord says, don't put your hand to the plough and look back. For then you will be unfit for the kingdom of heaven. . . . Rather, be careful. Continue to the end in the nakedness you professed before God and His angels. . . . You should not only continue in this humility and patience but also increase and go forward with them. For although you should move on from the early, beginning stages toward perfection, unfortunately you begin falling back from these to even worse things. It isn't those who begin these things who are saved, but those who continue in them to the end.

An Open Heart
Lactantius

Circumcision of the flesh was a figure of the second circumcision, signifying that the heart is to be laid bare. In other words, we ought to live with open and simple hearts since we are to treat it with reverence like the circumcised part of the body. As a result, God encourages us not to hide our hearts, that is, not to conceal any shameful act within the secret places of our consciences. This is the circumcision of the heart which the prophets speak about, which God transferred from the flesh to the soul, which alone will endure forever. Desiring to promote our lives and salvation according to His goodness, God has provided repentance in the circumcision of the heart. But forgiveness is denied to those who are obstinate and conceal their faults. But if we lay open our hearts (that is if we confess our sins and make amends with God), we will be pardoned by Him who regards not the outward appearance, as people do, but the innermost secrets of the heart.

Neither is there any creature that is not manifest in his sight: but all things are naked and opened unto the eyes of him with whom we have to do.

—Hebrews 4:13

> "God encourages us not to conceal any shameful act within the secret places of our consciences."

Armor of God

John Cassian

Wherefore take unto you the whole armour of God, that ye may be able to withstand in the evil day, and having done all, to stand.

—Ephesians 6:13

"Take," Paul says, "the shield of faith, wherewith ye may be able to quench all the fiery darts of the evil one." Faith, then, is what intercepts the flaming darts of lust. By the fear of future judgment and belief in the heavenly kingdom, it destroys them. "And take the breastplate," he says, "of charity." Certainly, this is what goes around the vital parts of the chest. Love protects what is vulnerable to the deadly wounds of prideful thoughts and keeps off fatal blows. The breastplate doesn't allow the devil's darts to penetrate to our hearts. For it "endureth all things, suffereth all things, beareth all things." "And for a helmet take the hope of salvation." The helmet protects the head. Since Christ is our head, we should protect it in every temptation and persecution, the hope of good things to come. Especially, we must keep our faith in Him complete and undefiled. . . . "And take the sword of the Spirit which is the word of God." For it is "sharper than any two-edged sword, and piercing even to the dividing of soul and spirit, and of the joints and marrow, and is a discerner of the thoughts and intents of the heart." It divides and cuts off any fleshly and earthly thing it finds in us. For whoever is protected by this armor will never be overcome by the weapons and devastation of the enemy. They won't be led away to the hostile land of frivolous thoughts bound in the enemy's chains as captives and prisoners. . . . But they will stand like triumphant conquerors in the land of thoughts they alone have chosen.

Loving the Sheep

Chrysostom

What could be greater than to be seen doing the things Christ declared to be proofs of love for Him? He said, addressing the leader of the apostles, "Peter, lovest thou Me?" When Peter confessed that he did, the Lord added, "if thou lovest Me tend my sheep." The Master didn't ask the disciple if he loved Him in order to get information (why would He when He already knows everyone's heart?), but to teach us how great an interest He has in the care of these sheep. Clearly, then, those who labor for these sheep that Christ values so highly will receive a great reward. For when we see anyone caring for members of our household, or our flocks, we consider that person's zeal for them to be a sign of love towards ourselves. Yet all these things can be bought with money. Imagine, then, how great a gift Christ will give to those who tend the flock He purchased, not with money nor anything of that kind, but by His own death. For He gave His own life to pay for the herd.

By this shall all men know that ye are my disciples, if ye have love one to another.

—John 13:35

> "Those who labor for the sheep Christ values so highly will receive a great reward."

Trouble Nears

Basil

For my thoughts are not your thoughts, neither are your ways my ways, saith the LORD.
—Isaiah 55:8

Bring out the gift of reason God has stored in our hearts. Then when troubles surround us, we will remember that we are only human, and as we have already seen and heard, that life is full of misfortunes. . . . Above all, reason will tell us according to God's command that we who trust Christ shouldn't grieve over those who have died.

For we hope in the Resurrection and in great crowns of which the Master has stored to reward our great patience. We must allow our wiser thoughts to speak to us in this melody. Then perhaps we might experience slight relief from our troubles. I urge you to stand firm, even if the blow is a heavy one. Don't fall under the weight of your grief. Don't lose heart. Be perfectly assured of this: although we can't understand why God ordained such troubles, the One who is wise and who loves us arranged them for us. We must accept them no matter how hard they are to endure. God knows that He is appointing what is best for each person. He knows why the terms of life that He fixes for us are unequal.

> "Although we can't understand the reasons why God ordained troubles, the One who is wise and who loves us arranged them for us."

God's Masterpiece

Basil

God doesn't judge the beauty of His work by how it charms the eyes. He doesn't have the same idea of beauty that we do. What He considers beautiful is that which perfectly demonstrates skillful artistry and tends to be useful toward its end. So then, God judged the design of His own works and approved each one of them. They fulfilled their ends according to His creative purpose. A hand, an eye, or any piece of a statue lying separate from the rest wouldn't look beautiful to anyone. But if each one is restored to its own place in beautiful proportion, although almost unperceived until now, they would strike even the most uncultured. Before uniting the parts of a work, artists distinguish between and recognize the beauty of each piece. They think of the object they have in hand. And Scripture depicts the Supreme Artist in the same way. It praises each one of His works. Soon, however, when His work is complete, He will give well-deserved praise to the whole.

Do ye look on things after the outward appearance? If any man trust to himself that he is Christ's, let him of himself think this again, that, as he is Christ's, even so are we Christ's.
—2 Corinthians 10:7

> "What God considers beautiful is that which perfectly demonstrates skillful artistry and tends to be useful toward its end."

The Names of Jesus

Origen

Wherefore God also hath highly exalted him, and given him a name which is above every name: That at the name of Jesus every knee should bow, of things in heaven, and things in earth, and things under the earth; And that every tongue should confess that Jesus Christ is Lord, to the glory of God the Father.

—*Philippians 2:9-10*

It is no wonder that Jesus is named after many good things in the Gospel. If we look at the names by which the Son of God is called, we will understand how many of these good things He is. The feet of those who preach His name are beautiful. One good thing is life. Jesus is the Life. Another good thing is the light of the world (when it is true light that enlightens people). And the Son of God is said to be all these things. Another good thing, in addition to life and light, is the truth. A fourth is the way that leads to truth. Our Savior teaches us that He is all these things. He says: "I am the Way and the Truth and the Life." Ah, isn't it good that the Lord shook off earth and mortality to rise again? And we have obtained this benefit from the Lord: that He is the Resurrection. He says, "I am the Resurrection." The door through which one enters into the greatest joy is also good. And Christ says, "I am the door." . . . We must not neglect mentioning the Word, who is God after the Father of all. For this another good, no less than the others. Happy, then, are those who accept these goods and receive them from those who announce their blessings, those whose feet are beautiful.

> "If we look at the names by which the Son of God is called, we will understand how many of these good things He is."

Jesus Really Died

Tertullian

Wasn't God really crucified? And, having been crucified, didn't He really die? And, having died, didn't He really rise again? If not, Paul would have falsely "determined to know nothing among us but Jesus and Him crucified." He would have falsely imposed on us that Christ was buried and rose again. Then our faith is also false. And all that we hope for from Christ is a dream. You who acquit the murderers of God from guilt are a disgrace! For Christ didn't suffer from them if He really never suffered. Will you spare the whole world from its only hope by destroying the essential dishonor of our faith? Whatever is unworthy of God is profitable to me. I am safe if I am not ashamed of my Lord. "Whosoever," He says, "shall be ashamed of Me, of him will I also be ashamed."

The Son of God was crucified. I am not ashamed because mankind must be ashamed of it. And the Son of God died. It is, by all means, to be believed because it is absurd. And He was buried and rose again. The fact is certain, because it is impossible. But how will all this be true if He wasn't true Himself, if He hadn't had within Himself that which might be crucified, might die, might be buried, and might rise again?

For to this end Christ both died, and rose, and revived, that he might be Lord both of the dead and living.
—Romans 14:9

The Loving Shepherd

Dionysius of Alexandria

Repent ye therefore, and be converted, that your sins may be blotted out, when the times of refreshing shall come from the presence of the Lord.

—Acts 3:19

"**Don't reject those who want to return in repentance.**"

Christ, who is the good Shepherd, goes in quest of one who wanders and is lost in the mountains. He calls this one back when it runs from Him, and when He has found it, troubles Himself to carry it on His shoulders. But we, on the other hand, harshly reject such a shepherd when He approaches us. Don't bring such misery on yourself and, by behaving this way, drive a sword into yourself. For when people set about doing evil or good to others, what they do doesn't just affect other people. Instead, depending on whether they attach themselves to wickedness or goodness, they themselves become controlled either by godly virtues or by unbridled passions. The former become the followers and friends of good angels. Both in this world and the next, they will enjoy perfect peace and immunity from all evil. They will obtain the most blessed destinies of eternity and will be in God's fellowship forever. But the latter will immediately fall away from the peace of God and from peace with themselves. Both in this world and after death, they will dwell with the murderous spirits. Therefore, don't reject those who want to return in repentance. Instead, receive the lost gladly, count them again among the faithful, and make up what is defective in them.

Saving Faith
Ignatius

Those who profess themselves to be Christ's are known not only by what they say, but also by what they practice. "For the tree is known by its fruit." It is better to be silent and be a Christian than to speak and not be a follower of Christ. "The kingdom of God is not in word, but in power." People "believe with the heart and confess with the mouth," the one "unto righteousness," the other "unto salvation."

What doth it profit, my brethren, though a man say he hath faith, and have not works? can faith save him?
—James 2:14

It is good to teach if the one who speaks also acts. For the one who shall both "do and teach, the same shall be great in the kingdom." Our Lord and God, Jesus Christ, the Son of the Living God, first did and then taught, as Luke testifies, "whose praise is in the Gospel through all the churches." There is nothing which is hidden from the Lord, but our secrets are near to Him. Let us, therefore, do all things as those who have Him dwelling in us, that we may be His temples and He may be in us as God. Let Christ speak in us, even as He did in Paul. Let the Holy Spirit teach us to speak the things of Christ in like manner as He did.

> "It is better for a man to be silent and be a Christian than to speak and not be a follower of Christ."

Satisfaction
Augustine

Not that we are sufficient of ourselves to think any thing as of ourselves; but our sufficiency is of God.
—*2 Corinthians 3:5*

Pride is the craving for undeserved glory. And this is undeserved glory: when the soul abandons the One it should cling to for sufficiency and becomes self-reliant. This happens when the soul is satisfied with itself. It falls away from the unchangeable good that would satisfy it more than itself. And this falling away is spontaneous. For the will should remain in love with the higher, changeless good that illumines it to intelligence and kindles it into love. Then it wouldn't become so dark and cold by turning to find satisfaction in itself. We didn't fall so far away that we became absolutely nothing. Instead, by turning toward ourselves, our souls became more secluded than when we clung to the Supreme One. Similarly, to exist in oneself, that is, to be one's own satisfaction after abandoning God, isn't to become a nobody. But, the holy Scriptures designate another name to proud people: "self-pleasers." Therefore, it is good to lift up the heart. But it isn't good to lift it up to oneself; that is pride. It is good only to lift our hearts up to the Lord, for that is obedience and humility.

> "This is deserved glory: when the soul abandons the One it should cling to for sufficiency and becomes self-reliant."

Ultimate Needs
Clement of Alexandria

If rulers don't terrify those who do good works, how will God, who is by nature good, terrify those who don't sin? Paul says, "If thou doest evil, be afraid," always using strict words with the churches after the Lord's example. Conscious of his own boldness and the hearers' weakness, he says to the Galatians, "Am I your enemy, because I tell you the truth?" Healthy people don't need doctors when they are strong, but those who are sick need a doctor's skill. In the same way, we who are sick from shameful lusts, excesses, and other flames of the passions need the Savior. And He administers not only mild but also stringent medicines. The bitter roots of fear then disintegrate the sores of our sins that eat us. Therefore, fear is beneficial if bitter. Being sick, we stand in need of the Savior; wanderers, of one to guide us; blind, of one to lead us to the light; thirsty, "of the fountain of life, of which whosoever partakes shall no longer thirst." Dead, we need life; sheep, we need a shepherd; children, we need a tutor. All of humanity stands in need of Jesus so that we may not remain as obstinate sinners to the end and be condemned.

I said, LORD, be merciful unto me: heal my soul; for I have sinned against thee.
—*Psalm 41:4*

> "All of humanity stands in need of Jesus so that we may not remain as obstinate sinners to the end."

Genuine Compassion
Sulpitius Severus

And the people asked [John], saying, What shall we do then? He answereth and saith unto them, He that hath two coats, let him impart to him that hath none; and he that hath meat, let him do likewise.

—Luke 3:10-11

In the middle of an unusually severe winter whose extreme cold killed many, St. Martin happened to meet a poor man without clothing at the gate of Amiens. He was begging those who passed by to have compassion upon him. However, everyone passed by the pitiful man without notice. Martin, a man full of God, recognized that because no one else showed pity to this man, he was left to him. But what could he do? He didn't have anything except the cloak he wore, for he had already given up the rest of his garments for similar reasons. Therefore, taking his sword, he divided his cloak into two equal parts. Martin gave one part to the poor man, while he again clothed himself with the rest of it. Some of the bystanders laughed at this, because now he looked hideous and stood out as being partly dressed. Many, however, who had better understanding, groaned deeply because they hadn't done anything like this. They especially felt shame because they owned more than Martin. They could have clothed the poor man without reducing themselves to nakedness. The following night, when Martin had gone to sleep, he had a vision of Christ dressed in that part of the cloak with which he had clothed the poor man.

Like the Sea
Athanasius

As with the faith of the disciples, we should speak frequently with our Master. For the world is like the sea to us, beloved. We sail on this sea, with our own free will acting like the wind. For we all navigate according to our will. If the Word is our pilot, we enter into rest. But if pleasure takes hold of us, we face the danger of storms and are shipwrecked. For just as the ocean has storms and waves, there are many afflictions and trials in the world. "When affliction or persecution ariseth, the unbeliever is offended," the Lord said. Because unbelievers aren't strengthened by the faith and because they favor temporal things, they can't stand up against difficulties. Like the foolish man's house built on sand, those without understanding fall under storms of temptation. The saints, however, have exercised their senses to be self-controlled. Because they are strong in faith and understand the Word, they don't faint under trials. From time to time, ever more powerful trials work against them, yet they continue to be faithful. They wake up the Lord who is with them and are delivered. Because they find relief as they pass through water and fire, they celebrate by offering up thankful prayers to God who has rescued them.

When thou passest through the waters, I will be with thee; and through the rivers, they shall not overflow thee: when thou walkest through the fire, thou shalt not be burned; neither shall the flame kindle upon thee.
—*Isaiah 43:2*

> "If the Word is our pilot, we enter into rest. But if pleasure takes hold of us, we face the danger of storms and are shipwrecked."

Loving God
Augustine

I love You, Lord, not with uncertainty, but consciously and with certainty. . . . But what do I love in loving You? Not physical beauty, the splendor of time, or the pleasant radiance of light. Not the sweet melodies of all kinds of songs or the fragrant smell of flowers, ointments, and spices. Not manna and honey. Not limbs that are pleasant for fleshly embraces. I don't love these things when I love my God. Yet, I love a certain kind of light, sound, fragrance, food, and embrace in loving my God. He is the light, sound, fragrance, food, and embrace of my inner person. In this love, the light shines that can't be contained into my soul. It is where those things resound that time can't snatch away, where there is a fragrance that no breeze can scatter, where there is a food which no amount of eating can cut into, and where there is a clinging to that no gratification can break apart. This is what I love when I love my God.

> "I love You,
>
> Lord, not with
>
> uncertainty, but
>
> consciously and
>
> with certainty."

Unselfish Giving
Lactantius

The greatest advantage of riches isn't using them for an individual's specific pleasure, but for the welfare of many people. They aren't for one's immediate enjoyment, but for the righteousness that never passes away. Therefore, by all means, we must not hope to receive something in return for showing mercy. We must expect the reward for such duty to come from God alone. If you expect it from others, then what you did wasn't kindness but lending something at interest. Those who act for themselves and not for the sake of others don't deserve to be rewarded. Yet, whenever people give to others without seeking their own advantage, they really give to themselves because God will reward them. God has also commanded us to invite those who cannot repay us to our dinners. For everything we do in life should be performed with mercy. Don't think, however, that this prevents you from interacting with friends or showing kindness to neighbors. But God has revealed to us what truly righteous behavior is: to live mercifully with our neighbors provided we know that one way of living relates to people and the other to God.

But when thou makest a feast, call the poor, the maimed, the lame, the blind: And thou shalt be blessed; for they cannot recompense thee.
—Luke 14:13–14a

"Those who act for themselves and not for the sake of others don't deserve to be rewarded."

God's Mercy

Chrysostom

Therefore also now, saith the LORD, turn ye even to me with all your heart, and with fasting, and with weeping, and with mourning.

—Joel 2:12

This is the loving-kindness of God: He never turns His face away from a sincere repentance. God accepts and welcomes anyone who has become wicked to the greatest extreme and chooses to return towards the path of holiness. He does everything to restore such people to their former position. But God shows an even greater mercy: For those who demonstrate incomplete repentance, He still won't pass by their small and insignificant turn. Instead, He even gives these people a great reward. This is evident from what Isaiah the prophet says concerning the Jews. He said, "On account of his sin I put him to pain for a little while, and smote him, and turned my face away from him, and he was pained, and walked sorrowfully, and then I healed him, and comforted him." And we can also cite that most ungodly king who sinned by the influence of his wife. However, when all he did was mourn, put on sackcloth, and condemn his sin, he received the mercy of God and was released from all the evils that threatened him.

> "God never turns His face away from a sincere repentance."

Avoiding Tricks
Lactantius

He who is both the Lord and most indulgent Parent promises that He will forgive the sins of the repentant. He will blot out all the iniquities of those who begin afresh practicing righteousness. For former uprightness is no use to those who live badly. The subsequent wickedness has destroyed their righteous works. In the same way, former sins don't stand in the way of those who have corrected their lives because the subsequent righteousness has erased the stain of their former lives. Those who repent of what they have done understand their former errors. Regarding this, the Greeks speak better and more significantly of *metanoia*, which we may speak of as a return to right understanding. Those who return to a right understanding and rescue their minds from madness, who grieve over their errors and rebuke themselves for madness, and commit their minds to a better course of life are guarded against being led into the same snares again. In short, even when dumb animals are ensnared by trickery but have untangled themselves and escaped, they become more cautious in the future. They will always avoid the things in which they have seen tricks, wiles, and snares. Therefore, repentance makes us cautious and diligent to avoid the faults which we once were tricked into.

Neither yield ye your members as instruments of unrighteousness unto sin: but yield yourselves unto God, as those that are alive from the dead, and your members as instruments of righteousness unto God.
—Romans 6:13

"Those who return to a right understanding and rescue their minds from madness are guarded against being led into the same snares again."

Resist Anger
Hermas

A fool uttereth all his mind: but a wise man keepeth it in till afterwards.
—*Proverbs 29:11*

Patience is great, mighty, strong, and calm. It is joyful, rejoicing, free from care, glorifying God at all times, having no bitterness, and abiding continually meek and quiet. Now this patience dwells with those who have complete faith. But anger is foolish, fickle, and senseless. Now folly gives birth to bitterness, bitterness to anger, and anger to frenzy. This frenzy, the product of so many evils, ends in great and incurable sin. For when all these spirits dwell in one vessel in which the Holy Spirit also dwells, the vessel cannot contain them, but overflows. The tender Spirit, then, not being accustomed to dwell with the wicked spirit nor with hardness, withdraws from such a man and seeks to dwell with meekness and peacefulness. Then, when the Spirit withdraws from the man in whom he dwelt, the man is emptied of the righteous Spirit, and being henceforward filled with evil spirits, he is in a state of anarchy in every action, being dragged here and there by the evil spirits, and there is a complete darkness in his mind as to everything good. This, then, is what happens to all angry people. Therefore, depart from that most wicked spirit, anger, and put on patience. Resist anger and bitterness, and you will be found in company with the purity that is loved by the Lord.

> "Resist anger and bitterness, and you will be found in company with the purity which is loved by the Lord."

In Process

Augustine

t Those who want to obey God, but can't, already possess a good will, although it is small and weak. But they are able to obey when they obtain a strong and robust will. When the martyrs obeyed the great commandments, they acted by a great will—that is, with great love. The Lord speaks of this great love: "Greater love hath no man than this, that a man lay down his life for his friends." . . . The Apostle Peter didn't possess this love when he fearfully denied the Lord three times. "There is no fear in love," says John the Evangelist in his first epistle, "but perfect love casteth out fear." Even though Peter's love was small and imperfect, it was still present when he said to the Lord, "I will lay down my life for Thy sake." Peter believed he could carry out what he felt he was willing to do by himself. . . . However, God works in us so that we can have the will to obey. Once we have this will, God works with us to perfect us. The apostle Paul says, "I am confident of this very thing, that He which hath begun a good work in you will perform it until the day of Jesus Christ." Therefore, God operates without us so that we can will to obey, but when we act on our will, He cooperates with us.

Jesus answered and said unto him, If a man love me, he will keep my words: and my Father will love him, and we will come unto him, and make our abode with him.

—John 14:23

"God works in us so that we can have the will to obey. Once we have this will, God works with us to perfect us."

Willingly Offer
Chrysostom

And Hannah was in bitterness of soul, and prayed unto the LORD, and wept sore.
—*1 Samuel 1:10*

Do you understand what watchfulness in prayer is? Listen to the words of Hannah, "Adonai Eloi Sabaoth." But hear even what preceded those words. The account says, "they all rose up from the table," but she didn't allow herself to sleep or rest. . . . But it says she stood "before the Lord." What did she say then? "Adonai, Lord, Eloi Sabaoth!" Interpreted, this means "O Lord, the God of Hosts." Hannah's tears went before her tongue. Through her tears she hoped to persuade God to follow her request. She continues, "If Thou wilt indeed look on the affliction of thine handmaid, and wilt give unto Thine handmaid a man child, then will I give him unto the Lord all the days of his life." Hannah didn't say "for one year" or "for two" as we do. Neither did she say, "If You will give me a child, I will give You money." But she said "I give back to You the very gift itself, my first-born, the son of my prayer." Here was a true daughter of Abraham. For Abraham gave when it was demanded of him. And Hannah offers even before it is demanded. . . . Let us all imitate her. . . . For prayer can accomplish great things.

> "Hannah's tears went before her tongue. Through her tears she hoped to persuade God to follow her request."

Be Worthy
Cyril of Jerusalem

A certain man in the Gospels went to a marriage feast. He put on unbecoming clothes, came in, sat down, and ate—for the bridegroom allowed it. However, when he saw everyone dressed in white, he should have found the same kind of clothes for himself. While he ate food like them, he wasn't like them in his fashion and purpose. And although the bridegroom was generous, he wasn't stupid. As he went around to each of the guests and observed them, he didn't care about their eating, but about their refined behavior. He saw a stranger who wasn't wearing wedding clothes and said to him, "Friend, how did you get in here? With what conscience? It wasn't because the doorkeeper didn't stop you, but because of the host's generosity. Were you ignorant of what clothes to wear to the banquet? You came in and saw the glittering style of the guests—shouldn't you have learned by what was right before your eyes? Shouldn't you have tactfully excused yourself so that you could come back again dressed appropriately?" . . . So he commands the servants, "Bind his feet which have boldly intruded. Bind his hands which didn't know how to put on bright clothes. And cast him into the outer darkness, for he is unworthy of the wedding celebration." You see what happened to that man, so be worthy of the feast.

And he saith unto him, Friend, how camest thou in hither not having a wedding garment? And he was speechless.
—Matthew 22:12

> "When he saw everyone dressed in white, he should have found the same kind of clothes for himself."

Hard Hearts
Clement of Alexandria

O the enormous evil of being ashamed of the Lord! He offers freedom; you flee into bondage. He grants salvation; you sink down into destruction. He gives everlasting life; you wait for punishment and prefer the fire the Lord "has prepared for the devil and his angels." Therefore the blessed apostle Paul says, "I testify in the Lord, that ye walk no longer as the Gentiles walk, in the vanity of their minds; having their understanding darkened, being alienated from the life of God through the ignorance that is in them, because of the hardness of their hearts, who, being past feeling, have given themselves over to lustfulness, to work all uncleanness and lewdness." . . . The Lord, with constant diligence, appeals, terrifies, urges, rouses, and reproves. Therefore, don't let anyone despise Jesus, for fear that he unwittingly despise himself. For the Scripture says, "Today, if ye will hear His voice, harden not your hearts." . . . Why, then, should we keep exchanging grace for wrath, not receive the Word with open ears, or entertain God as a guest in a pure heart? For His promise is full of grace, "if today we hear His voice." So, then, those who believe and obey will receive grace superabundantly.

> "The Lord, with constant diligence, appeals, terrifies, urges, rouses, and reproves."

Your Mind
Melito

God made you as perfect as seemed good to Him. He has given you a free mind. He has set many objects before you so that you can distinguish their nature and choose the good things for yourself. He has set the heavens before you and placed the stars in them. He has set the sun and the moon before you. They run their courses every day. He has set all of the waters before you and restrained them by His Word. He has set the whole wide world before you, which remains at rest and continues to thrive without changing. For fear that you might assume the earth continues because of its own nature, He makes it quake when He pleases. He has set the clouds before you, which, by His command, rain water from above and satisfy the earth. Consequently, you should know that the One who puts these things into motion is superior to them all. Accept His goodness with gratitude because He has given you a mind to distinguish these things from one another. Therefore, I advise you: know yourself and know God.

The heavens declare the glory of God; and the firmament sheweth his handywork.
—Psalm 19:1

> "I advise you:
> know yourself
> and know God."

Self-Denial

John Cassian

By humility and the fear of the LORD are riches, and honour, and life.
—Proverbs 22:4

Christian athletes who compete according to the rules . . . and desire to be crowned by the Lord should, by all means, fight to destroy the very fierce beast of pride. For it destroys every virtue. They must know that as long as pride remains in their hearts, they will never be free from evil, and will even lose any good qualities they seem to have by pride's influence. For no tower of righteousness (so to speak) can possibly be raised in our souls unless the foundation of true humility is first laid in our hearts. Being laid securely, it can bear the weight of perfection and love thrust on us in such a way that we can show true humility to others from the very bottom of our heart. And we won't be content to make others sad or injure them. But we can't possibly manage this unless the love of Christ implants true self-denial in us. This consists of stripping and depriving ourselves of all our possessions. Also, we must take up the yoke of obedience and subjection in humility and without show. Then . . . our own will won't be alive in us.

> "No tower of righteousness can possibly be raised in our souls unless the foundation of true humility is first laid in our hearts."

Spiritual Food

Athanasius

The soul is humbled when it doesn't follow wickedness, but feeds on righteousness. For righteousness and wickedness are the soul's food. According to what it wants, the soul can prefer and eat either of these meats. If it is bent toward righteousness, it will be nourished by righteousness, morality, self-control, meekness, and courage. For Paul said, "Being nourished by the word of truth." This was the case with our Lord. He said, "My meat is to do the will of My Father which is in heaven." But if the soul isn't like Him and prefers wickedness, it is nourished only by sin. The Holy Ghost described sinners and their food by referring to the devil. He said, "I have given him to be meat to the people of Ethiopia." For the devil is food for sinners. In the same way, our Lord and Savior Jesus Christ, the heavenly bread, is food for saints. For He said, "Except ye eat My flesh, and drink My blood." The devil is food for the impure and for those who do the deeds of darkness and not of light. Therefore, in order to turn them from wickedness, Christ commands these people to be nourished by the food of righteousness. This food is humility of mind, meekness that endures humiliations, and acknowledgment of God.

Then said they unto him, Lord, evermore give us this bread.
—John 6:34

> "The devil is food for sinners. In the same way, our Lord and Savior Jesus Christ, the heavenly bread, is food for saints."

Shared Love

Augustine

But I say unto you, Love your enemies, bless them that curse you, do good to them that hate you, and pray for them which despitefully use you, and persecute you.

—Matthew 5:44

If you are fond of a particular actor and consider his art to be one of the best, then you are fond of everyone else who admires him because of your common admiration. And the more fervent you are in your admiration, the harder you work to secure new admirers for him, and the more anxious you become to show him to other people. . . . Now if this is true, what is appropriate for us to do when we live in the love of God and find true happiness by enjoying Him? . . . When we aren't afraid that anyone who comes to know Him will be disappointed? When we know that everyone who actually does love Him will obtain an eternal reward—the very One they love? Then we must even love our enemies. For we aren't afraid of them. They can't take away what we love from us. Instead, we pity them, because the more they hate us, the more they are separated from the One we love. But if they turned to God, they would be forced to love Him the best. They would also love us because of our sharing such a blessing with them.

> "We pity our enemies because the more they hate us, the more they are separated from the One we love."

Easter Reflection

Lactantius

Does it please you to go through all of My pain and to experience grief with Me? Then consider the plots against Me and the irreverent price of My innocent blood. Consider the disciple's pretended kisses, the crowd's insults and abuse, and, even more, the mocking blows and accusing tongues. Imagine the false witnesses, Pilate's cursed judgment, the immense cross pressed on My shoulders and tired back, and My painful steps to a dreadful death. Study Me from head to foot. I am deserted and lifted high up above My beloved mother. See My hair clotted with blood, and My head encircled by cruel thorns. For a stream of blood is pouring down like rain on all sides of My Divine face. Observe My sunken, sightless eyes and My beaten cheeks. See My parched tongue that was poisoned with gall. My face is pale with death. Look at My hands that have been pierced with nails and My drawn-out arms. See the great wound in My side and the blood streaming from it. Imagine My pierced feet and blood-stained limbs. Then bow, and with weeping adore the wood of the cross. With a humble face, stoop to the earth that is wet with innocent blood. Sprinkle it with tears, and carry Me and My encouragement in your devoted heart.

Surely he hath borne our griefs, and carried our sorrows: yet we did esteem him stricken, smitten of God, and afflicted. But he was wounded for our transgressions, he was bruised for our iniquities: the chastisement of our peace was upon him; and with his stripes we are healed.

—Isaiah 53:4-5

> "Imagine My pierced feet and blood-stained limbs."

Holy Bodies
Chrysostom

And if thy right eye offend thee, pluck it out, and cast it from thee: for it is profitable for thee that one of thy members should perish, and not that thy whole body should be cast into hell.

—Matthew 5:29

"We have the power to make each part of us instruments of wickedness or righteousness."

Let us discipline our tongues to administer the Spirit's grace and rid our mouths of all bitterness, malice, and disgraceful words. For we have the power to make each part of us instruments of wickedness or righteousness. Hear how some people make the tongue an instrument of sin and others of righteousness! It is written about some, "Their tongue is a sharp sword." But about another, "My tongue is the pen of a ready writer." The former brought about destruction; the latter wrote God's law. Therefore, one was a sword and the other a pen not by nature, but by the choice of those who used it. . . . We see the same thing with the mouth. Those with mouths full of filth and wickedness were accused, "Their mouth is full of cursing and bitterness." But this wasn't the case with another: "My mouth shall speak of wisdom, and the meditation of my heart shall be of understanding." . . . So then, knowing these things, let us fortify ourselves on all sides with holiness to ward off God's wrath. Let us make the members of our body instruments of righteousness. Let us discipline our eyes, mouths, hands, feet, hearts, tongues, and entire bodies to be used only in holiness.

Finding Truth

Tertullian

Suppose the words "Seek, and ye shall find" were addressed to all people equally. One's aim is to carefully determine the sense of the words. I propose that there is something definite taught by Christ that the Gentiles are bound to believe. They must "seek" in order to believe when they have "found" it. However, there can be no indefinite seeking for the only definite thing. You must "seek" until you "find," and believe when you have found. You must not have anything else to do but to obey what you have believed (provided you believe that nothing else is to be believed, and, therefore, nothing else is to be sought). . . . Your Teacher instructs you not to seek anything other than that which He has taught.

But if from thence thou shalt seek the LORD *thy God, thou shalt find him, if thou seek him with all thy heart and with all thy soul.*
—*Deuteronomy 4:29*

> "You must 'seek' until you 'find,' and believe when you have found."

Spiritual People
Gregory of Nyssa

But let us, who are of the day, be sober, putting on the breastplate of faith and love; and for an helmet, the hope of salvation.
—1 Thessalonians 5:8

> "Someone who doesn't properly use these spiritual abilities, but uses them for opposite reasons, is inexpressibly strange and unnatural."

Courage and confidence are our weapons to deflect the enemy's surprise attacks. Hope and patience are the staffs to lean on when we are worn out by worldly trials. And we must stock up on sorrow and be ready to apply it, if need be, when we repent of our sins. At the same time, we must believe that it is only useful for serving our repentance. Righteousness will be our straightedge ruler, guarding us from stumbling in word or action, guiding us how to use our spiritual abilities, and teaching us to be considerate towards everyone we meet. . . . But someone who doesn't properly use these spiritual abilities, but uses them for opposite reasons . . . is inexpressibly strange and unnatural. Imagine someone putting on his armor the wrong way: reversing the helmet so that it covers his face, putting his feet into the breastplate, fitting the shin guards onto his chest, putting everything on the right side that belongs to the left and vice versa. How would such a soldier be likely to fare in battle? So then, this gives us an idea of the fate awaiting those who use their spiritual abilities contrary to their proper use.

Mysterious Cross

Ambrose

O the divine mystery of that cross! Weakness hangs on it, power is freed by it, evil is nailed to it, and triumphal trophies are raised toward it. One saint said: "Pierce my flesh with nails for fear of Thee." He doesn't mean nails of iron, but of fear and faith. For the chains of righteousness are stronger than those of punishment. Peter's faith bound him when he followed the Lord as far as the high priest's hall. No person had bound him and punishment didn't free him since his faith bound him. Again, when Peter was bound by the Jews, prayer freed him. Punishment didn't hold him because he hadn't turned from Christ.

Then said Jesus unto his disciples, If any man will come after me, let him deny himself, and take up his cross, and follow me.
—Matthew 16:24

Do you also crucify sin so that you can die to sin? Those who die to sin live to God. Do you live for Him who didn't even spare His own Son so that He could crucify our sins in His body? For Christ died for us that we could live in His revived body. Therefore, our guilt and not our life died in Him who, it is said, "bare our sins in His own body on the tree; that being set free from our sins we might live in righteousness, by the wound of whose stripes we are healed."

"Christ died for us that we could live in His revived body."

Guarded Souls
Athanasius

For to be carnally minded is death; but to be spiritually minded is life and peace.
—Romans 8:6

Let us dwell on the fact that while the Lord is with us, our enemies can't hurt us. When they approach us, they conform to the state they find us in. They adapt their delusions to the condition of our minds. Therefore, if they find us timid and confused, they will attack us like robbers, finding our minds unguarded. They think of us as we think about ourselves. For if they find us to be weak and cowardly, they increase our terror by delusions and threats; the unhappy souls are then tormented by these things. But if they see us rejoicing in the Lord, contemplating future bliss, mindful of the Lord, regarding all things to be in His hand, and knowing that no evil spirit has any strength against Christians, nor power over anyone—our enemies are defeated and turned backwards by the strength of these thoughts. Seeing Job fortified in this way, the enemy withdrew from him. But finding Judas unguarded, the enemy took him captive. Therefore, if we want to look down on the enemy, we must always think about the things of the Lord. Our souls must always rejoice in hope. Then we will see that the devil's snares are like smoke and the evil ones will flee rather than pursue us.

> "If we want to look down on the enemy, we must always think about the things of the Lord. Our souls must always rejoice in hope."

Fight for Faith

Cyprian

Behold a great and noble battle with the glorious reward of a heavenly crown. In so far as God observes us as we struggle and watches over those He has stooped to make His sons, He enjoys the spectacle of our contest. God watches us fight for our faith. His angels watch us, and Christ watches us. How great is the dignity, joy, and glory of competing and being crowned in the presence of God with Christ as the Judge! Beloved, let us be armed with our whole strength and let us be prepared for the struggle with uncorrupted minds, solid faith, and devoted courage. Let the army of God march forward to the appointed battle-field. Let the stable ones be armed, lest they be defeated. Let the backsliders also be armed, so that even they might regain what they lost. Let honor motivate all.

Wherefore gird up the loins of your mind, be sober, and hope to the end for the grace that is to be brought unto you at the revelation of Jesus Christ.
—1 Peter 1:13

> "Let us be armed with our whole strength and let us be prepared for the struggle with uncorrupted minds, solid faith, and devoted courage."

A Lamb to Slaughter

Origen

Ye are my witnesses, saith the LORD, and my servant whom I have chosen: that ye may know and believe me, and understand that I am he: before me there was no God formed, neither shall there be after me.

—Isaiah 43:10

It was a surprise, even to ordinary people, that someone who was accused and attacked by false testimony refused to protect Himself. He was able to defend Himself and to show that He wasn't guilty of any of the alleged charges. He could have listed the praiseworthy deeds of His own life and His miracles done by divine power in order to allow the judge to deliver a more honorable judgment concerning Him. But, by the nobleness of His nature, He condemned His accusers. Without hesitation, the judge would have set Him free if He had offered a defense. This is clear from his statement, "Which of the two do ye wish that I should release unto you, Barabbas or Jesus, who is called Christ?" and from what the Scripture adds, "For he knew that for envy they had delivered Him." Jesus, however, is continually attacked by false witnesses and, while wickedness remains in the world, is continually exposed to accusation. Yet, even now, He remains silent in the presence of these things and makes no audible answer. Instead, He places His defense in the lives of His genuine disciples. They are an outstanding testimony, one superior to all false witness, that refutes and overthrows all unfounded accusations and charges.

Final Reward

Eusebius

Is there genuine peace among us and untiring love for others? If we rebuke a fault, is our goal to encourage and not to destroy? Is our correction meant to save and not to be cruel? Do we exercise not only sincere faith towards God, but faithfulness in our social relationships? Do we pity the unfortunate? Do we have simple lives that hate concealing evil behind deceit and hypocrisy? Do we acknowledge the true God and His undivided sovereignty? This is real godliness and sincere, undefiled religion, . . . Those who confess allegiance to God aren't easily enraged. Instead, they stand nobly under the pressure of necessity. Trials that test their loyalty are, in effect, passports to God's favor. For we can't doubt that God is pleased with excellent human conduct. If both powerful and lowly people thank those who have helped them and serve them in return, it would be absurd if the supreme, Sovereign One, who is Good itself, neglected doing likewise. He follows us throughout our lives, is near to us in every one of our good acts, and accepts and rewards our righteousness and obedience. He postpones full compensation, however, until the time when He will review all of the actions of our lives. At that time, those who are clear will receive the reward of everlasting life, while the wicked will experience the penalties they deserve.

Cast not away therefore your confidence, which hath great recompence of reward. For ye have need of patience, that, after ye have done the will of God, ye might receive the promise.

—*Hebrews 10:35-36*

> "Trials that test their loyalty are, in effect, passports to God's favor."

Reach Ahead
Athanasius

That ye may approve things that are excellent; that ye may be sincere and without offence till the day of Christ; Being filled with the fruits of righteousness, which are by Jesus Christ, unto the glory and praise of God.
—*Philippians 1:10-11*

Having already begun to walk in righteousness, let us try all the harder to reach the things ahead of us. Don't turn to the things behind you like Lot's wife. For the Lord said, "No man, having put his hand to the plough, and turning back, is fit for the kingdom of heaven." This turning back is the feeling of regret and becoming worldly minded again. But don't be afraid of righteousness or be intimidated by it. It isn't far from us. For it isn't outside of us but is inside us. It is easy to walk in righteousness if we are willing. . . . On the other hand, when our minds swerve and turn away from their natural state, that is called vice of the soul. This isn't hard to understand. If we remain as we were made, we are righteous. But if we think of dishonorable things, we are evil. If we had to gain righteousness from outside of ourselves, it would be difficult. But if it is in us, we must keep ourselves from foul thoughts. Because the Lord has given us our souls as a deposit, we must preserve them. Then He will recognize the work He made.

> "Let us try all the harder to reach the things ahead of us. Don't turn to the things behind you like Lot's wife."

Groans and Tears

Augustine

It isn't wrong or unprofitable to spend much time in prayer as long as it doesn't hinder us from doing other good and necessary works duty calls us to. . . . For to spend a long time in prayer isn't, as some think, the same thing as praying "with much speaking." Multiplied words are one thing, but the sustained warmth of desire is another. It is written that the Lord continued all night in prayers and that His prayer was prolonged when He was in agony. Isn't this an example for us from our Intercessor who, along with the Father, eternally hears our prayers? . . .

If we are paying attention to our souls, far be it from us to use "much speaking" in prayer, or to refrain from prolonged prayer. To talk a lot in prayer is to cheapen and overuse our words while asking for something necessary. But to prolong prayer is to have our hearts throb with continual pious emotions toward the One we pray to. In most cases, prayer consists more of groaning than of speaking, of tears rather than words. He sees our tears. Our groaning isn't hidden from Him. For He made everything by a word and doesn't need human words.

> But when ye pray, use not vain repetitions, as the heathen do: for they think that they shall be heard for their much speaking.
>
> —Matthew 6:7

> "In most cases, prayer consists more of groaning than of speaking, of tears rather than words."

Great and Wonderful Love
Clement of Rome

Herein is love, not that we loved God, but that he loved us, and sent his Son to be the propitiation for our sins. Beloved, if God so loved us, we ought also to love one another.
—1 John 4:10-11

Who can describe the blessed bond of the love of God? What man is able to tell the excellence of its beauty as it ought to be told? The height to which love exalts is unspeakable. Love unites us to God. Love covers a multitude of sins. Love bears all things—is long-suffering in all things. There is nothing cruel, nothing arrogant in love. Love allows no divisions; love gives rise to no rebellions; love does all things in harmony. By love have all the elect of God been made perfect; without love nothing is well-pleasing to God. In love has the Lord taken us to Himself. On account of His love for us, Jesus Christ our Lord gave His blood for us by the will of God, His flesh for our flesh, and His soul for our souls.

You see, beloved, how great and wonderful a thing love is and that it is impossible to adequately declare its perfection. Who is fit to be found in it except those whom God has graciously privileged? Let us pray, therefore, and implore of His mercy, that we may live blameless in love, free from all human partialities for one above another.

> "By love have all the elect of God been made perfect; without love nothing is well-pleasing to God."

Who Is Good?
Gregory of Nyssa

The Lord, who sees the heart, discerned the young man's motives when he approached Him with a request. The youth did so, intently fixing his soul on God, but sought the *man*, calling Jesus "Good Master." He hoped to gain some knowledge about how to slow the approach of death. With good reason, Christ answered him in the same way He was addressed. For just as the question wasn't addressed to God the Word, the answer was given by the humanity of Christ. As a result, a double lesson was impressed on the youth through one answer. Christ taught him the duty of revering God, not by flattering speeches, but by his life. He taught the youth to honor God by keeping the commandments and buying eternal life by giving up every possession. But He also taught that humanity, having sunk in depravity through sin, is excluded from the title of "good." He said, "Why callest thou Me good?" The word "Me" implies the human nature that encompassed Him. But by attributing goodness to God, He expressly declared Himself to be good. For the Gospel says He is God.

And he said unto him, Why callest thou me good? there is none good but one, that is, God: but if thou wilt enter into life, keep the commandments. Jesus said unto him, If thou wilt be perfect, go and sell that thou hast, and give to the poor, and thou shalt have treasure in heaven: and come and follow me.

—Matthew 19:17-21

Jesus' Crown
Tertullian

And the soldiers platted a crown of thorns, and put it on his head, and they put on him a purple robe, And said, Hail, King of the Jews! and they smote him with their hands.

—John 19:2-3

What sort of garland did Christ Jesus . . . submit to on behalf of humanity? One made of thorns and thistles—a symbol of our sins, produced by the soil of the flesh. However, the power of the cross removed these thorns, blunting death's every sting in the Lord's enduring head. Yes, even beyond this symbol, contempt, shame, disgrace, and fierce cruelty disfigured and lacerated the Lord's temples. This was so that now you might be crowned with laurel, myrtle, olive, and any famous branch—with roses too—and both kinds of lily, violets of all sorts, and perhaps with gems and gold—garlands that will rival even the crown Christ obtained afterwards. For after the gall, He tasted the honeycomb. He was not greeted in heaven as the King of Glory until He had been condemned to the cross as King of the Jews. The Father first made Him a little lower than the angels for a time and then crowned Him with glory and honor. If you owe your own head to Him for these things, repay it if you can; He presented His for yours. Otherwise, don't be crowned with flowers at all; if you can't be crowned with thorns, you may never be crowned with flowers.

> "Jesus was not greeted in heaven as the King of Glory until He had been condemned to the cross as King of the Jews."

Thy Will
Cyprian

We say, "Thy will be done, as in heaven so in earth" not so that God will do what He wills, but that we may be able to do what God wills. For who resists God and prevents Him from doing what He wills? But since the devil hinders us from always obeying God's will with our thoughts and actions, we pray and ask that God's will may be done in us. . . . Now, if the Son was obedient to do His Father's will, the servant should be much more obedient to his Master's will! . . . This is the will of God which Christ both did and taught: humility in conversation; steadfastness in faith; modesty in words; justice in deeds; mercy in works; discipline in morals; inability to do a wrong, and ability to bear a wrong done; to keep peace with the brethren; to love God with all our hearts; to love Him as a Father; to fear Him as God; to prefer nothing above Christ (because He did not prefer anything above us); to adhere inseparably to His love; and to stand by His cross bravely and faithfully. When there is any battle against His name and honor, it is His will that we exhibit the consistency of confession; in torture, the confidence with which we do battle; in death, the patience with which we are crowned. This is to do the commandment of God. This is to fulfill the will of the Father.

I delight to do thy will, O my God: yea, thy law is within my heart.
—Psalm 40:8

> "If the Son was obedient to do His Father's will, the servant should be much more obedient to his Master's will!"

Hearts of Stone
Origen

Then said Jesus to those Jews which believed on him, If ye continue in my word, then are ye my disciples indeed.

—John 8:31

Consider the ignorant person who is feeling his disgrace. Either driven by someone's encouragement or moved by a desire to imitate other wise men, he hands himself over to someone he is sure will carefully train and competently instruct him. Then if he who had hardened himself in ignorance should faithfully surrender himself to a master and promise to obey him in everything, the master, seeing his determination, would promise to take away all ignorance and to fill his mind with knowledge. The master will not attempt this if the student refuses or resists his efforts, but only if he sacrifices and binds himself to complete obedience. In the same way, the Word of God promises to take away the stony heart of those who draw near to Him. God will not do this for those who don't listen to His word, but only for those who receive His commands.

> "The Word of God promises to take away the stony heart of those who draw near to Him."

Hope for the Future

Cyprian

Those who fight for God, having been placed in the heavenly army, should hope for the things prophesied. Since the Lord told us these things would come, we won't tremble at the storms and whirlwinds of the world and will have no cause for alarm. The encouragement of His foreseeing Word instructs, teaches, prepares, and strengthens the people of His church to endure the things to come. He predicted that wars, famines, earthquakes, and plagues would arise everywhere. For fear that an unexpected and new evil should shake us, He previously warned us that suffering would increase more and more in the last times. . . . The kingdom of God, beloved, is almost at hand. The reward of life, the rejoicing of eternal salvation, and the eternal joy and obtaining of Paradise are coming now with the passing away of the world. Already, heavenly things are taking the place of earthly, great things of small, and eternal things of things that fade away. What room is there here for anxiety and concern? Who, in the midst of these things, is trembling and sad except those without hope and faith? For it is those who aren't willing to go to Christ who fear death. It is those who don't believe that they are about to reign with Christ who aren't willing to go to Christ.

But take ye heed: behold, I have foretold you all things.
—Mark 13:23

"Those who fight for God, having been placed in the heavenly army, should hope for the things prophesied."

Divided Hearts
Gregory of Nyssa

Whosoever abideth in him sinneth not: whosoever sinneth hath not seen him, neither known him. Little children, let no man deceive you: he that doeth righteousness is righteous, even as he is righteous.
—1 John 3:6-7

Habit is always hard to resist. It possesses an enormous power of attracting and seducing the soul and of producing a counterfeit image of the good that can lead people into a certain habit and inclination. Nothing is so vile that people can't consider it desirable and praiseworthy once it has become fashionable. . . . For someone who has turned to the world, who feels its anxieties, and who engages his heart in pleasing people can't possibly fulfill the Master's first and greatest commandment. "Thou shall love God with all thy heart and with all thy strength." How can people fulfill that when they divide their heart between God and the world, when they exhaust the love they owe only to Him by using it for human affections? . . . If battling against pleasure seems tiring, have courage. This habit will produce a feeling of pleasure (even in the most irritating things) through the very effort of perseverance. And that pleasure will be the most noble and pure. This is a pleasure that the intelligent can embrace. Then no preoccupation with base trivialities will alienate them from the truly great things that "surpass all understanding."

Crucified with Christ
Origen

Notice that at the beginning it is said, "Whosoever will," but afterwards, "Whoso shall lose." If, then, we wish to be saved, let us lose our lives to the world as those who have been crucified with Christ. For our glory is in the cross of our Lord Jesus Christ. The world is to be crucified, to us and we to the world, so that we may gain the salvation of our lives. This salvation begins when we lose our lives for the sake of the Word. But if we think that the salvation of our life (or the salvation in God and joy of being with Him) is a blessed thing, then any loss of life should be a good thing. For the sake of Christ, death must precede the blessed salvation. Therefore, it seems to me that according to the analogy of self-denial, we should all lose our own lives. Let us all lose our own sinful lives, so that having lost what is sinful, we can receive that which is saved by righteousness. In no way will we profit from gaining the whole world. . . . But when we have the choice, it is much better to forfeit the world, and to gain our life by losing it for Christ, than to gain the world by forfeiting our life.

For whosoever will save his life shall lose it: and whosoever will lose his life for my sake shall find it.
—*Matthew 16:25*

"If we think that the salvation of our life is a blessed thing, then any loss of life should be a good thing."

Despise Doubt

Hermas

Therefore I say unto you, What things soever ye desire, when ye pray, believe that ye receive them, and ye shall have them.

—*Mark 11:24*

Those who are perfect in faith ask God for everything, trusting in the Lord. They obtain because they ask without doubting and without being double-minded. For double-minded people, even if they repent, will have difficulty being saved. Cleanse your heart from doubt, therefore, and put on faith because it is strong. Trust God that you will obtain from Him everything that you ask. If at any time after you have asked of the Lord, you are slower in obtaining your request than you expected, don't doubt. . . . Therefore, do not stop making the request of your soul and you will obtain it. But if you become weary and waver in your request, blame yourself and not Him who doesn't give to you. Consider the doubting mind. It is wicked and senseless and turns many away entirely from the faith even though they are very strong. For this doubting is the daughter of the devil, and acts extremely wickedly to the servants of God. Despise doubting, then, and gain mastery over it in everything. Clothe yourself with faith, which is strong and powerful. For faith promises all things and perfects all things, but doubt, having no thorough faith in itself, fails in every work which it undertakes.

> "Doubt, having no thorough faith in itself, fails in every work which it undertakes."

Noticed by God
Chrysostom

We shouldn't think of anything as our own. For even faith itself isn't our own, but more God's than ours. "For by grace are ye saved through faith; and this," said he, "not of ourselves; it is the gift of God." So then, we shouldn't think great things about ourselves or be puffed up, because we are human, dust and ashes, smoke and shadow. Why do you think great things about yourself? . . . Nothing is like humility. It is the mother, root, nurse, foundation, and bond of all good things. Without it we are detestable, cursed, and polluted. Say someone raises the dead, heals the lame, and cleanses the lepers, but acts with proud self-satisfaction. There can be nothing more cursed, nothing more impious, nothing more detestable than this. Don't attribute anything to yourself. Are you eloquent and do you have the grace of teaching? Don't think you should have more than other people as a result. But you especially should be humbled, because you have been trusted with more abundant gifts. For the one who was forgiven more will love more. If so, then you should also be humbled because God, having passed by others, noticed you. Be afraid because of this, for it will destroy you if you aren't careful.

John answered and said, A man can receive nothing, except it be given him from heaven.
—John 3:27

> "Nothing is like humility. It is the mother, root, nurse, foundation, and bond of all good things."

Our Cross
John Cassian

Knowing this, that our old man is crucified with him, that the body of sin might be destroyed, that henceforth we should not serve sin.

—Romans 6:6

The fear of the Lord is our cross. Those who are crucified no longer have the power to move or turn their limbs in any direction they please. Similarly, we shouldn't fix our wishes and desires on what pleases and delights us now, but according to how the Law of the Lord constrains us. Those who are fastened to the wood of the cross no longer consider present things or think about their preferences. They aren't distracted by anxiety and care for tomorrow and aren't disturbed by the desire for any possession. They aren't inflamed by pride, strife, or rivalry. They don't grieve during present pain and don't remember past injuries. For while they are still breathing in the body, they consider themselves dead to every earthly thing. Instead, they send the thoughts of their heart ahead to where they know they will shortly follow. So when we are crucified by fear of the Lord, we should definitely be dead to all these things. That is, we shouldn't only die to wickedness, but also to every earthly thing. We should fix the eye of our minds onto the place we constantly hope to reach. For in this way we can destroy all our desires and fleshly affections.

> "When we are crucified by fear of the Lord, we shouldn't only die to wickedness, but also to every earthly thing."

The Cause of Fear
Chrysostom

Christ sleeps. If He had been awake when the storm came on, either the disciples wouldn't have been afraid and wouldn't have sought His help, or else they wouldn't have thought He could do anything about it. Therefore, He sleeps. He makes them nervous and gives them a clearer perception of what was happening. People don't look at what happens to others in the same way as what happens to themselves. So when the disciples saw others benefiting and not themselves, they became apathetic. Because they couldn't see or enjoy their own blessings from Him, Christ allowed the storm. Then, by their deliverance from it, they could gain a better perception of their benefits. Christ doesn't do this in the presence of the crowd—they might be condemned as having little faith. Instead, He takes them aside, corrects them in front of stormy waters, and ends the storms raging in their souls. Christ rebukes His disciples, and says, "Why are ye fearful, O ye of little faith?" He teaches them that fear isn't caused by approaching trials, but by weakness of the mind.

And when he was entered into a ship, his disciples followed him. And, behold, there arose a great tempest in the sea, insomuch that the ship was covered with the waves: but he was asleep.
—*Matthew 8:23-24*

> "Fear isn't caused by approaching trials, but by weakness of the mind."

The Mind's Judgment
Basil

But let him that glorieth glory in this, that he understandeth and knoweth me, that I am the LORD which exercise lovingkindness, judgment, and righteousness, in the earth: for in these things I delight, saith the LORD.
—Jeremiah 9:24

> "The primary function of our minds is to know God, as much as the very small can know the infinitely great."

The primary function of our minds is to know God, as much as the very small can know the infinitely great. When our eyes first perceive visible objects, all visible objects aren't brought into sight at once. The hemisphere of heaven isn't seen with one glance. However, we are surrounded by the appearance of something, in reality, that is many things. Most, if not all of the things in it, are unperceived: the nature of the stars, their greatness, distances, movements, associations, size and other conditions, as well as the actual essence of the sky. . . . Nevertheless, no one would suggest that the heavens are invisible because of what is unknown. It is visible on account of our limited perception of it. This is the same with God. If demons have hurt the mind, it will be guilty of idolatry or will be perverted to some other form of wickedness. But if it has yielded itself to the Spirit's help, it will understand the truth and will know God. However, as the Apostle Paul says, it will know Him in part and more perfectly only in the life to come. For "when that which is perfect is come, then that which is in part shall be done away." The mind's judgment, therefore, is good. It has been given to us for a good purpose—to perceive God.

Shaping Clay

Anonymous

As long as we are on earth, let us practice repentance. We are like clay in the hand of the artist. For potters will reshape a vessel they have made if it becomes distorted or breaks in their hands. But if they have already put it into the furnace, it can never be fixed. In the same way, while we are in this world, we must repent of our fleshly, evil deeds while we have the chance to repent with our whole heart, so that the Lord can save us. For after we have left the world, we won't have any more power to confess or repent. Therefore, beloved, by doing the Father's will, keeping the flesh holy, and observing the Lord's commandments, we will obtain eternal life. For the Lord said in the Gospel of Luke, "If ye have not kept that which was small, who will commit to you the great? For I say unto you, that he that is faithful in that which is least, is faithful also in much." He means this: "Keep the flesh holy and the seal undefiled, that you may receive eternal life."

From that time Jesus began to preach, and to say, Repent: for the kingdom of heaven is at hand.

—Matthew 4:17

> "We must repent of our fleshly, evil deeds while we have the chance to repent with our whole heart, so that the Lord can save us."

Cursed for Jesus

Tertullian

In your patience possess ye your souls.
—Luke 21:19

You wound the violent more by enduring, for they will be beaten by Him for whose sake you endure. If a tongue breaks out in bitter curses or rebukes, remember the saying, "When they curse you, rejoice." The Lord Himself was "cursed" by the law, yet He is the only Blessed One. Therefore, let His servants follow our Lord closely and be cursed patiently so that we too may be blessed. If I strike back with my tongue, how can I be found to have obeyed the Lord? For He said that "a man is defiled, not by the defilements of vessels, but by the things which are sent forth out of his mouth."

In addition, I will touch on the pleasure of patience. Every injury, whether inflicted by tongue or hand, when handled with patience, will have the same fate as a weapon launched against and blunted on an immovably hard rock. For it will fall completely and lie there useless and fruitless. Therefore, when you have upset their enjoyment by not being pained, they are pained by the loss of enjoyment. Then you not only go away unhurt, which is enough, but gratified by your enemy's disappointment and revenged by his pain. This is the usefulness and the pleasure of patience.

> "If I strike back with my tongue, how can I be found to have obeyed the Lord?"

Good People
Testimonies of the Twelve Patriarchs

The minds of good people aren't empowered by the deceitful spirit of the devil. For the angel of peace guides their souls. They don't gaze passionately on corruptible things or gather riches for their pleasure. They don't delight in pleasure. They don't hurt their neighbors. They don't gorge themselves with food. They don't sin through prideful eyes, for the Lord is their portion. The good mind doesn't accept the glory and dishonor of people and it doesn't deceive, lie, fight, or curse. For the Lord dwells in these people and lights up their souls. They are always joyful towards everyone. The good mind doesn't have two tongues of blessing and cursing, insult and honor, sorrow and joy, quietness and trouble, hypocrisy and truth, or poverty and wealth, but they have one frame of mind toward everyone: pure and uncorrupted. They don't have double sight or double hearing because in everything they do, speak, or see, they know that the Lord is watching their souls. They cleanse their minds so that they won't be condemned by God or other people.

Doth a fountain send forth at the same place sweet water and bitter? Can the fig tree, my brethren, bear olive berries? either a vine, figs? so can no fountain both yield salt water and fresh.
—James 3:11-12

"Those of a good mind have one frame of mind toward everyone: pure and uncorrupted."

By Faith Alone
Gregory of Nyssa

Now faith is the substance of things hoped for, the evidence of things not seen.

—Hebrews 11:1

I boldly affirm that He who is above every name has many names in relation to us. And I receive them according to His various ways of dealing graciously with us. He is called the Light when He disperses the gloom of ignorance. He is the Life when He gives us the blessing of eternal life. He is called the Way when He guides us from error to the truth. Also He is called a "Tower of strength," a "City of encompassing," a Fountain, a Rock, a Vine, a Physician, and the Resurrection. All such terms refer to the various righteous blessings He gave to us. But those who set their sights on things beyond human understanding, who see the incomprehensible, but overlook what is comprehensible, use such titles to explain God. They are not only positive that they see Him, but measure Him whom no one has seen or can see. . . . And it seems fitting to warn young archers not to shoot at an impossible target while faith is available to them. We must warn them to drop their useless efforts to understand the incomprehensible, and not to lose the blessings at hand, which are found by faith alone.

Prayer and Effort

Augustine

Reject those who say we need only our own free will and not prayer to help us keep from sin. Even the Pharisee wasn't blinded by such darkness. For, although he mistakenly thought he only needed his own righteousness (and believed he was saturated with it), nevertheless, he thanked God that he wasn't "like other men, unjust, extortioners, adulterers, or even as the publican; for he fasted twice in the week, he gave tithes of all that he possessed." . . . Even so, God didn't approve him because he didn't ask for additional righteousness, as though he was full of it already. He also arrogantly preferred himself to the tax gatherer who hungered and thirsted for righteousness. So then, what about those who acknowledge they don't have righteousness, but believe they can find it within themselves instead of seeking their Creator, the source of all righteousness?

Yet it isn't a question of prayers alone, as if we don't need to include our willful efforts. For although God is "our Helper," we cannot be helped if we don't make some effort of our own. God doesn't work out our salvation in us as if we are dull stones or creatures without reason or will.

Sow to yourselves in righteousness, reap in mercy; break up your fallow ground: for it is time to seek the LORD, till he come and rain righteousness upon you.

—*Hosea 10:12*

> "Although God is 'our Helper,' we cannot be helped if we don't make some effort of our own."

Seek, Knock, and Ask

Tertullian

If I have believed what I was bound to believe and afterwards think there is something more to consider, I expect something else to be found. However, I shouldn't expect to find something new unless I had not really believed in the first place, although I appeared to, or have stopped believing. If I desert my faith, I then deny it also. No one seeks except the person who never possessed or has lost what he sought. In the Gospel of Luke an old woman lost one of her ten pieces of silver and began looking for it. When she found it, however, she stopped looking. A neighbor had no bread, so he knocked on a door. But as soon as the door opened and he was given bread, he stopped knocking. A widow kept asking to be heard by the judge because she was not admitted. However, when her lawsuit was heard, she stopped asking. So there is a limit to seeking, knocking, and asking. "For to every one that asketh," says Christ, "it shall be given, and to him that knocketh it shall be opened, and by him that seeketh it shall be found."

Foolish are those who always seek because they never find, for they seek where nothing can be found. Foolish are those who always knock because the door never opens, for they knock where there isn't a door to open. Foolish are those who always ask because they won't be heard. They ask of One who does not hear.

> "No man seeks except the person who never possessed or has lost what he sought."

Nothing Lasts
Theodoret

Why do we drink in the instruction of Scriptures as babies drink their mother's milk? So that when trouble falls on us, we can apply the Spirit's teaching to soothe our pain. I know how sad and distressing it is when someone has loved something and is suddenly deprived of it. In a moment, he falls from happiness to misery. But to those who have received good sense and who use discernment, trouble never comes completely unexpected. For nothing human is stable. Nothing is lasting—not beauty, nor wealth, health, dignity, or any of the things most people value. Some people fall from a summit of abundance to the lowest poverty. Some lose their health and struggle with various forms of disease. Some who are proud of their glorious heritage drag the crushing yoke of slavery. Beauty is spoiled by sickness and destroyed by old age. The Supreme Ruler hasn't allowed any of these things to remain. He hopes that those who possess these things will be afraid of change and lower their proud looks. Knowing how all possessions ebb and flow, they might stop putting their confidence in what is short-lived and fleeting and fix their hopes upon the Giver of all good.

For whatsoever things were written aforetime were written for our learning, that we through patience and comfort of the Scriptures might have hope.
—*Romans 15:4*

Everlasting Door

Ambrose

Give unto the LORD the glory due unto his name; worship the LORD in the beauty of holiness.
—Psalm 29:2

Go to those who are everlasting doors. As soon as they see Jesus, they are lifted up. Peter is an "everlasting door," whom the gates of hell can't conquer. James and John, the sons of thunder, are "everlasting doors." For the doors of the church are everlasting. There, the prophet who wants to proclaim Christ's praises says, "That I may tell all thy praises in the gates of the daughter of Sion."

Therefore, the mystery of Christ is great. Even angels stood before it amazed and bewildered. And, as a result, it is your duty to worship Him. Being a servant, you shouldn't demean your Lord. You can't plead ignorance, for He came down so that you could believe. If you don't believe, He hasn't come down for you, hasn't suffered for you. "If I had not come," Scripture says, "and spoken with them, they would have no sin: but now have they no excuse for their sin. He that hateth Me, hateth My Father also." Who, then, hates Christ? Those who dishonor Him— for just as love gives praise, hate withdraws honor. Those who hate, defame; those who love, pay reverence.

> "Who, then, hates Christ? Those who dishonor Him—for just as love gives praise, hate withdraws honor."

Have Pity
Lactantius

It is appropriate for the upright to support the poor and rescue captives, since the unrighteous esteem those who do these things. For it is deserving of the greatest praise for those to confer benefit from whom no one expected such conduct. For those who do good to relatives, neighbors, or friends deserve either no praise or at least no great praise, because they are bound to do it. They would be impious and detestable if they didn't do what both nature and relationship require. And if they do it, they do it not so much for the sake of obtaining glory as of avoiding a reprimand. But those who do it to a stranger and an unknown person are truly worthy of praise, because they were led to do it only by kindness. Justice exists where there is no obligation to be of service. . . . God promises a great reward for mercy: He will pardon all sins. He says, if you hear the prayers of those who appeal to you for help, I will also hear your appeal. If you pity those in distress, I will pity you in your distress. But if you don't regard or assist them, I will have the same mindset against you, and I will judge you by your own laws.

I have shewed you all things, how that so labouring ye ought to support the weak, and to remember the words of the Lord Jesus, how he said, It is more blessed to give than to receive.
—*Acts 20:35*

> "Justice exists where there is no obligation to be of service."

Perfected in Love

Augustine

But I say unto you, Love your enemies, bless them that curse you, do good to them that hate you, and pray for them which despitefully use you, and persecute you.

—Matthew 5:44

What is perfection of love? To love even our enemies and to love them so that they might become fellow Christians. For love shouldn't be fleshly. To wish people temporal, physical well-being is good. But when this fails, hope that their souls are safe. Do you wish life for your friend? You do well. Do you rejoice at your enemy's death? You do evil. However, even the life you wish for your friends may not be good for them. And the death of your enemies you rejoice over may have been for the good of them. It is uncertain whether this present life will be profitable or unprofitable for someone, but, without doubt, life with God is profitable. So love your enemies by wishing that they become Christians. Love your enemies so that they might fellowship with you. For Christ loved this way and, while hanging on the cross, said, "Father, forgive them, for they know not what they do." He didn't say, "Father, let them live long. Even though they kill Me, let them live." He was taking eternal death from them by His merciful prayer and by His supreme strength. . . . Therefore, if you have learned to pray for your enemy, you walk in the way of the Lord.

> "What is perfection of love? To love even our enemies and to love them so that they might become fellow Christians."

The Least of These

Chrysostom

If one of you says, "If I was supposed to entertain Paul as a guest, I would do it readily and eagerly," listen! It is in your power to entertain Paul's Master as your guest and you won't. For "he that receiveth one of these least," Christ said, "receiveth Me." The lower your neighbors may be, Christ comes to you through them all the more. For those that receive the great often do it out of vainglory. But those that receive the small do it purely for Christ's sake. It is in your power to entertain even the Father of Christ as your guest and you won't. For, "I was a stranger," He says, "And ye took Me in." And also, "Unto one of the least of these the brethren that believe on Me, ye have done it unto Me." Although they aren't Paul, if they are even the least of believers, Christ comes to you through them. Open your house. Take Him in. "He that receiveth a prophet," He said, "shall receive a prophet's reward." Therefore, those who also receive Christ will receive the reward of those who have Christ as their guest. Don't doubt His words, but believe.

Then shall they also answer him, saying, Lord, when saw we thee an hungred, or athirst, or a stranger, or naked, or sick, or in prison, and did not minister unto thee?
—Matthew 25:44

> "The lower your neighbors may be, Christ comes to you through them all the more."

His Watchful Eyes

Basil

The eyes of the LORD are in every place, beholding the evil and the good.

—Proverbs 15:3

Animals are deprived of reason but still contrive to preserve themselves. For example, a fish knows what kind of food to look for and what to avoid. So, then, what can we say when we are honored with reason, instructed by law, encouraged by the promises, made wise by the Spirit, and still are less reasonable about our own affairs than fish? They know how to provide for the future, but we deny our hope and spend our lives in brutal indulgence. A fish travels the whole length of the sea to find what is good for it, but what about those of us who are constantly idle? . . . Ignorance is no excuse. For there has been implanted in us natural reason. It tells us to identify ourselves with good and to avoid everything that is harmful. . . .

> "A fish travels the whole length of the sea to find what is good for it, but what about those of us who are constantly idle?"

Someone living near the sea said that the sea urchin, a little contemptible creature, often warns sailors of a coming calm or storm. When it sees a disturbance of the winds beforehand, it gets under a large stone, clings to it as if to an anchor, and tosses about in safety. The weight of the stone prevents it from becoming the plaything of the waves. . . . God has seen everything beforehand. He hasn't neglected anything. His eyes, which never sleep, watch over everything. He is present everywhere and gives to each being the means to preserve itself.

Look Ahead

Cyprian

Let all, acknowledging their own sins, put off the behavior of their old self. "For no man who looks back as he putteth his hand to the plough is fit for the kingdom of God." Lot's wife, who defiantly looked back when she was saved, lost the reward of her escape. Don't look to things behind us that the devil calls us back to. Instead, look to things ahead of us that Christ calls us to. Let us lift our eyes up to heaven, lest the earth deceive us with its delights and enticements. Let us pray not only for ourselves, but for all the people of God as the Lord taught us to pray. He calls us to pray for everyone in common prayer and agreement. If the Lord sees us as humble and peaceable, if He sees us joined together, if He sees us as fearful of His anger, if we are corrected by the present trials, then He will keep us safe from the enemy. Discipline comes first, but pardon will follow.

But now, after that ye have known God, or rather are known of God, how turn ye again to the weak and beggarly elements, whereunto ye desire again to be in bondage?

—*Galatians 4:9*

"Let us lift our eyes up to heaven, lest the earth deceive us with its delights and enticements."

Sincere Charity

Leo I

Cast thy bread upon the waters: for thou shalt find it after many days.

—*Ecclesiastes 11:1*

"The value of our charity is determined by the sincerity of our feelings."

We shouldn't be afraid that our worldly resources will decrease while we practice mercy. For Christian poverty is always rich because what it has is more valuable than what it doesn't have. In addition, the poor shouldn't be afraid of working in this world. For the Lord of everything has given them ownership of everything. Therefore, those who do good things must never be afraid lest they lose their power to do good. In the Gospel of Luke, Christ praised the widow's devotion because of her two coins. . . . For the value of our charity is determined by the sincerity of our feelings. And those who show mercy to others won't ever lack mercy for themselves. The widow of Zarephath discovered this. She offered Elijah one day's food during a famine. It was all she had, but she put the prophet's hunger before her own needs and gave up a handful of corn and a little oil with open hands. She didn't lose what she gave in faith, however. For in the jars she emptied by her godly generosity, a new source of abundance sprang up. Her sustenance didn't diminish because of the holy purpose she used it for. This is because she never dreaded being needy.

Sin's Cause
Augustine

There are two causes leading to sin: either we don't know our duty, or we don't perform the duty we know. The former is the sin of ignorance, the latter of weakness. Now, it is our duty to struggle against these things. But certainly we will be beaten in the fight unless God helps us to see our duty and to make our love of righteousness stronger than our love for earthly things. Our eager longing for temporal things and our fear of losing them leads us with open eyes into known sin. Then we aren't only sinners (for we are sinners even when we sin in ignorance), but we are transgressors of the Law. We leave undone what we know we should do and we do what we know we shouldn't do. Therefore, we should not only pray for pardon when we have sinned, saying, "Forgive us our debts, as we forgive our debtors," but we should pray for guidance to keep us from sinning. We should pray, "and lead us not into temptation." As the psalmist says, "The Lord is my light and my salvation." God is my light because He removes my ignorance. He is my salvation because He takes away my weakness.

Let the wicked forsake his way, and the unrighteous man his thoughts: and let him return unto the LORD, and he will have mercy upon him; and to our God, for he will abundantly pardon.
—Isaiah 55:7

"There are two causes leading to sin: either we don't know our duty, or we don't perform the duty we know."

Very God
Ambrose

Then said they unto him, What shall we do, that we might work the works of God? Jesus answered and said unto them, This is the work of God, that ye believe on him whom he hath sent.
—John 6:28-29

This is the foundation of our faith—to know that the Son of God is born. If He isn't born, then He isn't the Son. Neither is it sufficient to call Him Son unless you also distinguish Him as the Only-begotten Son. If He is a creature, He is not God. If He is not God, He is not the Life. If He is not the Life, then He is not the Truth . . . Therefore, faith is profitable when her brow is bright with a beautiful crown of good works. This faith . . . is contained in the following principles, which can't be overthrown. If the Son didn't have an origin, He isn't the Son. If He is a creature, He isn't the Creator. If He was made, He didn't make everything. If He needs to learn, He doesn't have foreknowledge. If He is a receiver, He isn't perfect. If He progresses, He isn't God. If He is unlike the Father, He isn't the Father's image. If He is Son by grace, He isn't one by nature. If He doesn't have a part in the Godhead, He has the capability to sin. "There is none good but God."

> "Faith is profitable when her brow is bright with a beautiful crown of good works."

Rebuke in Love
Augustine

We should rebuke in love—not eagerly hoping to injure the person, but earnestly taking care to improve him. If we have such a mindset, we practice what Christ commanded: "If thy brother shall sin against thee, rebuke him between thee and him alone." Why do you rebuke such people? Because you are grieved that they sinned against you? God forbid. If you do it out of love for yourself, you don't do anything. If you do it out of love for the other person, you act in excellence. Notice what these words say about whom you should love in doing so—yourself or the other person: "If he shall hear thee, thou hast gained thy brother." Do it for other people's sake then, so that you can "gain" them. If by doing so you "gain" them, they would also be lost if you hadn't done it. . . . Therefore, don't let anyone disregard it when he sins against a fellow Christian. For the Apostle Paul said, "But when ye sin so against the brethren, and wound their weak con-science, ye sin against Christ," because we have been all made members of Christ. How can you not sin against Christ if you sin against a member of Christ?

Take heed to your-selves: If thy brother trespass against thee, rebuke him; and if he repent, forgive him.
—Luke 17:3

> "Don't let anyone disregard it when he sins against a fellow Christian."

Single Purpose
Leo I

And fear came upon every soul: and many wonders and signs were done by the apostles.

—Acts 2:43

It is great and very precious in the Lord's sight, beloved, when all of Christ's people work together at the same duties and every rank and degree of both sexes cooperates with the same intent. How wonderful it is when one purpose motivates everyone to stay away from evil and do good. How excellent it is when God is glorified in His followers' work and the Author of godliness is blessed by heartfelt gratitude. The hungry are nourished, the naked are clothed, the sick are visited. People don't seek their own interests but "that which is another's," as long as they make the most of their own means to relieve others' misery. It is easy to find "a cheerful giver" when someone's performance is limited only by his means to give. By the grace of God, "which worketh all in all," we can enjoy all the benefits and the trials of being faithful. For those with different incomes can still think alike. And when people rejoice over other people's generosity, they are put on the same level with those who have a greater capacity to give. In such a community, there isn't disorder or diversity for the members of the whole body agrees on their one purpose—godliness. . . . For the excellence of every person's portion is the glory of the whole body. When we are all led by God's Spirit, we rejoice not only over the things we do on our own but also the things others do.

> "How wonderful it is when one purpose motivates everyone to stay away from evil and do good."

God, the Creator

Irenaeus

Having the truth as our guide and the evidence of God set clearly before us, we should not throw away the firm and true knowledge of God by running after numerous and diverse answers to questions. It is much better for us to investigate the mystery and authority of the living God and increase in the love of Him who has done, and still does, great things for us. We never should fall from the belief that this Being alone is truly God and Father who formed this world, fashioned humans, and gave His own creation the power to increase. He called man upwards from lesser things to those greater ones which are in His own presence just as He brings an infant which has been conceived in the womb into the light of the sun and puts wheat in the barn after He has given it full strength on the stalk. It is one Creator who fashioned the womb and created the sun and one Lord who raised the stalk of corn, increased and multiplied the wheat, and prepared the barn.

Thou, even thou, art LORD alone; thou hast made heaven, the heaven of heavens, with all their host, the earth, and all things that are therein, the seas, and all that is therein, and thou preservest them all; and the host of heaven worshippeth thee.

—*Nehemiah 9:6*

God Requires
Theodoret

And to love him with all the heart, and with all the understanding, and with all the soul, and with all the strength, and to love his neighbour as himself, is more than all whole burnt offerings and sacrifices.

—Mark 12:33

Our Savior, Lawgiver, and Lord was once asked, "What is the first commandment?" His reply was, "Thou shall love the Lord thy God with all thy heart, and with all thy soul, and with all thy mind." And He added, "This is the first commandment: and the second is like unto it, Thou shall love the neighbor as thyself." Then He said, "On these two commandments hang all the Law and the prophets." So then, those who keep these commands according to the Lord's definition plainly fulfill the Law. But those who violate them are guilty of violating the whole Law. So then, let us examine our conscience to see whether or not we have fulfilled the Divine commandments. We keep the first by guarding the faith, abhorring its enemies, and hating those who hate the beloved. We keep the second by caring for our neighbors and observing the laws of friendship in prosperity and misfortunes. On the other hand, those who look out for themselves, who belittle the laws of friendship and who disregard their suffering friends, are considered wicked. The Lord of all requires better things from His disciples.

"Let us examine our accurate conscience to see whether or not we have fulfilled the divine commandments."

Tough Times
Augustine

Not every gracious person is a friend. Neither is every one who strikes you an enemy. Better are the wounds of a friend than the tender kisses of an enemy. It is better to love with severity than to deceive with gentleness. . . . Those who restrain the frenzied and those who stir up the lethargic are both offensive and, in both cases, are motivated by love for the patient. Who can love us more than God does? And yet He not only gives us sweet instruction, but also continually stimulates us by healthy fear. God often adds the sharp medicine of suffering to the soothing remedies He comforts us with. He afflicts even the pious and devout patriarchs with famine, strikes a rebellious nation by even more severe punishments, and refuses to take away the apostle's thorn in the flesh (although asked to remove it three times) so that He may perfect His strength in weakness. Let us, by all means, love even our enemies, for this is right. God commands us to do so in order that we may be children of our heavenly Father "who maketh His sun to rise on the evil and on the good, and sendeth rain on the just and on the unjust." As we praise His gifts, let us also ponder His correction of those whom He loves.

As many as I love, I rebuke and chasten: be zealous therefore, and repent.

—Revelation 3:19

> "God not only gives us sweet instruction, but also continually stimulates us by healthy fear."

Refining Character

Minucius Felix

And he shall sit as a refiner and purifier of silver: and he shall purify the sons of Levi, and purge them as gold and silver, that they may offer unto the LORD an offering in righteousness.
—*Malachi 3:3*

Many of us are considered poor. However, this is not our disgrace but our glory. For as our mind relaxes through luxury, it is strengthened by frugality. Who can be poor who does not lack, who does not crave others' possessions, who is rich toward God? Instead, the poor are those who, although they have much, desire more. . . . We would rather despise riches than possess them. Instead, we desire innocence and ask for patience. We prefer being good above being extravagant. For to feel and suffer pain is not punishment—it is warfare. Stamina is strengthened by disease and misfortune often instructs us in virtue. In addition, both strength of mind and strength of body grow dull without exercise and hard work. . . . God isn't unable to help us, and He doesn't despise us. He is the ruler of all mankind and the lover of His own people. But through suffering He looks into and searches everyone. He weighs the character of every individual during danger, even death. Therefore, as gold is revealed in the fire, so our true selves are revealed in critical moments.

> Who can be poor who does not lack, who does not crave others' possessions, who is rich toward God?

Confess or Deny?
Tertullian

If it is our choice to confess or to deny Christ, why don't we choose the nobler thing and confess Him? If you aren't willing to confess, you aren't willing to suffer. And an unwillingness to confess is to deny. If suffering is completely in God's hands, don't we just leave it up to His will? Why don't we believe that, just as He can bring us back to a trial when we run away, He can also protect us when we don't run away? . . . How strange to try to honor God by fleeing from persecution (for He can bring you back to stand before the judgment seat) but to dishonor Him greatly by losing hope in His power to shield you from danger! Why, when witnessing, don't you be consistent, trust God, and say, "I will do my part. I won't run away. God, if He chooses, will be my Protector"? It is more filling to stay where we are in submission to God's will than to flee at our own will.

For the eyes of the LORD run to and fro throughout the whole earth, to shew himself strong in the behalf of them whose heart is perfect toward him.

—2 Chronicles 16:9

"If it is our choice to confess or to deny Christ, why don't we choose the nobler thing and confess Him?"

Bearing Fruit

Augustine

Herein is my Father glorified, that ye bear much fruit; so shall ye be my disciples.

—John 15:8

If Jesus had merely said, "Let your light so shine before men, that they may see your good works," it would appear that we should seek human praise. But those who are hypocrites, who cherish honors and covet emptiest glory, seek such praise. Scripture says about such people, "If I yet pleased men, I should not be the servant of Christ." . . . Also, "But let every man prove his own work, and then shall he have rejoicing in himself alone, and not in another." Therefore, our Lord didn't merely say, "that they may see your good works." But He added, "and glorify your Father who is in heaven." The mere fact that people please others by their good works doesn't make pleasing others an end in itself. Instead, please others so that God can be glorified in you. And those who offer praise should honor God, not other people. Our Lord demonstrated this when He healed the paralytic. Marveling at His powers, the multitude "feared and glorified God, which had given such power unto men." And Christ's imitator, the apostle Paul, says, "But they had heard only that he which persecuted us in times past now preacheth the faith which once he destroyed; and they glorified God in me."

> "Those who offer praise should honor God, not other people."

Using Gifts
Athanasius

The Lord doesn't allow unthankful people to have peace. "For there is no peace to the wicked, saith the Lord." They work in pain and grief. The Lord didn't even forgive the one owing ten thousand talents. For this man, who had been forgiven of great things, forgot to be kind in little things. Therefore, he paid the penalty even for his previous debt. This was definitely fair. For having experienced kindness himself he should have shown mercy to his fellow servant. Also, the one who received one talent, bound it up in a napkin, and hid it in the earth, was cast out for unthankfulness. . . . Of course, when he was required to deliver that which belonged to him to his master, he should have acknowledged the kindness of the one who gave it to him. He should have acknowledged how valuable the gift was. For the one who gave it wasn't a hard man. If he had been hard, he wouldn't have given the money in the first place. And the gift wasn't useless. He never found fault with it. For the giver was good and the gift was capable of bearing fruit. . . . Therefore, Christ praises those who enlarged their gifts. He said, "Well done, good and faithful servant; thou hast been faithful in a little, I will place thee over much; enter into the joy of thy Lord."

Then his lord, after that he had called him, said unto him, O thou wicked servant, I forgave thee all that debt, because thou desiredst me: Shouldest not thou also have had compassion on thy fellowservant, even as I had pity on thee?
—Matthew 18:32-33

> "The Lord doesn't allow unthankful people to have peace."

The Enemy's Plot

Gregory Nazianzen

Be patient therefore, brethren, unto the coming of the Lord. Behold, the husbandman waiteth for the precious fruit of the earth, and hath long patience for it, until he receive the early and latter rain.

—James 5:7

Will you be afraid of danger in persecution or of losing the most precious thing you have—Christ? . . . Perish the thought. For such fear isn't for the sane and such an argument argues insanity. If I may say so, it is incautious caution, a trick of the evil one! He is darkness and pretends to be light. And when he can't prevail in open war any longer, he lays secret snares. He gives apparently good advice (although it is really evil) to defeat us by a trick and trap us in His plotting. In this instance he is clearly aiming at defeating us. . . . This is his character. He will never cease from duplicity as long as he sees us pressing on towards heaven from which he has fallen. O beloved of God, why do you not recognize the plots of your enemy? For the battle is against him, and is concerned with the most important interests . . . The interests you are fighting for are great and you need great stability. Protect yourself with the shield of faith. The enemy fears you when you fight armed with this weapon. Therefore he wants to strip you of the Gift to make you unarmed and defenseless and defeat you more easily. He attacks every age and every form of life; everyone must resist him.

> "Protect yourself with the shield of faith. The enemy fears you when you fight armed with this weapon."

God's Discipline

Clement of Alexandria

Reproach is like the application of medicines, dissolving the calluses of the passions and purging the impurities of one's wickedness. In addition, it reduces pride and restores the patient to the healthy and true state of humanity. Admonition is the regimen of the diseased soul, prescribing what it must take and forbidding what it must not. And all this can lead to salvation and eternal health. For example, the general of an army, by inflicting offenders with fines, corporal punishments, chains, the most extreme disgrace, and sometimes even death, aims at goodness. He does so for the admonition of the officers under him. In the same way, He who is our great General, the Word, the Commander-in-Chief of the universe, admonishes those who reject the restraints of His law. In so doing, He peacefully brings them to the harmony of citizenship in order to release them from the slavery, error, and captivity of the enemy.

Blessed is the man whom thou chastenest, O LORD, and teachest him out of thy law.
—*Psalm 94:12*

A Fitting Life
Cyprian

That ye may be blameless and harmless, the sons of God, without rebuke, in the midst of a crooked and perverse nation, among whom ye shine as lights in the world.

—*Philippians 2:15*

Peacefulness, humility, and the tranquillity of a life well-lived is fitting for all Christians, according to the word of the Lord. He regards only those who are "poor and of a contrite spirit, and that tremble at" His word. Therefore, it is all the more necessary that you confess Christ and be an example to those who believe, observe, and fulfill this calling. Your character should provoke everyone to imitate your life and conduct. For the Jews were alienated from God because, on account of their behavior, "the name of God is blasphemed among the Gentiles." So also, God holds dear those who conform to the discipline involved in confessing and praising His name. The Lord warned us, "Let your light so shine before men that they may see your good works and glorify your Father which is in heaven." And the apostle Paul says, "Shine as lights in the world." Similarly, Peter urges, "As strangers and pilgrims, abstain from fleshly lusts, which war against the soul, having your conversation honest among the Gentiles; that whereas they speak against you as evil-doers, they may by your good works, which they shall behold, glorify the Lord." Your good works are, indeed, the greatest part of you. They are improved by the honor of your confession itself: guard and preserve your confessions by peaceful and virtuous lives.

> "Your character should provoke everyone to imitate your life and conduct."

Be an Example
Chrysostom

Live in a way that won't blaspheme the name of God. On the one hand, don't care about human reputation. On the other hand, don't give reason for others to speak poorly of you. But be moderate on both issues. As Scripture says, "Among whom ye shine as lights in the world." For Christ left us here to be lights. We are here to teach others and be like leaven in dough. We should go about as angels among people, as adults among children, as spiritual people among those who are natural. In this way they can profit as we become seeds bearing copious fruit. There is no need to speak if we shine through our lives. There is no need for teachers if we only demonstrate through our works. There would be no unbelievers if we were the Christians we should be. Everyone would convert to godliness if we generally kept the commandments of Christ, suffered through insults, allowed others to take advantage of us, blessed when we were cursed and did good when treated poorly. For example, Paul was only one man, yet how many followed him? If we were all like him, how many worlds could we have following us?

Let your light so shine before men, that they may see your good works, and glorify your Father which is in heaven.

—Matthew 5:16

> "If we were all like Paul, how many worlds could we have following us?"

Free from Snares

Cyprian

Not by works of righteousness which we have done, but according to his mercy he saved us, by the washing of regeneration, and renewing of the Holy Ghost.

—Titus 3:5

The one peaceful and trustworthy tranquillity, the one solid, firm, and constant security is this: to withdraw from the currents of a distracting world and to lift your eyes from earth to heaven, anchored in the harbor of salvation. Those who have received the gift of God and whose minds are very near to God can boast that they are completely unconcerned with the human things others elevate. One who is greater than the world can crave nothing, can desire nothing from the world. How stable, how free from all shocks that safeguard is! How heavenly is this protection and its constant blessings—to be freed from the snares of this entangling world, cleansed from earthly muck, and made suitable for the light of eternal life! By being allowed to know and condemn what we were, we are forced to love even more what we will be. However, it isn't necessary to pay with the elaborate effort of bribery or labor to gain dignity or power—these are free gifts from God and accessible to everyone. As the sun naturally shines, as the day gives light, as the fountain flows, as the rain produces moisture, so does the heavenly Spirit ingrain itself into us. When the soul, in its gaze into heaven, has recognized its Author, it rises higher than the sun and far exceeds all earthly power. It begins to be that which it believes itself to be.

"By being allowed to know and condemn what we were, we are forced to love even more what we will be."

Watch Your Words

Jerome

Beware of a blabbing tongue and itching ears. Don't gossip about others or listen to gossips. "Thou sittest," says the psalmist, "and speakest against thy brother; thou slanderest thine own mother's son. These things hast thou done and I kept silence; thou thoughtest wickedly that I was such an one as thyself, but I will reprove thee and set them in order before thine eyes." Keep your tongue from frivolously expressing disapproval and watch over your words. Know this: when you judge others, you are sentencing yourself. For you are also yourself guilty of the things you accuse them of. Isn't it an excuse to say, "If others tell me things, I cannot be rude to them"? For no one wants to talk to an unwilling listener. And an arrow never lodges itself in a stone. Instead, it often recoils on its shooter. Therefore, let the gossip learn not to be so quick to gossip because of your unwillingness to listen. Solomon says, "Meddle not with them that are given to gossip for their calamity shall rise suddenly; and who knoweth the destruction of them both?" That is, the person who knows the destruction of the gossip and of the person who listens to his gossip.

Whoso privily slandereth his neighbour, him will I cut off: him that hath an high look and a proud heart will not I suffer.
—*Psalm 101:5*

> "Keep your tongue from frivolously expressing disapproval and watch over your words."

Standing Firm
Anonymous

But the fruit of the Spirit is love, joy, peace, longsuffering, gentleness, goodness, faith, meekness, temperance: against such there is no law.
—*Galatians 5:22-23*

It is a great reward to have turned a wandering, dying soul to salvation. This is how we can repay the God who created us: by speaking and hearing with faith and love. Therefore, we must abide in our righteous, holy beliefs. Then we can make requests to God who says, "While thou art yet speaking, I will say, Lo, I am here." This is a great promise, for the Lord Himself said He is more ready to give than the asker is to ask. Since you have received this great kindness, don't envy one another's possessions. For as pleasing as these promises are for those that do them, those who are disobedient will be greatly condemned. Therefore, beloved, since we have a great chance to repent, we must turn to the God that called us while we still have the chance to be received by Him.

"God is more ready to give than the asker is to ask."

In Your Midst

Ambrose

Whatever two people have agreed on and asked for on earth will be done for them. For Christ says, "Where two or three are gathered together in My name, there am I in the midst of them." Imagine when an entire congregation is gathered in the name of the Lord . . . So then, make yourselves worthy so that Christ will be in your midst. For where peace is, there Christ is because Christ is Peace. And where righteousness is, Christ is there because Christ is Righteousness. Let Him be in the midst of you, so that you can see Him. Otherwise it will be said to you, "There standeth One in the midst of you, whom ye see not." The Jews didn't see Him whom they didn't believe in. We see Him by our devotion and notice Him by faith. Therefore, let Him stand in your midst. Then the heavens that declare God's glory will be opened to you and you will be able to do His will and work His works. As the heavens opened to Stephen, they will open to those who see Jesus. For Stephen said, "Behold I see the heavens opened and Jesus standing at the right hand of God." Jesus was standing as his advocate. He was standing as though He was anxious to help His athlete Stephen in his battle. He was standing as though He was ready to crown His martyr.

But he, being full of the Holy Ghost, looked up stedfastly into heaven, and saw the glory of God, and Jesus standing on the right hand of God.

—Acts 7:55

> "Let Him be in the midst of you, so that you can see Him."

139

Meaningful Names
Gregory of Nyssa

But glory, honour, and peace, to every man that worketh good, to the Jew first, and also to the Gentile.
—*Romans 2:10*

The weakest things are animals who reproduce in corrupt, damp elements. But the most honorable things are righteousness, holiness, and anything else that pleases God. So then, are flies, midges, and frogs . . . considered "holy" and "righteous" enough to be given honorable names, even though they don't have such high qualities? But up until now, we've never heard anything like this—the weak given dignified titles, or the great and honorable degraded by their names. For Scripture says Noah was a righteous man. Abraham was faithful, Moses meek, Daniel wise, Joseph pure, Job blameless, and David perfect in patience. So, then, were these people given these titles because they lived the contrary? Or consider those who are spoken of unfavorably, such as Nabal the Carmelite, Pharaoh the Egyptian, Abimelech the alien, and all who are mentioned for their evil. Did God honor them with dignified names? No! God judges and distinguishes between His creatures as they naturally and truly are. He doesn't call them names contrary to their natures, but gives them the appropriate titles with clear meanings.

> "God judges and distinguishes between His creatures as they naturally and truly are."

Avoiding Sin

Constitutions of the Holy Apostles

It is very important that the innocent remain innocent. Don't experiment with sin and bring on the trouble, sorrow, and weeping that come with forgiveness. For when you sin, how do you know that you will live long enough to have time to repent? It is uncertain when you will leave this world. And if you die in sin, you won't have another chance to repent. Through David, God says, "In the grave who will confess to Thee?" Therefore, we benefit by doing our duty readily, for then we can wait for our departure to another world without sorrow. Scripture urges us by Solomon, "Prepare thy works against thy exit, and provide all beforehand in the field." Otherwise, you will lack some of the necessary things for your journey. You would then be like the five foolish virgins mentioned in the Gospel of Matthew. Because they didn't have enough oil of piety, the lamps of Divine knowledge were extinguished and they were locked out of the bridal chamber. Therefore, those who care about their souls' security will be careful to stay out of danger by abstaining from sin and reserve the benefits of their former good works for themselves.

For what is your life? It is even a vapour, that appeareth for a little time, and then vanisheth away.
—James 4:14b

> "How do you know that you will live long enough to have time to repent?"

141

The Needy
Chrysostom

We should feel bound to Christ, even above the kingdom, because of His generosity. For servants, when calling their masters for a meal, consider themselves receivers and not givers. But in this case, the contrary is true. It wasn't the servant that called the Lord, but the Lord that first called the servant to His own table. And, still, you don't offer Him a place at the table? He brought you under His own roof first, and you don't take Him in afterwards? He clothed you when you were naked, but even after this, you don't receive Him as a stranger? He first gave you a drink out of His own cup, so won't you give Him so much as cold water? He has made you drink of the Holy Spirit, and do you even soothe His bodily thirst? . . . Don't you consider it a great thing to hold out the cup Christ is to drink from and to put it to His lips? . . . Consider whom you are giving a drink to and tremble. Imagine that you have become a priest of Christ, giving Him with your own hand, not flesh, but bread, and not blood, but a cup of cold water. He clothed you with a robe of salvation. And He clothed you by Himself. At least clothe Him through your service. Christ made you glorious in heaven, so save Him from shivering, nakedness, and shame. . . . Let us be generous to those in need.

> "Christ made you glorious in heaven, so save Him from shivering, nakedness, and shame."

Grafted In

Leo I

The Lord says, "Thou shalt love the Lord thy God, from all thy heart and with all thy mind: and thou shalt love thy neighbour as thyself." Therefore, faithful souls should put on the unfading love of their Author and Ruler. They should submit entirely to His will, for His works and judgments are true and His justice and tender-hearted compassion will never fail. Although we can be worn out by labor and misfortunes, there is good reason for us to endure everything. For we know that struggles will either prove us to be good or make us to be better. But such godly love can't be perfect unless we also love our neighbors. We must not only include those connected to us by friendship or our neighborhood, but must include everyone. For we have a common nature with every person, whether they be enemies or allies, slaves or free. . . . But the extent of Christian grace gives us even a greater reason to love our neighbor. This grace, which reaches every part of the whole world, doesn't look down on anyone. It teaches us not to neglect anyone. So He rightly commands us to love our enemies and to pray to Him for our persecutors. By grafting shoots of wild olive trees from every nation daily onto the holy branches of His own olive tree, Christ makes people reconciled instead of enemies, adopted children instead of strangers, righteous instead of ungodly.

But I say unto you, Love your enemies, bless them that curse you, do good to them that hate you, and pray for them which despitefully use you, and persecute you.
—Matthew 5:44

> "We know that struggles will either prove us to be good or make us to be better."

Run Swiftly
Gregory Nazianzen

My son, walk not thou in the way with them; refrain thy foot from their path: For their feet run to evil, and make haste to shed blood.

—Proverbs 1:15-16

Take my advice, my friend, and be slow to do evil, but swiftly run toward your salvation. For readiness to do evil and tardiness in doing good are equally bad. If you are invited to a revelry, don't be quick to go. If you are tempted to backslide, leap away. If a group of evildoers says to you, "Come with us, share our bloodguiltiness, let us hide in the earth a righteous man unjustly," don't even listen to them. Then you will benefit greatly in two ways: you will make the other people realize their sin, and you will save yourself from keeping evil company. David said to you, "Come and let us rejoice in the Lord," and a prophet said, "Come and let us ascend into the Mountain of the Lord." Our Savior Himself said, "Come unto me all ye that labour and are heavy laden, and I will give you rest." Don't resist them and don't delay. Instead, be like Peter and John, and hurry to the tomb and the Resurrection.

> "Readiness to do evil and tardiness in doing good are equally bad."

Spotless
Chyrosostom

How can the body become a sacrifice? If you don't let your eye look at anything evil, it has become a sacrifice. Don't let your tongue say anything filthy, and it has become an offering. By not letting your hand do anything lawless, it has become a burnt offering. . . . For a sacrifice can't be unclean. Sacrifice is a first-fruit of all other actions. So then, let us give the first-fruit of our hands, feet, mouth, and all other parts to God. Such a sacrifice is well pleasing. Those from the Jews, however, were unclean. "Their sacrifices," it says, "are unto them as the bread of mourning." But ours are not. They presented a dead sacrifice. But by subduing our bodies we present a living sacrifice and are able to live ourselves. . . . For He doesn't say to offer our bodies as a sacrifice, but to "present" them. It is though He said not to have any interest in them ever again. . . . He also shows something else through this: we must make our bodies acceptable if we intend to present them. For we aren't presenting them to any mortal being but to God, the King of the universe. Since, then, it is to be presented and is a sacrifice, clean it from every spot. For if it has a spot, it won't be a sacrifice any longer.

I beseech you therefore, brethren, by the mercies of God, that ye present your bodies a living sacrifice, holy, acceptable unto God, which is your reasonable service.
—Romans 12:1

> "Let us give the first-fruit of our hands, feet, mouth, and all other parts to God. Such a sacrifice is well pleasing."

Seeing the Father
Augustine

No man hath seen God at any time. If we love one another, God dwelleth in us, and his love is perfected in us.
—1 John 4:12

God is invisible. He can't be seen with eyes but with the heart. If we want to see the sun, we should purge the physical eye. In the same way, if we want to see God, we must purify the eye that we see God with. Where is this eye? Listen to the Gospel of Matthew: "Blessed are the pure in heart, for they shall see God." We shouldn't imagine God according to what we want to see. For then we would make God out to be some huge form or an immense expanse. His figure would extend in all directions like the light we see with our eyes. So either we would make God out to be as big as we could imagine or else picture Him as a benevolent old man. Don't imagine any of these things. But imagine this if you want to see God: "God is love." What sort of face does love have? What shape does it take? What stature? What feet or hands? No one can say. And yet it has feet that carry people to church. It has hands that reach out to the poor. It has eyes that show us those in need. For it is said, "Blessed is the man who considereth the needy and the poor." Love also has ears which the Lord spoke about, saying, "He that hath ears to hear let him hear." These aren't separate parts of love, but bring complete understanding and sight to those who have it. Live in love, and love will live in you. Dwell, and you will be dwelt in.

> "Imagine this if you want to see God: 'God is love.'"

Unspeakable and Invisible

Theophilus

The soul of a person is not seen, being invisible to humans, but is observed through the motion of the body. Likewise, God cannot be seen by human eyes, but is known through His providence and works. In the same way, any person who sees a ship on the sea rigged, in sail, and headed for the harbor will conclude that there is a pilot in her who is steering her. So we must perceive that God is the Pilot of the whole universe, even though He is incomprehensible and not visible to the eyes of the flesh. For if a person cannot look at the sun on account of its exceeding heat and power, although it is a very small heavenly body, how can a mortal person face the unspeakable glory of God? Like the pomegranate, contained by its rind, which has many cells and compartments separated by tissues, and many seeds dwelling in it, the whole creation is contained by the Spirit of God. And the containing Spirit is, along with the creation, contained by the hand of God. . . . People believe an earthly king exists, even though he isn't seen by everyone. He is recognized by his laws and ordinances, authorities, forces, and statutes. Are you unwilling to recognize God by His works and mighty deeds?

The heavens declare his righteousness, and all the people see his glory.
—*Psalm 97:6*

A Holy Fear

Hermas

The fear of the LORD is the beginning of knowledge: but fools despise wisdom and instruction.

—Proverbs 1:7

Fear the Lord and keep His commandments. For if you keep the commandments of God, you will be powerful in every thing you do. . . . This is the fear that is necessary to be saved. But do not fear the devil. By fearing the Lord, you will have dominion over him, for he has no power. Satan shouldn't be an object of fear for any reason, but He in whom there is glorious power is truly to be feared. . . . As you fear the Lord, you will not do the wicked deeds of the devil, but will refrain from them.

Fears are of two kinds. If you do not wish to do that which is evil, fear the Lord, and you will not do it. But if you wish to do that which is good, fear the Lord, and you will do it. Thus, the fear of God is strong, great, and glorious. Fear God and you will live to Him. For as many as fear Him and keep His commandments, they will live to God.

> "Satan shouldn't be an object of fear for any reason."

Persecution Coming

Cyprian

No one is free from the risk of persecution. . . . But how serious it is for Christians who are unwilling to suffer for their own sins when He who had no sin suffered for us! The Son of God suffered in order to make us children of God, but people won't suffer to continue being children of God! If we suffer from the world's hatred, Christ first endured the world's hatred. If we suffer rebukes in this world, if exile or torture, the Maker and Lord of the world experienced harder things than these. He also warns us, "If the world hates you, remember that it hated Me before you. If ye were of the world, the world would love their own: but because ye are not of the world, but I have chosen you out of the world, therefore the world hateth you. Remember the word that I said unto you, 'The servant is not greater than his lord.' If they have persecuted Me, they will also persecute you." Whatever our Lord God taught, He did so that disciples who learn have no excuse not to do what they learn.

Choosing rather to suffer affliction with the people of God, than to enjoy the pleasures of sin for a season.

—Hebrews 11:25

> "How serious it is for Christians who are unwilling to suffer for their own sins when He who had no sin suffered for us!"

God's Omnipotence

Augustine

God is greater than our heart, and knoweth all things.
—1 John 3:18-20

If "we assure our hearts," we must do so "before Him." Because "if our heart thinks ill of us" or accuses us that we aren't doing something with the right attitude, "greater is God than our heart, and knoweth all things." You may hide your heart from people, but try to hide it from God! How can you hide it from Him? For a fearing, confessing sinner said to God, "Whither shall I go from Thy Spirit? and from Thy face whither shall I flee?" He looked for a way to run away from God's judgment, but he couldn't find any escape. For where isn't God present? "If I shall ascend," he said, "into heaven, Thou art there: if I shall descend into hell, Thou art there." So where will you go? Will you listen to this advice? If you are going to run from Him, run to Him. Run to Him by confessing, not from Him by hiding. . . . So say to Him, "Thou art my place to flee unto," and be nourished by His love that leads to life. Let your conscience prove to you that your love is from God. And if it is from God, don't desire to display it to people. For human praises can't lift you to heaven, nor can their condemnations bring you down from there. Let Him who crowns you see. Let Him who judges and rewards you be your witness.

> "Run to God by confessing, not from Him by hiding."

Pleasure's Reward

Lactantius

Those who are anxious for the truth and don't want to deceive themselves must lay aside hurtful and detrimental pleasures which bind the mind to the body. . . . True things they must prefer to the false, eternal things to short-term things, useful things to those that are pleasant. Don't let anything be pleasing to the sight but those things that are done with piety and righteousness. Don't let anything be agreeable to the hearing but that which nourishes the soul and makes you a better person. The sense of hearing especially shouldn't be distorted into wickedness, since it is given for us to gain the knowledge of God. Therefore, if it is pleasurable to hear melodies and songs, let it be pleasant to sing and hear the praises of God. This is true pleasure, the attendant and companion of moral excellence. It isn't frail and brief like the things those who are slaves to the body desire, but lasting and providing uninterrupted delight. If people pass its limits and seek nothing from pleasure but pleasure itself, they plan their own deaths. . . . For those who choose temporal things will go without things eternal. Those who prefer earthly things will not have heavenly things.

Ye have lived in pleasure on the earth, and been wanton; ye have nourished your hearts, as in a day of slaughter.
—James 5:5

> "If people seek nothing from pleasure but pleasure itself, they plan their own deaths."

Winds of Heresy
Tertullian

For there are many unruly and vain talkers and deceivers, specially they of the circumcision: Whose mouths must be stopped.

—Titus 1:10-11a

Let us keep in mind the sayings of the Lord and the letters of the apostles. They have both told us beforehand that there will be heresies, and in anticipation have given us warnings to avoid them. Since we aren't surprised that they exist, we shouldn't doubt that they are capable of doing shameful things. The Lord teaches us that many "ravening wolves shall come in sheep's clothing." Now, what is this sheep's clothing but the external surface of a profession for Christ? Who are the ravening wolves but deceitful spirits lurking within the church to waste the flock of Christ? Who are the false prophets but deceptive predictors of the future? Who are the false apostles but the preachers of a false gospel? Who also are the Antichrists, both now and forever, but those who rebel against Christ? Heresies today won't tear apart the church by their perversion of doctrine any less than the Antichrist will persecute her by his cruel attacks (except persecution makes martyrs, but heresy only apostates). . . . For the Apostle Paul says, "Prove all things; hold fast that which is good." He considers heretics "not approved" and urges people to turn away from them.

Living Sacrifices

Augustine

This is true sacrifice: every work that unites us in holy fellowship to God performed for His supreme good. For He alone can bless us in the end. Therefore, even our merciful acts aren't sacrifices if they aren't done for God's sake. For sacrifice is a Divine thing even though we make or offer it. Those who have vowed themselves to God and are consecrated in His name are sacrifices in that they die to the world in order to live for God. . . . Encouraging us to make this sacrifice, the apostle says, "I beseech you, therefore, brethren, by the mercy of God, that ye present your bodies a living sacrifice, holy, acceptable to God, which is your reasonable service." When the soul uses the body as a servant or instrument, it is a sacrifice if used rightly for God. But the soul itself becomes much more of a sacrifice when it offers itself to God. It is inflamed by the fire of His love in order that it can receive His beauty, become pleasing to Him, lose the shape of earthly desires, and be remolded into permanent loveliness.

The gold for things of gold, and the silver for things of silver, and for all manner of work to be made by the hands of artificers. And who then is willing to consecrate his service this day unto the LORD?
—1 Chronicles 29:5

> "Those who have vowed themselves to God and are consecrated in His name are sacrifices in that they die to the world in order to live for God."

Gentle Rebukes
Chrysostom

Preach the word; be instant in season, out of season; reprove, rebuke, exhort with all longsuffering and doctrine.

—2 Timothy 4:2

Those who are rebuked must not become angry, for we are all human and have faults. Those who rebuke must not rejoice over the person and make a scene, but do it privately and with gentleness. Those who rebuke need to be very gentle, in order to persuade them to bear the cut. Don't you see how gently surgeons treat their patients when they must burn and cut them? Those who rebuke must act this way even more. For rebukes are even sharper than fire and knifes. They make people react. As a result, surgeons take great care to make the patients bear the cutting quietly. They cut as tenderly as possible, even giving in a little, and giving time for the patient to take a breath. So should we offer rebukes, so that the rebuked won't run away. . . . For those also who are cut by the surgeons wail against those who are cutting them. The surgeons, however, ignore these things and consider only the health of the patients. We should also do all these things so that our rebukes may be effective. We must bear everything and look to the reward ahead. "Bear ye one another's burdens," Paul said, "and so fulfill the law of Christ." So then, both rebuking and bearing with one another, we will be able to fulfill the call to edify one another.

> "Rebukes are even sharper than fire and knifes. They make people react."

True Harmony
Clement of Rome

Let us consider those who serve under our generals and the order, obedience, and submissiveness with which they perform the things commanded them. All are not prefects or commanders of a thousand, or of a hundred, or of fifty, or the like, but each one in his own rank performs the things commanded by the king and the generals. The great cannot exist without the small, nor the small without the great. There is a kind of mixture in all things from which rises mutual advantage. Take our body, for example. The head is nothing without the feet, and the feet are nothing without the head. The very smallest members of our bodies are necessary and useful to the whole body, but all work harmoniously together and are under one common rule for the preservation of the whole body. Let our whole body, then, be preserved in Christ Jesus, and let everyone be subject to his neighbor, according to the special gift bestowed upon him. Let the strong not despise the weak, and let the weak show respect to the strong. Let the rich man provide for the wants of the poor; and let the poor man bless God, because God has given him one to supply his need. Let the wise man display his wisdom, not by words, but through good deeds. Let us consider, then, brethren, of what matter we are made.

Be of the same mind one toward another. Mind not high things, but condescend to men of low estate. Be not wise in your own conceits.

—Romans 12:16

God Revealed
John of Damascus

The secret things belong unto the LORD our God: but those things which are revealed belong unto us and to our children for ever, that we may do all the words of this law.

—Deuteronomy 29:29

No one has seen God at any time. But the Only-begotten Son, who is in the Father's heart, is indescribable and incomprehensible. . . . He didn't leave us in absolute ignorance, however. He implanted evidence of His existence into nature. Creation, its maintenance, and its operation proclaim the majesty of God's nature. Moreover, He disclosed knowledge of Himself to us that was possible for us to understand. First through the Law and the prophets and later by His Only-begotten Son, our Lord, God, and Savior Jesus Christ. Therefore, everything the Law, prophets, apostles and evangelists have given us we receive, know, and honor. We don't seek anything beyond them. For God, being good, is the cause of all good. He isn't subject to envy or any passion. Envy is far removed from the Divine nature, for it is passionless and good. Therefore, knowing everything and providing what is beneficial for each person, God revealed what was profitable for us to know. What we couldn't bear, however, He kept secret. Let us be satisfied with these things. Let us live by them, and not remove eternal boundaries or go beyond divine tradition.

> "Knowing everything and providing what is beneficial for each person, God revealed what was profitable for us to know."

Redeemed with Blood

Ambrose

Don't trust in riches, for such things are left here on earth. Only faith will accompany you. Righteousness will also go with you if faith has led the way. Why do riches entice you? "Ye were not redeemed with gold and silver," possessions, or silk garments, "from your vain conversation, but with the precious blood of Christ." So then, the rich are those who are heirs of God, joint heirs with Christ. . . . Don't reject a poor man. For when Christ was rich, He became poor. He became poor because of you so that, by His poverty, He could make you rich. So then, don't praise yourself as though you were rich. He sent out even His apostles without money and the first of them said: "Silver and gold have I none," but I have faith. I am rich enough in the name of Jesus, "which is above every name.". . . I don't have silver and I don't need any. I don't have gold and I don't desire it. But I have what you rich don't have. I have what even you would consider more valuable and I give it to the poor. I say in the name of Jesus: "Be strengthened, ye weak hands, and ye feeble knees." But if you want to be rich, you must be poor.

Hearken, my beloved brethren, Hath not God chosen the poor of this world rich in faith, and heirs of the kingdom which he hath promised to them that love him?

—James 2:5

Turn to God
Augustine

And I will bring the blind by a way that they knew not; I will lead them in paths that they have not known: I will make darkness light before them, and crooked things straight. These things will I do unto them, and not forsake them.

—Isaiah 42:16

God doesn't help us carry out sin, but without His help, we can't do what is right or fulfill every part of the law of righteousness. Just as light doesn't help us shut or avert our eyes, it helps us to see. In fact, the eye can't see at all unless the light helps it. In the same way, the light of our souls helps our mental sight through His light and we can do good through His righteousness. But if we turn away from Him, it is our own doing. We are then acting according to the wisdom of the flesh and have given in to our fleshly, lawless desires. Therefore, when we turn to God, He helps us; when we turn away from Him, He turns His back on us. Even then, He helps us turn to Him. Certainly, this isn't something the light does for the eyes. Therefore, when He commands, "Turn ye unto Me, and I will turn unto you," what else can we say but, "Help us follow Your commands"?

> "When we turn to God, He helps us. When we turn away from Him, He turns His back on us."

Dangerous Opinions
Origen

A man will abandon other habits (although it may be hard to tear himself from them) more easily than he will surrender his opinions. Even the former aren't easily put aside by those who have become accustomed to them. Houses, cities, villages, and intimate acquaintances are not willingly given up when we favor them. This, therefore, was a reason why many of the Jews at that time disregarded the clear testimony of the prophecies, the miracles Jesus did, and the sufferings it has been said He endured. People who favor their ancestors' and fellow-citizens' most contemptible traditions lay them aside with difficulty. As a result, one can see that human nature is affected.

Can the Ethiopian change his skin, or the leopard his spots? then may ye also do good, that are accustomed to do evil.
—*Jeremiah 13:23*

Reconcile First
John Cassian

And when ye stand praying, forgive, if ye have ought against any: that your Father also which is in heaven may forgive you your trespasses.
—Mark 11:25

The Lord doesn't allow us to offer the spiritual sacrifices of prayer if we are aware of someone's bitterness against us. He said, "If then thou bringest thy gift to the altar and there rememberest that thy brother hath aught against thee, leave there thy gift at the altar and go thy way; first be reconciled to thy brother, and then come and offer thy gift." So then, how can we stay angry with our neighbor, and not only for several days but even until sunset, if we're not even allowed to pray when someone has something against us? For Paul commands us, "Pray without ceasing," and "in every place lifting up holy hands without wrath and disputing." Therefore, we must never pray at all if we treasure such poison in our hearts. Then we will become guilty of disobeying Paul's command to pray everywhere and without ceasing. But if we deceive ourselves and venture to pour out our prayers contrary to His command, we aren't really offering God prayer but a stubborn temper and a rebellious spirit.

> "The Lord doesn't allow us to offer the spiritual sacrifices of prayer if we are aware of someone's bitterness against us."

Knowledge Puffs Up

Irenaeus

It is better and more profitable to belong to the simple and ignorant class, . . . than by imagining ourselves learned and skillful, to be found among those who blaspheme against their own God by making up another god as the Father. Paul exclaimed, "Knowledge puffeth up, but love edifieth." He did not mean to attack a true knowledge of God, for in that case he would have accused himself. He knew that some, puffed up by a false claim to knowledge, fall away from the love of God. They imagine that they are perfect because they propose the idea of an imperfect Creator. . . . Now, there can be no greater conceit than this: that anyone should imagine he is better and more perfect than He who made and fashioned him, gave him the breath of life, and commanded him into existence. It is therefore better that one have no knowledge whatsoever of any reason why a single thing in creation has been made, believe in God, and continue in His love, than to fall away, puffed up through knowledge of this kind, from that love which is the life of man. Instead of searching after no other knowledge than the knowledge of Jesus Christ the Son of God who was crucified for us, such a person falls into impiety by subtle questions and hair-splitting expressions.

And if any man think that he knoweth any thing, he knoweth nothing yet as he ought to know. But if any man love God, the same is known of him.
—1 Corinthians 8:2-3

> "Some, puffed up by a false claim to knowledge, fall away from the love of God."

Disciplined Prayer

Cyprian

Be not rash with thy mouth, and let not thine heart be hasty to utter any thing before God: for God is in heaven, and thou upon earth: therefore let thy words be few.
—Ecclesiastes 5:2

When we pray let our words and requests be disciplined, maintaining quietness and modesty. Let us consider ourselves as standing in God's sight. We must please the divine eyes both with the use of our body and with the tone of our voice. For, as it is characteristic for a shameless person to be noisy with his cries, it is fitting for the modest man to pray with calm requests. Moreover, the Lord told us to pray in secret, which is best suited to faith—in hidden and remote places and in our very bedrooms. Then we can know that God is present everywhere and hears and sees everything. In His abundant majesty, He enters even into hidden and secret places. It is written, "I am a God at hand, and not a God afar off. If a man shall hide himself in secret places, shall I not then see him? Do not I fill heaven and earth?" And again: "The eyes of the Lord are in every place, beholding the evil and the good." When we meet with believers in one place and celebrate God's sacrifice with Christ, His Priest, we should be modest and disciplined. We shouldn't throw about our prayers indiscriminately with untamed voices, nor cast a request to God with overbearing wordiness when it should be mentioned modestly. For God isn't the hearer of the voice, but of the heart.

> "As it is characteristic for a shameless person to be noisy with his cries, it is fitting for the modest man to pray with calm requests."

Bond of Peace
Chrysostom

What is the "unity of Spirit"? In the human body there is a spirit that holds all the different parts together. It is the same here. The Spirit was given to unite those separated by race and manners. For young and old, rich and poor, children and youth, women and men, and every soul becomes more completely one than in the human body. This spiritual relationship is far greater than the other natural one and the perfection of the union is even more complete in its simplicity. How is this unity maintained? "In the bond of peace." . . . This is a glorious bond. Let us bind ourselves to one another and to God with it. For this bond won't bruise us or cramp the hands it binds. It leaves them free and gives them more room to play and greater courage than those who aren't restrained have. The strong will support the weak if they are bound to them. They won't allow the weak to perish. Also, if they are tied to the lazy, the strong will arouse and animate them. For it is said, "Brother helped by brother is as a strong city."

There is one body, and one Spirit, even as ye are called in one hope of your calling.
—Ephesians 4:4

> "Let us bind ourselves to one another and to God with the bond of peace."

Fishing for the Lost

Ephraim Syrus

The Lord didn't hunger for the Pharisees' food, but for the sinful woman's tears. And when He was satisfied and refreshed by the tears He turned and rebuked those who called Him to eat perishable food. He did this to show that He didn't become a guest for food for the body, but to help the soul. For our Lord didn't mingle with gluttons and drunkards for pleasure, as the Pharisee supposed. But He did so in order to mingle His medical teaching with their mortal food. For just as the evil one gave his deadly counsel to Adam and Eve, so through eating, the Lord gave His life-giving counsel to the sons of Adam through eating. For He was the Fisherman who came down to fish for the lost lives. The tax collectors and harlots rushing into self-indulgence and drunkenness ran to spread His nets where they assembled. Then He could rescue these people from food that fattens bodies and bring them fasting that fattens souls.

God Avenges
Lactantius

The most treacherous persecutors, who are disgraced and mocked by the name of God, must not think they will escape with forgiveness, because they have administered God's wrath to us. For those who received power but severely abused it and have arrogantly insulted God by impiously and wickedly trampling His eternal name beneath their feet will be punished with the judgment of God. He promises that He will quickly take revenge on them and exterminate the evil monsters from the earth. But also, although He usually avenges the persecutions of His people in the present world, God commands us to wait patiently for the day of heavenly judgment when He Himself will honor or punish all according to what they deserve. Therefore, don't let sacrilegious people expect that those whom they trample will be unavenged. Those ravenous and hungry wolves who have tormented righteous people . . . will surely meet with their reward. But let us work hard so that people will punish nothing in us but our righteousness. Let us strive with all our might so that we can deserve the avenging of our suffering and a reward at the hands of God.

Thus saith the Lord GOD; Because that Edom hath dealt against the house of Judah by taking vengeance, and hath greatly offended, and revenged himself upon them.
—Ezekiel 25:12

"**God commands us to await patiently for the day of heavenly judgment.**"

Ready to Hear
Chrysostom

Therefore seeing we have this ministry, as we have received mercy, we faint not.
—2 Corinthians 4:1

See how God allows trials, and, by them, stirs up, awakens, and energizes the disciples? So then, we shouldn't sink down under trials because He will "also make the way of escape, that we may be able to bear them." Nothing makes friends as well and holds them as firmly as affliction does. Nothing fastens and compacts the souls of believers as well. Nothing is as timely for us teachers so that the things we say will be heard. For when hearers are in an easy time, they become listless and lazy and seem to be annoyed with the speaker. But when they are in affliction and distress, they long deeply to listen. When a soul is distressed, it looks for comfort everywhere. . . . The afflicted soul doesn't want to be concerned about many things. It only wants peace and stillness. It is content to be done with the present things, even if nothing else follows. . . . Paul says, "Tribulation worketh patience, and patience experience, and experience hope, and hope maketh not ashamed." So then, don't sink in your afflictions, but give thanks in everything so that you may profit from them and please God.

> "The afflicted soul doesn't want to be concerned about many things. It only wants peace and stillness."

Jesus' Humility
Jerome

While the disciples were arguing about who was most important, our Lord, the teacher of humility, took a little child and said: "Except ye be converted and become as little children ye cannot enter the kingdom of heaven." And, lest it appear that He preached more than He practiced, Christ fulfilled His own command. For He washed His disciples' feet. He received the traitor with a kiss. He spoke with the Samaritan woman. He talked about the kingdom of heaven with Mary at His feet. And when He rose again from the dead, He showed Himself to some poor women first. Pride is opposed to humility, and through it Satan lost his high position as an archangel. The Jewish people perished in their pride. For, while they claimed that they deserved the most important seats and greetings in the market place, the Gentiles, who used to be considered "a drop in a bucket," displaced them. Also, it was two poor fishermen, Peter and James, who were sent to refute the sophists and the wise men of the world. As Scripture says: "God resisteth the proud and giveth grace to the humble." Beloved, think what a great sin it must be to have God as its opponent. For in the Gospels, the Pharisee is rejected because of his pride but the publican is accepted because of his humility.

For the day of the LORD of hosts shall be upon every one that is proud and lofty, and upon every one that is lifted up; and he shall be brought low.

—Isaiah 2:12

Die Daily
Athanasius

And I will say to my soul, Soul, thou hast much goods laid up for many years; take thine ease, eat, drink, and be merry. But God said unto him, Thou fool, this night thy soul shall be required of thee: then whose shall those things be, which thou hast provided?
—Luke 12:19-20

Children, let us cling to self-discipline and not be careless. For the Lord is our fellow-worker. As it is written, "to all that choose the good, God worketh with them for good." But to avoid carelessness, we should consider Paul's words, "I die daily." If we also live as though dying daily, we won't sin. This means that, as we rise day by day, we should think that we won't live through the evening. Also, when we are about to lie down to sleep, we should think that we won't wake up. For our life is naturally uncertain, and Providence gives it to us daily. By living our daily lives in this way, we won't fall into sin, lust after anything, cherish wrath against anyone, or heap up earthly treasure. But daily expecting death, we will abandon wealth, forgive everyone for everything, and won't harbor lust for women or any other foul pleasure. But we will turn from it as past and gone, always working and looking forward to the Day of Judgment. For the dread and danger of torment always destroys the ease of pleasure. It lifts up the soul that is likely to fall.

"If we live as though dying daily, we won't sin."

A Thirst for Knowledge
Hilary of Poitiers

O Lord God Almighty, I know that I owe You the devotion of all my words and thoughts as my main duty. The greatest reward of speech You have given me is the opportunity to serve by preaching You and displaying You as You are to a blind and rebellious world. For you are our Father and Father of God the Only-begotten Son. But I am only expressing my own desires. I must also pray for your help and compassion. Then Your Spirit's breath will fill the sails of faith and confession which I have spread out, and a favorable wind will move me forward on my voyage of instruction. We can trust the promise of Christ who said, "Ask, and it shall be given you, seek, and ye shall find, knock, and it shall be opened unto you." In whatever we lack, we will pray for the things we need. We will be untiring and energetic as we study Your prophets and apostles. We will knock to enter every gate of hidden knowledge. But You are the One who answers these prayers, who gives us the things we seek, who opens the door we beat on.

For every one that asketh receiveth; and he that seeketh findeth; and to him that knocketh it shall be opened.
—*Matthew 7:8*

"We will be untiring and energetic as we study Your prophets and apostles."

Allowed by God
Origen

My brethren, count it all joy when ye fall into divers temptations; Knowing this, that the trying of your faith worketh patience.
—James 1:2-3

God is faithful and won't allow us to be tempted beyond what we are able. Notice how the Son of God forced the disciples to enter the boat and cross over to Gennesaret. The boat was stronger than they were and able to get as far as the middle of the sea. Notice how He forced them to endure and struggle with the waves until they became needful of divine assistance—then Jesus came to them. And I would say with confidence that, because of the prayer of Jesus to the Father for the disciples, they suffered nothing when the sea, waves, and hostile winds were fighting against them. The simpler student might be satisfied only with the narrative, but let us remember that if we ever fall into distressful temptations, Jesus has forced us to enter their boat. He wants us to go ahead of Him to the other side. For it is impossible for us to reach the other side unless we have endured the temptations of waves and hostile winds. When many difficulties attack us, and, with a moderate struggle we have swum through them to some extent, let us consider that our boat is in the midst of the sea. It is distressed by waves that want to shipwreck our faith or some other virtues. But when we see the spirit of the evil one striving against us, let us conceive that then the wind is contrary to us.

> "It is impossible for us to reach the other side unless we have endured the temptations of waves and hostile winds."

The Crafty Crab

Basil

Look at the tricks and cunning of weak animals and learn not to imitate those that do wicked. The crab loves the flesh of the oyster which is sheltered by its shell. The shell is a solid refuge that nature has provided for its soft and delicate flesh. Therefore, it is a difficult prey to conquer. . . .

Thanks to the two shells which envelop it and which adapt themselves perfectly to each other, the crab's claws are quite powerless. So what does the crab do? When it sees the clam sheltered from the wind, warming itself with pleasure, and half-opening its shells to the sun, it secretly throws in a pebble. This prevents the shell from closing and the crab takes by cunning what it couldn't take by force. Such is the malice of these animals, even though they are deprived of reason and speech. But you should rival the crab in cunning and productiveness while keeping from hurting your neighbor. This animal is like the one who craftily approaches his brother, takes advantage of his neighbor's misfortunes, and finds his delight in other people's troubles. But don't copy them! Be content with your own lot. For poverty, while having only necessities, is more valuable in the eyes of the wise than only pleasure.

And the soldiers likewise demanded of [John], saying, And what shall we do? And he said unto them, Do violence to no man, neither accuse any falsely; and be content with your wages.
—Luke 3:14

> "You should rival the crab in cunning and productiveness while keeping from hurting your neighbor."

Finding Forgiveness

Augustine

Bless the LORD, O my soul, and forget not all his benefits: Who forgiveth all thine iniquities; who healeth all thy diseases.

—Psalm 103:2-3

"What shall I render unto the Lord," that while I remember these things my soul isn't appalled at them? I will love You, Lord, thank You, and confess my sins to Your name. You have wiped out my wicked and sinful acts. Because of Your grace and mercy, You have melted away my sin as though it were ice. Whatever evils I haven't committed, I attribute to Your grace. For what wouldn't I have committed, by loving sin for sin's sake? Yes, everything that I confess You have pardoned, both those things which I did by my own perverseness, and those which I didn't carry out because of Your guidance. Who would dare to attribute their purity and innocence to their own strength when they consider their own weakness? Why would they love You any less, as if they had less of a need for Your merciful forgiveness given to those who turn to You? For when whoever You call obeys Your voice and despises the things I confess, don't let them despise me. I am sick but was healed by the same Physician that healed them or rather made them better. Because of this let them love You much more. Let them see that You have restored me from such great sin. Let them see themselves as weak and in need of help.

> "Who would dare to attribute their purity and innocence to their own strength when they consider their own weakness?"

Christian Responsibility

Gregory Nazianzen

If the one who loves deserves the most, how can I measure how much you owe me for my love to you? Instead, show respect for yourselves—the image of God committed to your care. Hold tightly to the faith you have received and were brought up in. You are being saved by it. Trust that it will save others (but, be assured, not many can boast of what you can). Realize that piety consists, not in speaking about God often, but in silence for the most part. For the tongue is a dangerous thing if it isn't governed by reason. Believe that listening is always safer than talking, just as learning about God is more pleasant than teaching. Leave the deeper study of these questions to those who are the stewards of the Word. And, for yourselves, worship a little through words, but even more by your actions. Worship more by keeping the Law than by admiring the Lawgiver. Show your love for Him by running from wickedness, pursuing righteousness, living and walking in the Spirit, drawing your knowledge from Him, and building on the foundation of faith. Don't use wood, hay, or stubble. They are weak materials and are easily burnt up when the fire tries our works or destroys them. But use gold, silver, and precious stones, which will remain standing.

Now if any man build upon this foundation gold, silver, precious stones, wood, hay, stubble; Every man's work shall be made manifest: for the day shall declare it, because it shall be revealed by fire; and the fire shall try every man's work of what sort it is.

—1 Corinthians 3:12-13

Reconciliation
Chrysostom

At that time Jesus answered and said, I thank thee, O Father, Lord of heaven and earth, because thou hast hid these things from the wise and prudent, and hast revealed them unto babes.
—Matthew 11:25

Forgive wicked offenses so that you can receive a royal pardon for your own offenses. The greater the wrongs you forgive, the greater the pardon you will receive. Therefore, we have been told to say, "Forgive us, as we forgive." This teaches us that the measure of our forgiveness begins with us. As a result, the degree to which we benefit from the enemy's attacks is proportionate to their severity. So then, let us eagerly seek reconciliation with those who have hurt us, whether or not they were right. . . . Christ tells us to go to those who provoke us. He said, "Forgive your debtors in order that your Father may also forgive your trespasses." Christ didn't offer us a small reward, but an exceedingly great one. So then, reflecting on all of this, considering the reward, and remembering that wiping away sins doesn't take much work and passion, let us forgive those who have wronged us.

> "The greater the wrongs you forgive, the greater the pardon you will receive."

The Hidden Course
Origen

When a field has brought good, rich crops to perfect maturity, no one would logically say that the farmer made those fruits. Everyone would acknowledge that the crops had been produced by God. In the same way, our own perfection isn't brought about by inactivity and idleness, but by some activity on our part. Yet we aren't credited with its perfection. God is. He is the first and primary cause of the work. Take, for example, a ship that has overcome the dangers of the sea through hard working sailors, the aid of navigation, a pilot's zeal and carefulness, favorable breezes, and the careful observation of the signs of the stars. No one in his right mind would attribute the vessel's safety to anything else than the mercy of God when, after being tossed by the waves, and wearied by the billows, it has at last reached the harbor. Not even any of the sailors or the pilot would venture to say, "I have saved the ship," but would refer entirely to the mercy of God. This isn't because these men feel that they haven't contributed skill or labor to save the ship, but because they know that while they did work hard, the vessel's safety was ensured by God. Similarly, in the race of life, we must work diligently and passionately.

Who hath saved us, and called us with an holy calling, not according to our works, but according to his own purpose and grace, which was given us in Christ Jesus before the world began.
—2 Timothy 1:9

Wisdom
Clement of Alexandria

And unto man he said, Behold, the fear of the Lord, that is wisdom; and to depart from evil is understanding.
—Job 28:28

"Be not elated on account of thy wisdom," says Proverbs. "In all thy ways acknowledge her, that she may direct thy ways, and that thy foot may not stumble." By these remarks the author means to show that our actions should be reasonable. In addition, he demonstrates that we should select and possess useful things out of the entire culture. For there are various ways of wisdom that lead directly to the way of truth. Faith is the way of truth. Proverbs says, "Thy foot shall not stumble," referring to anyone who rejects God's guiding power. The author adds, "Be not wise in thine own eyes," referring to irreverent ideas that revolt against God's authority. "But fear God," who alone is powerful. Consequently, we should not oppose God. The verse continues clearly, "the fear of God is departure from evil." It also says, "and depart from all evil." Such is the discipline of wisdom. It causes pain in order to produce understanding and restores peace and eternal life.

"Wisdom causes pain in order to produce understanding and restores peace and eternal life."

Satan's Tricks

Augustine

We must use all our discernment when Satan acts as an angel of light. For by his trickery, he could lead us into harm's way. But while he only deceives our physical senses, he doesn't distort our minds. He can't pervert the pure judgment that enables us to lead a life of faith. Therefore, our religion isn't in danger. If, pretending to be good, he does or says the things fitting for good angels, and we believe he is good, our error won't hurt our Christian faith. But when he leads us onto his own path through these good things that go against his nature, we must be very careful to detect and refuse to follow him. How many people could actually escape from all of the devil's deadly tricks, without God restraining and watching over them? The difficulty of the matter prevents us from trusting in ourselves or in one another. It leads everyone to place their confidence in God alone. Certainly, no pious person can doubt that this is very useful for us.

Be sober, be vigilant; because your adversary the devil, as a roaring lion, walketh about, seeking whom he may devour.
—1 Peter 5:8

> "Satan can't pervert the pure judgment that enables us to live a life of faith."

Marriage
Jerome

But and if thou marry, thou hast not sinned; and if a virgin marry, she hath not sinned. Nevertheless such shall have trouble in the flesh: but I spare you.
—*1 Corinthians 7:28*

What is ordered is also commanded. What is commanded must be done. And that which must be done implies punishment if it isn't done. For it is useless to order someone to do something but leave them free to do it or not do it. If the Lord had commanded virginity, it would have seemed as though He condemned marriage. And that would do away with humanity's seed-plot, from which virginity itself grows. If He had cut off the root, how could He expect fruit? If the foundations weren't laid first, how could He build the structure and put on the roof to cover everyone?

Excavators work hard to remove mountains. The bowels of the earth are pierced in search for gold. And when the tiny particles have been formed into jewelry, first by the furnace's fire and then by the craftsman's hand, the one is not considered blessed who wears the beautiful gold, but the one who separated the gold from the dross. So then, don't marvel if the angelic life of celibacy isn't demanded of us, but merely advised as we face fleshly temptations and evil promptings. For if advice is given, one is free to offer obedience. But if there is a command, a servant is bound to comply.

No Revenge
Augustine

You have heard an insult, like the wind. You are angry, like a wave. When the wind blows, and the wave swells, the ship is then endangered, the heart is in jeopardy, and the heart is tossed back and forth. When you were insulted, you longed for revenge. But if you have been avenged and so rejoice in the person's pain, you have suffered shipwreck. Why is this? Because Christ is asleep in you. What does it mean that Christ is asleep in you? That you have forgotten Christ. Rouse Him then. Call Christ to mind and let Him wake up in you. Pay attention to Him. What do you want? Revenge. Have you forgotten that, when He was being crucified, Christ said, "Father, forgive them, for they know not what they do?" The one who was sleeping in your heart didn't want revenge. Wake Him up then. Remember Him. Remember Him through His word, for He commands us to remember Him. Then if Christ wakes up in you, you will say, "What kind of person am I who wants revenge? Who am I to threaten other people? I might die before I am avenged, . . . therefore, I will restrain my anger and return to a calm heart." For when Christ commanded the sea, peace was restored.

Thou shalt not avenge, nor bear any grudge against the children of thy people, but thou shalt love thy neighbour as thyself: I am the LORD.

—Leviticus 19:18

> "Have you forgotten that Christ said, 'Father, forgive them, for they know not what they do?'"

Watch Out!

Gregory I

He saith unto him the third time, Simon, son of Jonas, lovest thou me? Peter was grieved because he said unto him the third time, Lovest thou me? And he said unto him, Lord, thou knowest all things; thou knowest that I love thee. Jesus saith unto him, Feed my sheep.

—John 21:17

Watch out! The wolf doesn't attack the Lord's flock stealthily at night anymore, but in open daylight. We see him move toward slaughtering the sheep, yet we oppose him without caution and without darts of words. So then, what fruits of a growing flock can we show the Lord if we calmly watch a wild beast mangle those we have been caring for? But we must study to make our hearts passionate by imitating earthly shepherds. They often keep watch through winter nights, nipped by rain and frost, lest even one sheep should perish. And if the prowler does bite one greedily, they busy themselves to save it. They pant with rapid heartbeats, leap to rescue the sheep with loud cries, and are stimulated by the urgency, lest the lord of the flock require what they lost carelessly. Watch then, lest anything perish. And if anything is seized by chance, bring it back to the Lord's flock by cries of godly instruction. Then the Shepherd of shepherds may mercifully approve of us in His judgment for having watched over His flock.

> "The wolf doesn't attack the Lord's flock stealthily at night anymore, but in open daylight."

Abandoning Sin

Clement of Alexandria

People working and toiling by themselves for freedom from passion achieve nothing. But if they show themselves to be very earnest and longing for this, they attain it by the power of God. For God works with willing souls. If they abandon their eagerness, however, the Spirit given by God is restrained. For only one exercising compulsion saves the unwilling. But one showing grace saves the willing. The kingdom of heaven doesn't belong to sleepers and lazy people, "but the violent take it by force." . . . He yields and grants entrance to those He knows persevere vigorously or violently. For God delights in being conquered in such things. On hearing those words, Peter, the chosen, outstanding, and first of the disciples . . . quickly seized and comprehended the saying. And what does he say? "Lo, we have left all and followed Thee." Now if by "all" he means his own property, . . . he forgets that the kingdom of heaven is their compensation. If they throw away the old mental possessions and soul diseases and follow in the Master's footsteps, they are joined to those enrolled in heaven. One truly follows the Savior by aiming at sinlessness and His perfection, adorning and fashioning the soul in front of the mirror of His holiness, and arranging everything to be like Him.

And he said unto them, Verily I say unto you, There is no man that hath left house, or parents, or brethren, or wife, or children, for the kingdom of God's sake, who shall not receive manifold more in this present time, and in the world to come life everlasting.
—Luke 18:29-30

> "One truly follows the Savior by arranging everything to be like Him."

181

Self-inflicted Harm
Chrysostom

And be ye kind one to another, tenderhearted, forgiving one another, even as God for Christ's sake hath forgiven you.
—Ephesians 4:32

God requires two things from us: to condemn ourselves for our sins and to forgive others. The former is for the sake of the latter. For those who consider their own sins are more lenient toward their fellow-servants. It's easier, then, to forgive from the heart and not merely with the lips.

Therefore, don't thrust the sword into yourself by being revengeful. For how does the grief you have been afflicted with compare to the ones you will face by remaining angry and bringing on God's condemnation? If you are careful, and keep yourself under control, the evil will come upon the head of your afflictors. They will suffer harm. But if you continue to be indignant and displeased, then you will suffer harm from yourself. . . . See how much you gain by meekly bearing the spite of your enemies. First and greatest, you gain deliverance from sins. Secondly, strength and patience. Thirdly, gentleness and goodness. For those who don't know how to be angry with their afflictors that grieve them will be much readier to serve those that love them. Fourthly, you will always be free from anger. Nothing can equal this. For those who are free from anger are clearly delivered from discouragement too. They won't spend their lives on useless burdens and sorrows. . . . They will enjoy pleasure and ten thousand blessings.

> "Those who are free from anger are clearly delivered from discouragement too."

Seal of
Salvation
Cyril of Jerusalem

Those who think they can test God's grace deceive themselves. They don't know the power of His grace. Keep your soul free from hypocrisy, because He reins and searches hearts. For those who are going to enlist people for war examine the ages and bodies of those taking service. In the same way, the Lord examines the purpose of enlisting souls. He rejects as unfit for His service anyone who has a secret hypocrisy, but He readily gives His grace to those whom He finds to be worthy. He doesn't give holy things to the dogs, but when He recognizes a good conscience, He gives it the seal of salvation. That seal is wonderful. Demons tremble at it and angels recognize it. Some are compelled to run from it while others notice that it is kindred to them. Therefore, those who receive this spiritual, saving seal also need to have a compatible disposition with it. For just as a writing reed or a pen needs someone to use it, grace also needs believing minds.

Even so ye also outwardly appear righteous unto men, but within ye are full of hypocrisy and iniquity. Woe unto you, scribes and Pharisees, hypocrites! because ye build the tombs of the prophets, and garnish the sepulchres of the righteous.
—Matthew 23:28-29

> "Those who think they can test God's grace deceive themselves."

183

Plain Words
Origen

So that thou incline thine ear unto wisdom, and apply thine heart to understanding; If thou seekest her as silver, and searchest for her as for hid treasures; Then shalt thou understand the fear of the LORD, and find the knowledge of God.
—*Proverbs 2:2,4-5*

If a Greek wished to teach people who understood only Egyptian or Syriac, the first thing that he would do is learn their language. He would rather have the Greeks consider him a barbarian by speaking like the Egyptians or Syrians in order to be useful to them, than to remain always Greek and have no means of helping them. In the same way, the Divine nature intended to teach not only those who were learned in the literature of Greece, but also the rest of mankind. Jesus adapted Himself in order to be understood by the simple multitudes whom He addressed. He sought to win their attention by using language familiar to them. This is so that after their first introduction, they might be easily persuaded to strive after an understanding of the deeper truths hidden in Scripture. For even the ordinary reader of Scripture can see that it contains many things too deep to understand at first. But these things are understood by those who devote themselves to carefully studying the divine Word. In proportion to the pains and zeal they spend on its investigation, these things become plain to them.

Store Up Mercy

Chrysostom

Let us stop fighting and pray in a becoming way. We should put on the mildness of angels instead of the demons' brutality. No matter how we've been injured, we must soften our anger by considering our own case and our reward. Let us quiet the storms; we can pass through life calmly. Then, upon our departing, the Lord will treat us as we treated our neighbors. If this is a heavy, terrible thing to us, we must let Him make it light and desirable. What we don't have strength to carry out because of our struggle against sin, let us accomplish by becoming gentle to those who sinned against us. Surely this is not painful or burdensome. But let us, by being kind to our enemies, store up mercy for ourselves. For in this present life everyone will love us, and above all, God will befriend and crown us. He will count us worthy of the good things to come. And we will gain them all.

Be kind and compassionate to one another, forgiving each other, just as in Christ God forgave you.

—*Ephesians 4:32*

> "Let us, by being kind to our enemies, store up mercy for ourselves."

Obtaining Faith

Hilary of Poitiers

Jesus saith unto him, I am the way, the truth, and the life: no man cometh unto the Father, but by me.
—John 14:6

He who is the Way doesn't sidetrack us or lead us into spacious wastelands. He who is the Truth doesn't mock us with lies. He who is the Life doesn't betray us with deathly delusions. Christ chose these winsome names for Himself to indicate His methods for our salvation. As the Way, He will guide us to the Truth. And the Truth will root us in the Life. Therefore, it is vital that we know the mysterious way (which He reveals) of attaining this life. "No man cometh to the Father but through Me." The way to the Father is through the Son. Now we must ask whether the way is by obedience to His teaching or by faith in His Godhead. For it is conceivable that our way to the Father could be by obeying the Son's teaching, rather than by believing that the Father dwells in the Son. Therefore, we must next seek out the true meaning of this instruction. For it isn't by cleaving to a preconceived opinion, but by studying the force of the words, that we can possess this faith.

> "As the Way, He will guide us to the Truth. And the Truth will root us in the Life."

Crucified with Christ

Gregory of Nyssa

If a single sin is so awful that you think it's safer not even to aim for a holy life, how much more awful it is for an entire life to practice sin, and remain absolutely ignorant of the purer way! How can you, in your indulgent life, obey the Crucified? . . . How can you obey Paul when he urges you "to present your body a living sacrifice, holy, acceptable unto God," when you are "conformed to this world," and not transformed by renewing your mind? How can you do this when you aren't "walking" in this "newness of life," but still pursue the routine of "the old man?" . . . Does all this seem insignificant to you—being crucified with Christ, presenting yourself as a sacrifice to God, becoming a priest to the most high God, making yourself worthy for the Almighty to look upon? What greater blessings can we imagine for you, if you make light of the consequences of these things? For the consequence of being crucified with Christ is that we will live with Him, be glorified with Him, and reign with Him. . . . Therefore, we want you also to become crucified with Christ, a holy priest standing before God, and a completely pure offering. Prepare yourself for God's coming by holiness. Then you too will have a pure heart to see God with.

I beseech you therefore, brethren, by the mercies of God, that ye present your bodies a living sacrifice, holy, acceptable unto God, which is your reasonable service. And be not conformed to this world: but be ye transformed by the renewing of your mind, that ye may prove what is that good, and acceptable, and perfect, will of God.

—Romans 12:1-2

The Wolf
Chrysostom

Be sober, be vigilant; because your adversary the devil, as a roaring lion, walketh about, seeking whom he may devour.

—1 Peter 5:8

The devil's attacks are frequent and fierce and he surrounds our salvation on all sides. Therefore, we must watch and be sober. We must fortify ourselves against his assault. For if he gains even a slight advantage, he will enter in easily and introduce all his forces to a great degree. So then, if we care about our salvation at all, we must not allow him to even approach slightly, but must restrain him in important matters beforehand. It would be a horrible mistake if we didn't defend our salvation as eagerly as he seeks to destroy our souls. I say this because I am afraid that the wolf might be standing in the flock even now unseen. He preys on the sheep who are carelessly led away from the flock and from instruction by his craftiness. If such wounds were sensible, or the body had received the blows, we could easily discern his plots. But since the soul is what receives the wounds and is invisible, we all need to watch carefully. For no one knows a person's heart as well as that person's own spirit. For the Word is spoken to everyone and is offered as a general remedy to anyone who needs it. But each individual hearer must accept the remedy that is appropriate for his own ailments.

> **"I am afraid that the wolf might be standing in the flock even now unseen."**

Perfect Holiness
Augustine

We are renewed day by day by making progress in our righteousness and true holiness through the knowledge of God. For those who do so transfer their love from temporal things to eternal things, from visible things to invisible things, from fleshly things to spiritual things. . . . They do this in proportion to their help from God. For God said, "Without me ye can do nothing." When the last day of life finds them holding on tightly to their faith in the Mediator through such progress and growth, they will be welcomed by the holy angels. They will be led to God, whom they have worshiped, and will be perfected by Him. As a result, they will receive an immortal body at the end of the world. They won't be led to punishment, but to glory. For our likeness of God will be perfected into His image when our sight of God is perfected. The Apostle Paul speaks of this. He says, "Now we see through a glass, in an enigma, but then face to face." And also: "But we with open face, beholding as in a glass the glory of the Lord, are changed into the same image, from glory to glory, even as by the spirit of the Lord." This is what happens from day to day in those who make good progress.

For which cause we faint not; but though our outward man perish, yet the inward man is renewed day by day.
—2 Corinthians 4:16

> "We are renewed day by day by making progress in our righteousness and true holiness through the knowledge of God."

Heavenly Crowns

Tertullian

Henceforth there is laid up for me a crown of righteousness, which the Lord, the righteous judge, shall give me at that day: and not to me only, but unto all them also that love his appearing.

—2 Timothy 4:8

To those who conquer, God says, "I will give a crown of life." So be faithful to the point of death, and fight the good fight. The apostle Paul felt confident that this crown had been laid up for him. The angel also receives a crown of victory as he rides on a white horse to conquer. Another is adorned with an encircling rainbow of beautiful colors—a heavenly meadow. Similarly, the elders sit around crowned, too, with golden crowns, and the Son of Man glimmers above the clouds. If these things merely appear in the vision of John, what will it really be like when they are actually displayed? Look at the crowns. Inhale the fragrances. Why do you condemn the brow destined for a crown to a little garland or a twisted headband? For Christ Jesus has even made us kings for God, His Father. What do you have in common with a flower that will die? For you have a flower in the Branch of Jesse, Jesus Christ, upon which the Spirit rested—a flower undefiled, unfading, everlasting.

Train to Run
John Cassian

"One who strives in the games is not crowned unless he has contended lawfully." Those who want to conquer their natural, fleshly desires should first try to overcome the evil that resides outside of their nature. If we want to test the force of Paul's saying, we should first learn the laws and discipline of the world's contest. Then, by comparing these things, we will be able to understand what Paul meant to teach those competing in a spiritual contest. . . . People must first be tested carefully and prove that they aren't stained by a bad reputation. Then, by the yoke of slavery, they must be judged worthy to join this training and those who practice it. Thirdly, they must produce sufficient evidence of their ability and prowess. . . . Then, at last, they will be allowed to enter the most distinguished conflict of all the games. They will gain permission to contend for what only victors and those decked out with many crowns and prizes receive. For if we understand this illustration from a worldly perspective, we should know the system and method of our spiritual conflict by comparison as well.

Know ye not that they which run in a race run all, but one receiveth the prize? So run, that ye may obtain.
—1 Corinthians 9:24

"If we want to test the force of Paul's saying, we should first learn the laws and discipline of the world's contest."

Knowledge and Joy
Augustine

And the grace of our Lord was exceeding abundant with faith and love which is in Christ Jesus.
—*1 Timothy 1:14*

You can't blame any human faults on God, for pride causes all human offenses. Their remedy, however, the conviction and removal of sin, comes from heaven. In mercy, God humbles Himself. He descends from above and displays to us pure, visible grace in human form. He becomes a Man of great love for those who join with Him. For even though the Word of God was so united with God as to be called His Son, He was also the Son of Man, and never acted according to His own will. . . . This is an important example for us. It is the divine lesson taught by and learned from the treasures of wisdom and knowledge hidden in Christ. Now we all know, now we don't know; now we rejoice, now we don't rejoice—in order to begin, continue, and complete our good work. Then we will understand that our knowledge and joy aren't a result of our own wills, but are gifts of God. We will be cured of our vanity and understand the spiritual truth that "The Lord will give kindness and sweet grace, and our land shall yield her fruit."

> "In mercy, God humbles Himself. He descends from above and displays to us pure, visible grace in human form."

Chain of Command
Theodoret

Whenever something happens to the helmsman, either the officer in command at the bow or the highest-ranked seaman takes his place. This isn't because they become self-appointed helmsmen, but because they look out for the ship's safety. It is the same in war. When the commander falls, the chief official assumes the command. This isn't an attempt to violently seize power, but because he cares for his men. And Timothy, when sent by Paul, took his place. Therefore, it is righteous to accept the responsibilities of helmsman, captain, or shepherd, and to gladly risk everything for the sake of Christ's sheep, not leaving His creatures abandoned and alone. . . . Let us, then, bravely bear the evils that confront us, for heroes are discovered in war, athletes are crowned in contests, the art of the helmsman is shown in the surge of the sea and in fire. I beg of you, don't think only about yourselves. Rather, consider everyone else. Think about the sick even more than the well. For the apostle Paul commanded, "Comfort the feeble-minded, support the weak." Stretch out your hands to those who are struck down. Tend to their wounds and set them at their post to fight the devil. Nothing will annoy the devil as much as seeing them fighting again.

Feed the flock of God which is among you, taking the oversight thereof, not by constraint, but willingly; not for filthy lucre, but of a ready mind.
—1 Peter 5:2

Double-Minded
Clement of Rome

The all-merciful and giving Father has tenderness toward those that fear Him and kindly and lovingly gives good things to those who come to Him with a trusting mind. Therefore, let us not be double-minded; neither let our souls be proud on account of His exceedingly great and glorious gifts. It is written, "Wretched are they who are of a double mind and of a doubting heart, who say, These things we have heard even in the times of our fathers; but, behold, we have grown old, and none of them has happened unto us." Far be it from us, you foolish ones! Instead, compare yourselves to a tree: for instance, the vine. First of all, it sheds its leaves, then it buds, next it puts forth leaves, and then it flowers; after that comes the sour grape, and then follows the ripened fruit. You see how in a little time the fruit of a tree comes to maturity. So shall God's will be accomplished, soon and suddenly, as the Scripture also bears witness saying, "Speedily will He come, and will not tarry," and "The Lord shall suddenly come to His temple, even the Holy One, for whom ye look."

> "The all-merciful and giving Father lovingly gives good things to those who come to Him with a trusting mind."

Good Counsel
Dionysius of Alexandria

How great is the example You showed of enduring evil! How great, too, is Your model of humility! How is it that the Lord gave us this example to show us that we shouldn't give up counseling our neighbors even if they aren't affected by our words? For incurable wounds are wounds that can't be healed by harsh medications or by more pleasant ones. Similarly, the soul, when it has been taken captive, gives itself up to wickedness, refuses to consider what is profitable for it, and won't accept goodness despite great counsel. As if it is deaf, it won't benefit from any advice. Not that it can't, but it won't. This happened in Judas's case. Nevertheless, Christ, although He knew this beforehand, didn't ever stop doing everything to counsel him. Since we know that Jesus practiced this, we also should never stop striving to set the careless right even if it seems no good comes from our counsel.

But they mocked the messengers of God, and despised his words, and misused his prophets, until the wrath of the LORD arose against his people, till there was no remedy.

—2 Chronicles 36:16

"We shouldn't give up counseling our neighbors even if they aren't affected by our words."

Watchful Prayer
Cyprian

Seek the LORD and his strength, seek his face continually.
—*1 Chronicles 16:11*

Let us pray urgently and groan with continual requests. For not long ago, I was scolded in a vision because we were sleepy in our prayers and didn't pray with watchfulness. Undoubtedly, God, who "rebukes whom He loves," rebukes in order to correct and corrects to preserve. Therefore, let us break away from the bonds of sleep and pray with urgency and watchfulness. As the Apostle Paul commands us, "Continue in prayer, and watch in the same." For the apostles continually prayed day and night. Also, the Lord Jesus Himself, our teacher and example, frequently and watchfully prayed. We read in the Gospel of Luke, "He went out into a mountain to pray, and continued all night in prayer to God." Certainly, what He prayed for He prayed on our behalf since He wasn't a sinner but bore the sins of others. In another place we read, "And the Lord said to Peter, 'Behold, Satan has desired to sift you as wheat: but I have prayed for thee, that thy faith fail not.'" If He labored, watched, and prayed for us and our sins, we should all the more be continually in prayer. First of all, pray and plead with the Lord. Then, through Him, be restored to God the Father!

> "Let us break away from the bonds of sleep and pray with urgency and watchfulness."

Fishing for Compliments
Jerome

Don't fish for compliments, lest you defy God while you are applauded. "If I yet pleased men," Paul says, "I should not be the servant of Christ." He stopped pleasing men when he became Christ's servant. For Christ's soldiers march on through good talk on the right hand and evil talk on the left. No praise excites them. No criticism crushes them. They aren't puffed up by riches, nor do they withdraw because of poverty. They despise both joy and sorrow. The sun doesn't burn them during the day nor the moon by night.

Don't pray on the street corners for fear that human applause would interrupt the straight course of your prayers. Don't flaunt your fringes, wear phylacteries for show, or wrap yourself up in the self-interest of Pharisees. Do you know what kind of dress the Lord requires? Wisdom, justice, self-control, courage. Let these be the four edges of your horizon. Let them be a four-horse team to carry you, Christ's charioteer, to your goal at full speed. No necklace can be more precious than these. No gems can form a brighter galaxy. You are decorated by them, you are fastened in, you are protected on every side. They are your defense as well as your glory. For every gem is turned into a shield.

For they loved the praise of men more than the praise of God.
—John 12:43

> "Christ's soldiers march on through good talk on the right hand and evil talk on the left."

Heavenly Speech
Sulpitius Severus

The words of a wise man's mouth are gracious; but the lips of a fool will swallow up himself.
—Ecclesiastes 10:12

Restrain your tongue from speaking evil. Put the bridle of the law on your mouth so that, if you speak at all, you will speak only when it would be sinful to be silent. Beware lest you say anything others can rightly find fault with. For once a word is spoken, it is as if you threw a stone. Therefore, we must think over our words for a long time before we speak them. The lips that never say what they wish they could recall are blessed. And the speech of a pure mind must also be pure. It must always edify rather than injure the hearers. The Apostle Paul commanded, "Let no corrupt communications proceed out of your mouth, but that which is good for the edification of faith, that it may convey grace to them that hear." The tongue that doesn't form any words but these about Divine things is precious to God. And the mouth which flows continually with heavenly speech is holy. . . . Accustom your tongue to always speak about good people. Use your ears to hear the praises of good people rather than the condemnation of wicked people. Make sure that all your good actions are done for God's sake. For you know that every such deed only brings you as much of a reward as you have done it out of fear and love for Him.

> "The speech of a pure mind must also be pure. It must always edify rather than injure the hearers."

True Righteousness
Lactantius

Although righteousness unites all the virtues, two in particular can never be separated from it—piety and equity. . . . If piety is knowing God and the culmination of knowing God is worshiping Him, then obviously those who don't know God don't know righteousness. For how can we know righteousness if we don't know its source? . . .

Say ye to the righteous, that it shall be well with him: for they shall eat the fruit of their doings.
—Isaiah 3:10

The other part of justice is equity. Obviously I'm not talking about the equity of judging well (although this is praiseworthy), but of making oneself equal to others. . . . For God, who produces and gives breath to people, desired that all should be equally matched. He has placed the same life conditions on everyone; He has given everyone wisdom. No one is prevented from receiving His heavenly benefits. For He gives light, water, food, and the most pleasant rest of sleep to everyone. In the same way, He grants everyone equity and virtue. In His eyes, no one is a slave and no one is a master. For, if we all have the same Father, by an equal right we are all His children. No one is poor in God's sight except the unrighteous. No one is rich except those filled with virtue.

> "No one is poor in God's sight except the unrighteous. No one is rich except those filled with virtue."

Three Temptations

Augustine

Love not the world, neither the things that are in the world. If any man love the world, the love of the Father is not in him. For all that is in the world, the lust of the flesh, and the lust of the eyes, and the pride of life, is not of the Father, but is of the world.

—1 John 2:15-16

Human desires are tempted only by the lust of the flesh, the lust of the eyes, or the pride of life. The devil tempted the Lord by these three. He was tempted by the lust of the flesh when, while hungry from fasting, He was told, "If thou be the Son of God, speak to these stones that they become bread." Listen to His response: "Not by bread alone doth man live, but by every word of God." He was also tempted by the lust of the eyes to perform a miracle, when He was told, "Cast thyself down: for it is written, He shall give his angels charge concerning thee: and in their hands they shall bear thee up, lest at any time thou dash thy foot against a stone." . . . Listen to His answer and, when you face similar temptations, say the same thing: "Get thee behind me, Satan; for it is written, Thou shall not tempt the Lord thy God." . . . How else was the Lord tempted? By the "pride of life." When the devil carried Him up to a high place and said to Him, "All these will I give thee, if thou wilt fall down and worship me." . . . What answer did the Lord teach us to give by His answer to the devil? "It is written, Thou shall worship the Lord thy God, and Him only shall thou serve." Holding these things fast, you won't have the strong desires of the world. Because you won't have the strong desires of the world, the lust of the flesh, the lust of the eyes, and the pride of life won't change you. . . . For if you love the world, you cannot love God.

The Strait Way
Basil

"Here is the strait and narrow way which leadeth unto life." Here are the teachers and prophets "wandering in deserts and in mountains and in dens and caves of the earth." Here are apostles, evangelists, and wanderers' lives remote from cities. I have embraced this with all my heart so that I can win what was promised to Christ's martyrs and all His saints. Then I can truly say, "Because of the words of thy lips I have kept hard ways." . . . Our Savior was crucified for our sakes so that by His death He could give us life, train us, and motivate us to endure. I press on towards Him and to the Father and the Holy Spirit. I work hard to be found faithful and consider myself unworthy of worldly goods. . . . Think about all these things in your heart. Follow them with passion. As you have been commanded, fight for truth to the point of death. For Christ was "obedient" even "unto death." The Apostle Paul says, "Take heed lest there be in any of you an evil heart . . . in departing from the living God. But exhort one another . . . (and edify one another) while it is called to-day." Today means our entire lifetime. If you live like this, beloved, you will save yourself. You will make me glad and you will glorify God forever.

For we which live are alway delivered unto death for Jesus' sake, that the life also of Jesus might be made manifest in our mortal flesh.

—2 Corinthians 4:11

> "As you have been commanded, fight for truth to the point of death."

The Greatest Thing

Gregory Nazianzen

And unto man he said, Behold, the fear of the Lord, that is wisdom; and to depart from evil is understanding.

—Job 28:28

We have received the grace to run from superstitious error, be joined to the truth, serve the living and true God, and rise above creation. . . . Therefore, let us look at and think about God and heavenly things according to the grace given us. We must begin discussing them at a suitable point. And Solomon says this starting point, the beginning of wisdom, is to get wisdom. He tells us that the beginning of wisdom is fear. We must not neglect fear in our contemplation (for unbridled contemplation would, perhaps, push us over a cliff). Instead, we must be grounded, purified, and lightened by fear to be raised up high. For where there is fear there is the keeping of commandments. And where there is keeping of commandments there is purifying of the flesh. . . . Where there is purifying there is illumination. And illumination satisfies the desire of those who long for the greatest things and the Greatest Thing.

> "Let us look at and think about God and heavenly things according to the grace given us."

Good Persecution
Augustine

If suffering persecution was always praiseworthy, the Lord could have said, "Blessed are they which are persecuted," without adding "for righteousness' sake." In addition, if inflicting persecution was always blameworthy, Scripture wouldn't say, "Whoso privily slandereth his neighbour, him will I persecute." Therefore, in some cases, the one who suffers persecution is wrong and the one who inflicts it is right. The truth is, however, that the bad have always persecuted the good, and the good have persecuted the bad. The former harm by their unrighteousness, the latter seek to do good by administrating discipline. The former act with cruelty, the latter with peace. The former are compelled by lust, the latter by love. Those who aim to kill aren't careful about how they inflict wounds, but those who aim to cure are cautious with their dagger. For one seeks to destroy what is healthy, but the other, that which is decaying. . . . The Jews scourged Christ; Christ also scourged the Jews. People handed the apostles over to national powers and the apostles handed people over to the power of Satan. In all these cases, one thing is important to observe: who was on the side of truth, and who on the side of iniquity? Who acted from a desire to hurt, and who from a desire to correct what was wrong?

Every branch in me that beareth not fruit he taketh away: and every branch that beareth fruit, he purgeth it, that it may bring forth more fruit.

—John 15:2

Always Present
Lactantius

Finally, brethren, farewell. Be perfect, be of good comfort, be of one mind, live in peace; and the God of love and peace shall be with you.

—*2 Corinthians 13:11*

> "Justice and kindness are as immortal as the mind and soul, which become like God through good works."

Remove irreverence and disagreements. Calm turbulent and deadly disagreements that invade, divide, and disperse human societies and the divinely unified commonwealth. As far as we can, let us aim at being good and generous. If we have a large supply of wealth and resources, let us not devote it to a single person's pleasure but offer it for the welfare of many. For pleasure is as short-lived as the body it pleases, but justice and kindness are as immortal as the mind and soul, which become like God through good works. Let us worship God not in temples but in our hearts. For all handmade things are destructible. Therefore, let us cleanse this temple. It isn't defiled by smoke or dust, but by evil thoughts. It isn't lit by blazing torches, but by the brightness and light of wisdom. If we believe that God is always present in this temple and knows the secrets of the heart, we will always seek His favor and never fear His anger.

The Beginning of Virtue

Ambrose

We can say the ways of the Lord are the courses of a good life, guided by Christ. He says, "I am the Way, and the Truth, and the Life." The way, then, is the immense power of God. For Christ is our way—and a good way, too. He is the way that has opened the kingdom of heaven to believers. In addition, the Lord's ways are straight. It is written: "Make Thy ways known unto me, O Lord." . . . Christ, then, is the beginning of our righteousness. He is the beginning of purity. He taught maidens not to seek men's embraces, but to serve the Holy Spirit rather than a husband with the purity of their bodies and minds. Christ is the beginning of frugality, for He became poor even though He was rich. Christ is the beginning of patience, for when He was abused verbally, He didn't lash back. When He was struck, He did not strike back. Christ is the beginning of humility, for He took the form of a servant even though He was equal with God the Father in the majesty of His power. Every virtue has its origin in Christ. As a result, we should learn these diverse virtues, for "a Son was given us, whose beginning was upon His shoulder."

Jesus saith unto him, I am the way, the truth, and the life: no man cometh unto the Father, but by me.
—John 14:6

> "Every virtue has its origin in Christ. As a result, we should learn these diverse virtues."

Only One Church

Cyprian

For we being many are one bread, and one body: for we are all partakers of that one bread.

—1 Corinthians 10:17

The church is one but has fruitfully spread out far and wide. In the same way, there are many rays of the sun, but one light. There are many branches of a tree, but one strength from its root. And many streams flow from one spring. So, although multiplicity seems diffused by its abundance, unity is preserved in the source. You may try to separate a ray of the sun from its body of light, but its unity doesn't allow a division of light. Break a branch from a tree and, when broken, it won't be able to bud. Cut off a stream from its source, and the separated portion dries up. So also, the church, shining with the light of the Lord, sheds her rays over the whole world. Yet it is one light that is scattered everywhere. The unity of the body isn't separated. Her fruitful abundance spreads her branches over the whole world. She flows liberally, broadly expanding her rivers. Yet her head is one, her source one. She is one mother that produces much fruit. From her womb we are born, by her milk we are nourished, and by her spirit we are given life.

> "The church, shining with the light of the Lord, sheds her rays over the whole world. Yet it is one light that is scattered everywhere."

Objects of
Enjoyment
Augustine

To enjoy something is to rest with satisfaction in it for its own sake. On the other hand, to use something is to employ whatever means we can to obtain what we desire. . . . Suppose that we were travelers in a foreign country and couldn't live happily away from our native country. Our traveling was miserable and, wanting to end our misery, we decided to go home. We find out, however, that we must use some form of transportation, either by land or water, in order to reach our native country, where we will be happy. The beauty of the land we pass through and the pleasurable motion charms our hearts. Those pleasures turn things we should use into objects of enjoyment and as a result we don't hurry to end our journey. Becoming engrossed in imagined delight, our thoughts are diverted from the delights of home that would *truly* make us happy. This is a picture of our condition in our mortal lives. We have wandered far from God. If we want to return to our Father's home, this world must be used and not enjoyed, so that the invisible things of God may be clearly seen and understood by the things that are made. By means of material and temporary things, we may grasp that which is spiritual and eternal. But the true objects of enjoyment are the Father, Son, and Holy Spirit.

For we know that if our earthly house of this tabernacle were dissolved, we have a building of God, an house not made with hands, eternal in the heavens.

—*2 Corinthians 5:1*

Belong to God
Gregory Nazianzen

For none of us liveth to himself, and no man dieth to himself. For whether we live, we live unto the Lord; and whether we die, we die unto the Lord: whether we live therefore, or die, we are the Lord's.
—Romans 14:7-8

Even fearful things are useful and very valuable to the wise. For although we pray that they wouldn't happen, when they do they instruct us. The afflicted soul, as Peter says, is near to God. Those who escape danger are brought closer to the One who preserved them. So then, don't be frustrated that we had to struggle, but give thanks that we were saved. Don't be one thing to God in the time of peril and another when the danger is over. Instead, resolve to follow the One who preserved you whether you are at home or away, in private life or in public office. Attach yourself to His side and don't think much of earth's little concerns. Let those who come after us, tell our story not only for our glory and the benefit of our soul, but as a very useful lesson to everyone else—that danger is better than security and misfortune is preferable to success. For if we belonged to the world before our fears, after them we belong to God.

> "Those who escape danger are brought closer to the One who preserved them."

Save the Wounded
Cyprian

John demonstrates that Jesus Christ the Lord is our Advocate and the Intercessor for our sins. He says, "My little children, these things write I unto you, that ye sin not. And if any man sin, we have an Advocate with the Father, Jesus Christ the Supporter: and He is the propitiation for our sins." . . . Considering His love and mercy, we shouldn't be bitter, cruel, or inhuman toward believers. Instead, we should mourn with those who mourn, weep with those who weep, and raise them up by the help and comfort of our love as much as we can. We should be neither too rigorous in rejecting their repentance nor too lax in allowing communion. A wounded brother lies in the battlefield stricken by the enemy. There is the devil trying to kill the one he has wounded. Here is Christ encouraging the one He has redeemed not to perish completely. Which one do we assist? On whose side do we stand? Do we favor the devil, allowing him to destroy while we pass by our lifeless brother as the priest and Levite did in the Gospel? Or, rather, as priests of God and of Christ, do we imitate Christ's teachings and actions, and snatch the wounded man from the jaws of the enemy to save him for God the Judge?

And of some have compassion, making a difference: And others save with fear, pulling them out of the fire; hating even the garment spotted by the flesh.

—Jude 1:22-23

> "Considering His love and mercy, we shouldn't be bitter, cruel, or inhuman toward believers."

Sources of Sin
Clement of Alexandria

And it shall be with him, and he shall read therein all the days of his life: that he may learn to fear the LORD his God, to keep all the words of this law and these statutes, to do them.

—Deuteronomy 17:19

> "Sin has only two sources: ignorance and inability."

Although human actions are countless, sin has only two sources: ignorance and inability. Both depend on ourselves since we either will not learn, or else will not restrain lust. Ignorance leads to poor judgment, and inability yields a failure to comply with correct judgments. For those who are deceived won't act correctly, although perfectly able to do so. Neither will those incapable of acting remain blameless even though they are capable of discernment. Consequently, two kinds of correction are applicable to the two kinds of sin: for ignorance, knowledge and understanding from Scripture; for inability, training according to the Word that is regulated by the discipline of faith and fear. Both remedies develop into perfect love.

Obedience into Action

Gregory of Nyssa

If we live in the "the winds" of spiritual life above and are rooted in His ways, then we joyfully become fathers to other people. . . . The lives of those who are established like this are truly blessed. For Wisdom always agrees and rejoices with them. They find happiness daily in her alone. For the Lord rejoices in His saints. There is joy in heaven over those who are being saved, and Christ, like the father of the prodigal son, makes a feast for His rescued child.

Now therefore hearken unto me, O ye children: for blessed are they that keep my ways.
—*Proverbs 8:32*

"There is joy in heaven over those who are being saved, and Christ, like the father of the prodigal son, makes a feast for His rescued child."

Partakers of God
Origen

Apply yourself diligently to the reading of the sacred Scriptures. Pay close attention to them, I say. For we who read the things of God need to study them diligently, lest we say or think anything too rashly about them. While studying the things of God diligently . . . knock at their locked door. Then it will be opened for you by the doorkeeper. (Jesus says, "To him the doorkeeper opens.") As you discipline yourself to study these things with an unwavering trust in God, seek the true meaning of the Scriptures, which so many have missed. But don't be satisfied with knocking and seeking. For prayer is essential for knowing the things of God. The Savior not only said, "Knock, and it shall be opened to you; and seek, and ye shall find," but also, "Ask, and it shall be given unto you." My fatherly love to you has made me thus bold; but whether my boldness be good, God will know, and His Christ, and all partakers of the Spirit of God and the Spirit of Christ. May you also partake, and always increase your inheritance, so that you can say not only, "We are become partakers of Christ," but also partakers of God.

> "Do you diligently examine your reading of the sacred Scriptures? Pay close attention to them, I say."

Dangerous Thorns

Chrysostom

Let us kindle the light of knowledge and not plant among thorns. You know what the thorns are, even though I haven't told you. For you often heard the Lord call the cares of this life and the deceitfulness of riches by this name. For just as thorns are unfruitful, so are these things. Just as thorns tear up those who handle them, so do these passions. Just as thorns catch on fire easily and are hated by farmers, so are the things of the world. Just as wild beasts, snakes, and scorpions hide in thorns, so do they hide in the deceitfulness of riches. But let us kindle the fire of the Spirit to burn up these thorns, drive away the beasts, and make the field clear for the farmer. After cleansing it, let us water the field with streams of the Spirit. Let us plant fruitful olive trees and evergreens. Let us plant light-giving, nutritious, and wholesome trees. For giving to the poor has these qualities and places a seal on those who do so. Even when death comes, charity won't wither. But it always stands tall to enlighten the mind, feeds the sinews of the soul, and gives even mightier strength. And if we constantly possess it, we will be able to approach the Bridegroom with confidence and enter into the bridal chamber.

> *And the cares of this world, and the deceitfulness of riches, and the lusts of other things entering in, choke the word, and it becometh unfruitful.*
> —Mark 4:19

> "Let us kindle the light of knowledge and not plant among thorns."

Faithful Witness
Hilary of Poitiers

Canst thou by searching find out God? canst thou find out the Almighty unto perfection?
—Job 11:7

All existence originates from the Father. In Christ and through Christ, God is the source of everything. In contrast to everything else, He is completely self-existent. He doesn't receive His being from the outside, but possesses it from and in Himself. He is infinite, for nothing can contain Him and He contains everything. He is eternally unrestricted by space, for He can't be limited. He is eternally prior to time, for time is His creation. Imagine what you think might be God's farthest limit, and you will find Him present there. Strain to see as far as you can, for there is always a further horizon to strain toward. He owns infinity, just as you own the power to make such efforts to comprehend Him. Words will fail you, but His being will not be restrained. Turn back the pages of history and you will always find Him present. If numbers fail to express the old ages you have penetrated, God's eternity still isn't diminished. Exercise your intellect to comprehend Him as a whole, but He will elude you. . . . Therefore, since no one knows the Father but the Son, let our thoughts of the Father be one with the thoughts of the Son. He is the only faithful Witness who reveals God to us.

> "Imagine what you think might be God's farthest limit, and you will find Him present there."

Two Cities
Augustine

Humility enables us to submit to what is above us, and nothing is higher above us than God. By making us submit to God, humility lifts us up. But pride, a defect of nature, is refusing to submit to and opposing the Supreme One. As a result, pride falls to a low state. It is written, "Thou castedst them down when they lifted up themselves." The writer doesn't say, "when they had been lifted up," as if first they were raised up and then thrown down. But "when they lifted up themselves," they were thrown down—that is, the very lifting up was already a fall. Therefore, humility is especially valuable to the city of God. It is exhibited in the city of God and in the person of Christ its King. On the other hand, the Scriptures say that the wickedness of pride rules over Christ's enemy, the devil. Certainly this is the difference between the cities of godly people and of ungodly people . . . one guided and formed by the love of self, the other by love of God.

A man's pride shall bring him low: but honour shall uphold the humble in spirit.
—*Proverbs 29:23*

> "Humility is especially valuable to the city of God."

Form of a Slave
Leo I

Wherefore, my beloved, as ye have always obeyed, not as in my presence only, but now much more in my absence, work out your own salvation with fear and trembling. For it is God which worketh in you both to will and to do of his good pleasure.

—Philippians 2:12-13

We must not pursue foolish and vain things or yield to fear in the midst of trouble. We are, no doubt, flattered by deception and weighed down by troubles, but because "the earth is full of the mercy of the Lord," Christ's victory is ours. He fulfills what He said: "Fear not, for I have overcome the world." So then, whether we fight against the world's ambition, the lusts of the flesh, or against the darts of heresy, we must always arm ourselves with the Lord's cross. . . . We should remember the Apostle Paul's instruction, "Let this mind be in you which was also in Christ Jesus: who being in the form of God counted it not robbery to be equal with God, but emptied Himself, taking the form of a bond-servant, being made in the likeness of men and found in fashion as a man. Wherefore God also exalted Him, and gave Him a name which is above every name, that in the name of Jesus every knee should bow of things in heaven, of things on earth, and of things below, and that every tongue should confess that the Lord Jesus Christ is in the glory of God the Father."

> "We must always arm ourselves with the Lord's cross."

Understanding Christ

Clement of Alexandria

The Savior teaches nothing in a merely human way, but teaches His own with Divine and mystic wisdom. Therefore, we must not listen to His words with worldly ears. We must search out and learn the meaning hidden in them. For what the Lord seems to have simplified for the disciples requires even more attention than puzzling statements because of its overabundance of wisdom. In addition, the things He explained to His children require even more consideration than the things which seem to have been simply stated. Those who heard such explanations didn't ask questions, because the Lord's words pertaining to the entire design of salvation were meant to be contemplated with awe and a deep spiritual mind. We must not receive these words superficially with our ears, but must apply our minds to understanding the Spirit of the Savior and the unspoken meaning of His words.

It is the spirit that quickeneth; the flesh profiteth nothing: the words that I speak unto you, they are spirit, and they are life.

—John 6:63

Believe, Hope, Love
Augustine

Likewise, ye younger, submit yourselves unto the elder. Yea, all of you be subject one to another, and be clothed with humility: for God resisteth the proud, and giveth grace to the humble.

—1 Peter 5:5

In the Old Testament there is a veiling of the New, and in the New Testament there is a revealing of the Old. According to that veiling, fleshly people . . . once were and continue to be dominated by fear of punishment. But according to the revealing, spiritual people . . . have been freed by the gift of love. They knocked in holiness and even hidden things opened up to them. And now they seek without pride, fearing lest even revealed things be closed up to them. There is nothing more contrary to love than envy, and envy comes from pride. Consequently, the Lord Jesus Christ, the God-Man, both discloses Divine love towards us and serves as an example of human humility for us. As a result, our great swelling can be cured by a greater counteracting remedy. For in pride there is great misery. But there is even greater mercy in God's humility. Therefore, make this love your goal. Refer all that you say to it. Whatever you speak, speak it in such a way that those you converse with may believe when they hear you, upon believing they might hope, and upon hoping they might love.

> "There is nothing more contrary to love than envy, and envy comes from pride."

Gradual Adjustments
Origen

Suppose someone gradually became acquainted with an art or science, such as geometry or medicine, until he reached perfection. Having trained himself in its principles and practice for a long time, he attained complete mastery over the subject. Such a person could never go to sleep with such mastery only to wake up ignorant of his subject. So then, as long as that mathematician or physician continues to study his art and to practice its principles, the knowledge of his profession remains with him. But if he stops practicing it and neglects his diligent habits, a few things will gradually escape him. By and by he will forget more and more until everything is forgotten and completely erased from memory. Of course, it is possible that when he first began to fall away and to give in to negligence, he could be aroused and return quickly to his senses. He could recover recent losses and regain the knowledge that had only been slightly erased from his mind. Now let us apply this example to those who have devoted themselves to the knowledge and wisdom of God and whose learning and diligence incomparably surpass all other training. For those who are perfect will see the glory of the Lord face to face as He reveals His mysteries to them.

I press toward the mark for the prize of the high calling of God in Christ Jesus. Let us therefore, as many as be perfect, be thus minded.

—Philippians 3:14-15a

Consuming Fire

Athanasius

Bring forth therefore fruits meet for repentance.
—Matthew 3:8

Our will should keep up with the grace of God and not fall behind. Otherwise, while our will is idle, the grace given to us might begin to leave us. The enemy, finding us empty and naked, would then enter into us. This happened to a man in the Gospel of Matthew. The devil went out of the man. However "having gone through dry places, he took seven other spirits more wicked than himself; and returning and finding the house empty, he dwelt there, and the last state of that man was worse than the first." . . . But Paul orders us not to let the grace we received be unprofitable. He wrote these things particularly to his disciple Timothy but enforces them on us through him. He said, "Neglect not the gift that is in thee. For he who tilleth his land shall be satisfied with bread; but the paths of the slothful are strewn with thorns." The Spirit forewarns us not to fall into these thorns. He says, "Break up your fallow ground, sow not among thorns." When we despise the grace given to us, and, as a result, fall into worldly concerns, we give ourselves over to our lusts. Then in times of persecution we are offended and become completely unfruitful. . . . Servants of the Lord should be diligent and careful. Moreover, they should burn like a flame. Then, when they have passionately destroyed all their fleshly sin, they can draw near to God. For according to the saints' expression, He is "a consuming fire."

> "Paul orders us not to let the grace we received be unprofitable."

Eternal Beauty

Cyprian

Be constant in prayer as well as in reading. Speak with God, and let God speak with you. Let Him instruct you in His commands; let Him direct you. No one can make poor those He makes rich, for those who have been supplied with heavenly food can't be poor. When you know that it is you who will be perfected, golden ceilings and houses with costly marble mosaics will seem dull to you in comparison to the dwelling in which God has lived and in which the Holy Spirit has begun to make His home. Let us then decorate this house with the colors of innocence. Let us illuminate it with the light of justice. Then it will never decay with the wear of age, nor will its wall colors or its gold become tarnished. Those things made artificially beautiful are perishing. Things that can't really be owned can't provide abiding assurance for their possessors. But remain in a beauty that is continually vivid, in perfect honor, in permanent splendor. It can neither decay nor be destroyed. It can only be fashioned into greater perfection.

I will greatly rejoice in the LORD, my soul shall be joyful in my God; for he hath clothed me with the garments of salvation, he hath covered me with the robe of righteousness, as a bridegroom decketh himself with ornaments, and as a bride adorneth herself with her jewels.
—Isaiah 61:10

"No one can make poor those He makes rich, for those who have been supplied with heavenly food can't be poor."

The Great Physician

Irenaeus

For there is not a just man upon earth, that doeth good, and sinneth not.

—*Ecclesiastes 7:20*

What doctor, anxious to heal a sick person, would prescribe medicine according to the patient's whims and not according to medical necessity? The Lord came as the physician of the sick, saying, "They that are whole need not a physician, but they that are sick; I came to call not the righteous but the sinners to repentance." Then how can the sick be strengthened, or how can sinners come to repentance? Is it by continuing in the same direction? Or is it by undergoing a great change and reversing their former mode of living, which brought them much sickness and many sins? But ignorance, the mother of all these sins, is driven out by knowledge. As a result, the Lord would disclose knowledge to His disciples. It was also His practice to heal those who were suffering and to keep sinners from sin. Therefore, through knowledge He didn't address his listeners according to their fresh ideas and He didn't respond in harmony with the opinion of His questioners. Instead, He spoke according to the doctrine that leads to salvation, without hypocrisy or respect of persons.

Tried by Fire
Cyril

Is this what the Lord teaches us to pray, not to be tempted at all? Then how is it said elsewhere, "a man untempted is a man unproved," and "count it all joy when you fall into various temptations"? But does entering into temptation mean being overwhelmed by temptation, perhaps? For temptation is like a raging winter stream that is difficult to cross. Therefore, those who aren't overwhelmed by temptations pass through. They show themselves to be excellent swimmers and aren't swept away at all. Those who aren't like this, however, enter into the waters of temptations and are overwhelmed. For example, Judas entered into the temptation of loving money. He didn't swim through it but was overwhelmed, and both his body and spirit were strangled. . . . On the other hand, a group of uninjured saints gave thanks for being delivered from temptation: "O God, you have tested us. You have tried us by fire, like silver is tried. You brought us into the net. You laid afflictions on us. You made people to ride over our heads. We went through fire and water, but You brought us a place of rest." For these saints can say boldly that they have passed through and not been pierced. But You have brought us to a place of rest, and coming to a place of rest is being delivered from temptation.

And lead us not into temptation, but deliver us from evil: For thine is the kingdom, and the power, and the glory, for ever. Amen.
—*Matthew 6:13*

> "Temptation is like a raging winter stream that is difficult to cross."

A Clean Conscience

Lactantius

Let us cleanse our conscience, which is open to the eyes of God. As the philosopher Tully says, "Let us always so live as to remember that we shall have to give an account." Remember that we are being watched at every moment . . . by the One who will be both Judge and Witness. When He demands an account of our lives, we won't be allowed to deny his actions. Therefore, it is better either to run from our conscience or to open our mind of our own accord, and tear open our wounds to pour out those things that would destroy us. No one can heal these wounds but He who made the lame to walk, restored sight to the blind, cleansed the impure limbs, and raised the dead. He will quench restless desires, He will root out lusts, He will remove envy, He will relieve anger. He will give true and lasting health. Everyone should seek this remedy since the soul is harassed by greater danger than the body. A cure should be applied as soon as possible to secret diseases.

> "Remember that we are being watched at every moment by the One who will be both Judge and Witness."

The Best Offering

Jerome

The poor widow only put two mites into the treasury. However, because she put in everything that she had, Scripture says her gifts to God were much more valuable than what the wealthy offered. For such gifts aren't evaluated by their weight, but by the willingness of the giver. You may have spent your money on many people and a few of your friends might have benefited from your generosity. Yet there are even more who haven't received anything from you. . . . But if you give yourself to the Lord and resolve to follow the Savior in righteousness, then you will see what you once were. You will realize how you have lagged behind in Christ's army. . . . Therefore, I wouldn't want you to offer to the Lord only what a thief can steal from you or an enemy can capture. Don't give Him what a law could confiscate or what is liable to fluctuate in value. Don't offer what belongs to a long line of owners who follow each other as fast as wave follows wave in the sea. To sum this all up, don't offer what you must leave behind when you die. Instead, offer to God that which no enemy can carry off and no tyrant can take from you. Give Him that which will go down to the grave— rather, will go with you to the kingdom of heaven and the enchantments of Paradise.

And he called unto him his disciples, and saith unto them, Verily I say unto you, That this poor widow hath cast more in, than all they which have cast into the treasury: For all they did cast in of their abundance; but she of her want did cast in all that she had, even all her living.
—Mark 12:43-44

> "Offer to God that which no enemy can carry off and no tyrant take from you."

The Right Path
Gregory of Nyssa

See then that ye walk circumspectly, not as fools, but as wise.
—Ephesians 5:15

There is only one right path. It is narrow and constricted. It doesn't have any way to turn on one side or the other. No matter how we step away from it, there is always the danger of straying hopelessly away. As a result, we must correct the habit many people have gotten into as much as possible. I mean those who fight strenuously against the more wicked pleasures, yet who still hunt for pleasure in worldly honor and positions of power. They act like slaves who longed for freedom, but, instead of working to get away, they only changed masters. They thought freedom was in that change. But all people are slaves even though they may not be ruled by the same masters. . . . This same thing happens when any emotion, instead of righteous reason, controls the course of a life. For the Lord's commands are exceedingly far-reaching. They "enlighten the eyes" even of "the simple" and declare that good belongs only to God. But God isn't pain, but He is pleasure. He isn't cowardice, but boldness. He isn't fear, anger, or any other emotion that sways the unguided soul. But, as the Apostle Paul says, He is Wisdom, Sanctification, Truth, Joy, Peace, and everything like that.

Live under Control

Justin Martyr

If the flesh does not rise again, then why is it guarded and why do we not allow it to indulge its desires? Why don't we imitate physicians, who, it is said, when they get a patient that is beyond hope and incurable, allow him to indulge his desires? For the physician allows the patient this kind of life because the patient is dying and will shortly become a corpse. But if our physician, God in Christ, having rescued us from our desires, regulates our flesh with His own wise and temperate rule, it is evident that He guards it from sins because it has a hope of salvation, just as physicians do not allow people whom they hope to save to indulge in whatever pleasures they please.

Let not thine heart envy sinners: but be thou in the fear of the LORD all the day long. For surely there is an end; and thine expectation shall not be cut off.

—Proverbs 23:17-18

Honor the King
Theonas

Submit yourselves to every ordinance of man for the Lord's sake: whether it be to the king, as supreme; Or unto governors, as unto them that are sent by him for the punishment of evil-doers, and for the praise of them that do well.

—1 Peter 2:13-14

Perform the duties you are officially appointed to with the utmost fear of God, affection for your prince, and perfect carefulness. Consider all commands of the emperor that doesn't offend God as having proceeded from God Himself. Execute them in love as well as fear and cheerfulness. For nothing refreshes a person who is wearied by weighty cares as well as the timely cheerfulness and gentle patience of an intimate servant. On the other hand, nothing annoys and distresses a person as much as the gloomy disposition, impatience, and grumbling of a servant. Far be it from you Christians who walk passionately for the faith to behave in such a way. In order to honor God, suppress and stamp down all the wickedness of your minds and bodies. Be clothed with patience and courtesy. Be nourished by the morality and hope of Christ. Bear everything for your Creator's sake. Endure everything, overcome and get above everything, so that you can win the favor of Christ the Lord. These duties are numerous and require great effort. But those that seek to master them are self-controlled in everything. They do it to gain a corruptible crown, but we an incorruptible.

> "Perform the duties you are officially appointed to with the utmost fear of God, affection for your prince, and perfect carefulness."

Not of This World

Anonymous

The Lord said, "No servant can serve two masters." If we desire to serve both God and money, it will be unprofitable for us. "For what will it profit if a man gain the whole world, and lose his own soul?" This world and the next are enemies. One encourages us to commit adultery and be corrupt, greedy, and deceptive. The other says good-bye to these things. Therefore, we can't be friends of both. Rightly, by renouncing the one, we commit to the other. We must recognize that it is better to hate present things, since they are trifling, short-lived, and corruptible, and love the things to come that are good and incorruptible. For if we do Christ's will, we will find rest, but if we disobey His commandments, nothing will save us from eternal punishment. . . . Therefore, beloved, we must compete earnestly, knowing that the battle is close at hand. For although many undertake long voyages, striving for a corruptible reward, not all of them are crowned. Only those that have labored hard and contended gloriously receive the reward. So then, we should contend in this way so that we may be crowned. We must run the straight course. May many people join the incorruptible race and work hard so that we may all be rewarded.

No man can serve two masters: for either he will hate the one, and love the other; or else he will hold to the one, and despise the other. Ye cannot serve God and mammon.

—Matthew 6:24

> "This world and the next are enemies. Therefore, we can't be friends of both."

Live Like Saints

Athanasius

Having therefore these promises, dearly beloved, let us cleanse ourselves from all filthiness of the flesh and spirit, perfecting holiness in the fear of God.
—2 Corinthians 7:1

In order to search Scripture and truly understand it, we must have an honorable life, a pure soul, and Christ's righteousness. Then our minds can understand the word of God as much as human nature allows. Without a pure mind and a life modeled after the saints, we couldn't possibly understand the words of the saints. For people who want to see a city or country go to the place to see it. In the same way, if we want to understand those who wrote about God, we must begin by washing and cleansing our souls. We must live like the saints themselves and imitate their works. When we become like them and live the common life, we can understand what God has revealed to them. And by being closely knit to them, we can escape the danger of sinners and fire at the Day of Judgment. We can receive what is stored up in the kingdom of heaven for the saints. Such treasure, "Eye hath not seen, nor ear heard, neither have they entered into the heart of man." These things are prepared for those who live a righteous life and who love God and Christ Jesus our Lord.

> "If we want to understand those who wrote about God, we must begin by washing and cleansing our souls."

Keep from Idols

Tertullian

When the apostle Paul commands, "Flee idolatry," he certainly means everything related to idolatry. Think about how many thorns are hidden in idolatry—what a thicket it is. Nothing must be given to an idol, nothing must be taken from one. If it is inconsistent with faith to recline in an idol's temple, what is it to appear in an idol's dress? What communion have Christ and Belial? Therefore flee from it, for John urges us to keep at a distance from idolatry—to have no close dealings of any kind with it. Even an earthly serpent sucks in men at some distance with its breath. Going still further, John says, "My little children, keep yourselves from idols,"—not now from idolatry, as if from the service of it, but from idols—that is, from any resemblance to them, for it is an unworthy thing that you, the image of the living God, should become the likeness of an idol and a dead man.

Little children, keep yourselves from idols.
—1 John 5:21

A Better Choice

John Cassian

And Jesus answered and said unto her, Martha, Martha, thou art careful and troubled about many things: But one thing is needful: and Mary hath chosen that good part, which shall not be taken away from her.
—Luke 10:41-42

Our main effort should be to always cling to God and to heavenly things. Anything other than this, no matter how great it may be, should be given second place, treated as having no consequence, or perhaps considered hurtful. The Gospel account of Martha and Mary gives us an excellent illustration of this state of mind. Martha's service was certainly a sacred one since she was ministering to the Lord and His disciples. But Mary, intent only on spiritual instruction, was clinging close to the feet of Jesus. . . . The Lord says she chose the better part and that wouldn't be taken away from her. When Martha was working with careful piety and was weighed down by her service, . . . she asked the Lord for her sister's help. She said: "Carest Thou not that my sister has left me to serve alone? Bid her therefore that she help me." Certainly it wasn't unworthy work, but she called Mary to a praiseworthy service. Yet what does the Lord say? "Martha, Martha, thou art anxious and troubled about many things: but few things are needful, or only one. Mary hath chosen the good part, which shall not be taken away from her." You see, then, that the Lord considers meditation (i.e., pondering divine things) the supreme good. Therefore, all other virtues should be put in second place. We admit, however, that they are necessary, useful, and excellent because they exist for the sake of this one thing.

Constant Thoughts
Chrysostom

If we always see God in our minds, and always remember Him, everything appears tolerable to us. We can bear everything easily and be above it all. For when we see or remember a loved one, our spirits are aroused and our thoughts elevated. We bear everything easily while delighting in the recollection. So then when we call to mind and remember the One who actively loved us, would we feel pain, or dread any terrifying, fearful or dangerous thing? Would we be cowardly? Never. For things appear difficult to us only when we don't remember God as we should, when we don't always carry Him in our thoughts. When we don't, He can rightly say, "Thou hast forgotten Me, I also will forget thee." Then the evil would be doubled: we forget Him and He us. . . . For the effect of God's memory is great. But so is the effect of our remembering Him. The result is that we choose good things and accomplish them. . . . Therefore, if we want to obtain good things, let us seek the things of God. For those who seek the things of this world will fail, but those who prefer the things of God will obtain them.

When my soul fainted within me I remembered the LORD: and my prayer came in unto thee, into thine holy temple.
—*Jonah 2:7*

> "If we always see God in our minds, and always remember Him, everything appears tolerable to us."

233

The Remedy
Ambrose

O wretched man that I am! who shall deliver me from the body of this death? I thank God through Jesus Christ our Lord. So then with the mind I myself serve the law of God; but with the flesh the law of sin.
—Romans 7:24-25

Death is not only an evil but also a good thing . . . For we see that death is advantageous and life is a penalty. Therefore, Paul says: "To me to live is Christ and to die is gain." What is living to Christ but the body's death and the breath of life? We must die with Him in order to live with Him. So then, let us daily practice and incline ourselves toward dying. Then, by separating our souls from bodily desires, we can learn to withdraw, appear dead, and not provoke death (as though it was lifted to heaven where earthly lusts can't approach it or attach themselves to it). For the law of the flesh wars against the law of the mind and gives it over to the law of error. The Apostle Paul said, "For I see a law of the flesh in my members warring against the law of my mind, and bringing me into captivity in the law of sin." We are all attached and feel it. But we aren't all delivered from sin. Therefore, I am miserable unless I seek the remedy. . . . Our remedy is the grace of Christ, and the body of death is our body. Therefore, let us be like strangers to our body, lest we become strangers to Christ.

> "We must die with Him in order to live with Him."

Lasting Truth

Augustine

By genuine holiness, the people of God cast out the enemy of godliness. They do so by rejecting him, not by pacifying him. And they overcome all of the enemy's temptations by praying to God against him. For the devil can only conquer or master those who are allied with sin. Therefore, he is conquered in the name of the One who became human but lived without sin. . . . But we are separated from God by sin. And in this life, we aren't cleansed from sin by our own good deeds or our own power, but by God's compassion and forgiveness. For God, in His goodness, has given us any holiness we might have. While in the flesh, we might tend to attribute too much to ourselves if we don't live under God's pardon until the end. The Mediator offered us this grace so that we who are polluted by sinful flesh could be cleansed by one representing sinful flesh. And by this compassionate grace of God, we are governed by faith both in this life and after this life. We are led toward perfection by the vision of unfading truth.

How much more shall the blood of Christ, who through the eternal Spirit offered himself without spot to God, purge your conscience from dead works to serve the living God?
—*Hebrews 9:14*

> "God, in His goodness, has given us any holiness we might have."

Fight for Truth
Basil

Looking for that blessed hope, and the glorious appearing of the great God and our Saviour Jesus Christ.

—Titus 2:13

Are we called to fight for the truth through temptations? Yes, for the righteous Rewarder won't allow us to be tried beyond what we can bear. Instead, in return for our previous struggles, He will crown us with patience. Therefore, don't flinch from fighting a good fight on behalf of truth. Don't despairingly fling away the work we have already achieved. For the soul's strength isn't shown by one brave action or by short-term effort. But He who tests our hearts wants us to win crowns of righteousness after long, drawn-out trials. Keep your spirit from breaking. Maintain the unshaken firmness of your faith in Christ. And, before long, our Champion will appear. He will come and won't delay. Expect tribulation after tribulation and hope upon hope, yet only for "a little while, a little while." In this way, the Holy Spirit knows how to comfort His children by a promise for the future: after tribulation comes hope. What we are hoping for is not far off, for the complete human existence is only a tiny interval compared with the endless age our hopes rest in.

> "He who tests our hearts wants us to win crowns of righteousness after long, drawn out trials."

Model Repentance

Jerome

We can see the complete repentance of a sinner in the fifty-first psalm. It was written by David after he lay with Bathsheba, the wife of Uriah the Hittite. When the prophet Nathan rebuked him, David replied, "I have sinned." Because he confessed his sin immediately, he was comforted by the words: "The Lord also hath put away thy sin." David had added murder to his adultery. Yet bursting into tears he said, "Have mercy upon me, O God, according to Thy loving-kindness: according unto the multitude of Thy tender mercies blot out my transgressions." A sin so great needed great mercy. Consequently, he went on to say: "Wash me throughly from mine iniquity, and cleanse me from my sin. For I acknowledge my transgressions: and my sin is ever before me. Against Thee, Thee only have I sinned"—as a king, he didn't have anyone to fear but God— "and done this evil in Thy sight; that Thou mightest be justified when Thou speakest and be clear when Thou judgest." For "God hath concluded all in unbelief, that He might have mercy upon all." And this was how David progressed: although he was once a sinner, he became a model for us after his repentance. For he was able to say, "I will teach transgressors Thy ways; and sinners shall be converted unto Thee." For just as "confession and beauty are before God," sinners who confess their sins and say, "my wounds stink and are corrupt because of my foolishness" are cleansed from their infections. But "he that covereth his sins shall not prosper."

The sacrifices of God are a broken spirit: a broken and a contrite heart, O God, thou wilt not despise.

—Psalm 51:17

Worthwhile Questions
Clement of Alexandria

Why dost thou strive against him? for he giveth not account of any of his matters.
—Job 33:13

Now we know that certain things aren't worth questioning. For example, we don't investigate subjects that are already evident, such as whether it is daytime when it is the day. Neither do we study things unknown that are never destined to become clear, such as whether the stars are even or odd in number. We don't examine subjects that can be argued equally well on opposite sides, such as whether what is in the womb is a living creature or not. Nor is there any point in investigating when irrefutable logic establishes one or the other position. If, then, we reject inquiry due to these reasons, faith is established. For we acknowledge that it is God who speaks regarding each one of the unanswerable points we investigate and comes to our help through Scripture. Who, then, is so irreverent as to disbelieve God and to demand proofs from God as from men? Again, some questions demand the evidence of the senses, like whether fire is warm or snow is white. Other questions demand admonition and rebuke, such as the question of whether you should honor your parents. In addition, there are those questions that deserve punishment, such as asking for proof that there is such a thing as providence.

Sovereign God

Eusebius

When people praise my acts of service, which are inspired by heaven, don't they confirm that God caused the deeds I have done? Certainly they do. For God does whatever is best, and humans perform the commands of God. Surely everyone knows that the holy service these hands have done came from a pure, genuine faith towards God. Whatever has been done for the common good was carried out through active effort combined with supplication and prayer. As a result, individuals and the public have benefited greatly. . . . For righteous prayer is invincible. Everyone who makes a holy request will receive what they asked God for. A refusal is impossible, except when faith wavers. For God is always favorable and ready to approve of human righteousness. While it is natural for us to err occasionally, God doesn't cause human error. Therefore, righteous people should thank God for their own individual security and the happy state of public affairs. At the same time, however, they should respond to Christ's favor with holy prayers and constantly ask that He would continue to bless us.

And he said unto him, Why callest thou me good? there is none good but one, that is, God: but if thou wilt enter into life, keep the commandments.
—Matthew 19:17

"Whatever has been done for the common good was carried out through active effort combined with supplication and prayer."

God Rejoices
Chrysostom

I say unto you, that likewise joy shall be in heaven over one sinner that repenteth, more than over ninety and nine just persons, which need no repentance.

—Luke 15:7

If God rejoices over the little one that is found, how do you despise those God earnestly cares for? We should give up even our lives for one of these little ones. But are the lost ones weak and contemptible? Then it is even more important that we do everything we can to preserve them. Even Christ left the ninety-nine sheep and went after the one. He took advantage of the safety of so many to prevent the loss of one. Luke says that He even brought the lost one home on His shoulders. And "There was greater joy over one sinner that repenteth, than over ninety and nine just persons." By His leaving the saved ones for it, and by His taking more pleasure in this one, He showed how greatly He valued it. So then, don't be careless about such souls. . . . For our neighbors' sake, don't refuse to do any of the tasks that seem lowly and troublesome. Although we have to do the service for someone small and shabby, although the work is hard and we must pass over mountains and valleys, endure everything for your neighbor's salvation. For a soul is so important to God that "He spared not His own Son."

> "Endure everything for your neighbor's salvation."

Work Hard
Clement of Alexandria

The duty of the Word is to supervise our instruction and discipline. Therefore, work hard and don't faint. . . . Just as there is one way of training philosophers, another for public speakers, and another for athletes, a certain character results from the training of Christ. Those who have been trained in this way become dignified above all else in their walk, their sitting at the table, their food, their sleep, their going to bed, their regimen, and the rest of their way of life. For training guided by the Word is not too strained, but has the right tension. . . . Christ devotes Himself to watching for the favorable moment, reproving evil, exposing the causes of evil affections, and striking at the roots of irrational lusts. He points out what we should abstain from and supplies salvation's antidote to the diseased. . . . How can we not acknowledge the Divine Instructor with the highest gratitude? He isn't silent, but discloses things that threaten to destroy us and instructs us in living righteously. Therefore, we must confess our deepest obligations to Him. . . . It is essential to think about human nature, to live as the truth directs, and to admire the Instructor and His counsel. These things are all suitable and harmonious with each other. We must live a real life conforming ourselves to the image of the Instructor and making the Word and our deeds agree.

For the commandment is a lamp; and the law is light; and reproofs of instruction are the way of life.

—Proverbs 6:23

> "How can we not acknowledge the Divine Instructor with the highest gratitude?"

Strength to Survive

Athanasius

I gave my back to the smiters, and my cheeks to them that plucked off the hair: I hid not my face from shame and spitting.
—Isaiah 50:6

If one day we will receive comfort from afflictions, rest from labor, health after sickness, and eternal life from death, it isn't right to agonize over temporal, human pain. To be agitated by the trials we face is inappropriate. And it isn't right to fear mobs who fight against Christ and conspire against godliness. Instead, we should please God all the more through these things. We should consider such matters to be the test and exercise of a righteous life. For how can we have patience if there isn't previous labor and sorrow? Or how can our strength be tested without attacks from the enemy? . . . Finally, how can we see righteousness unless the sin of very wicked people appears previously? As a result, our Lord and Savior Jesus Christ reminds us how to suffer. When He was beaten, He bore it patiently. Although verbally abused, He didn't lash out in return. When He suffered, He didn't speak threats but gave His back to the torturers and His cheeks to buffetings. He didn't turn His face away from the spitting but was willingly led to His death so that we could see the image of righteousness in Him. By following these examples, we can tread on serpents, scorpions, and all of the enemy's power.

> "Our Lord and Savior Jesus Christ reminds us how to suffer."

Spiritual Maturity

Vincent of Lérins

Religion's growth in the soul corresponds with the body's growth. Although over the years it develops and reaches its full size, it still remains the same. There is a wide difference between the flower of youth and the maturity of age. However, those who were young once are still the same now that they are old. As much as their height and individual, outward form changes, their nature remains the same. They are the same person. An infant's limbs are small and a young adult's are large, but the infant and the young adult are the same. For when people are full-grown, they have the same number of joints they had as children. And if maturer age has given birth to anything within the body, it was already present in the embryo. Nothing new is produced in old people that wasn't already hidden in them as children. This, then, is undoubtedly the genuine, legitimate rule of progress, the established and most beautiful order of growth: mature age always develops a person's parts and forms which the wise Creator already framed in the infant. In a similar way, Christian doctrine follows the same laws of progress. Religion may be solidified by years, strengthened by time, and refined by age. However, it will continue to be innocent and simple, complete and perfect in all its parts and, so to speak, in all its senses. It won't allow change, won't throw away its distinctiveness, and won't vary within its limits.

But speaking the truth in love, may grow up into him in all things, which is the head, even Christ.

—*Ephesians 4:15*

Our Head
Gregory I

I am the vine, ye are the branches: He that abideth in me, and I in him, the same bringeth forth much fruit: for without me ye can do nothing.
—John 15:5

Our Head, which is Christ, has willed us to be His members. As a result, by the bond of love and faith He makes us one body in Himself. It is fitting for us to adhere our hearts to Him, since without Him we can't be anything. But through Him we can be what we are called to be. Don't let anything divide us from our well-established Head, lest by refusing to be His members, we be left separated from Him and wither like branches fallen from the vine. Therefore, in order to be considered the worthy dwelling place of our Redeemer, we must abide in His love with completely resolved minds. For He Himself says, "He that loveth Me will keep My word, and My Father will love him, and We will come unto him, and make Our abode with him." But we can't stay close to the Author of good unless we cut covetousness—for it is the root of all evil. . . . Therefore, we eliminate greed from the temple of faith. It only serves idols. Then we won't face anything hurtful or disorderly while in the house of the Lord.

> "Don't let anything divide us from our well-established Head."

The Reason for Love
Chrysostom

Some love because they are loved; others love because they have been honored. Still others show love because the person was useful to them in some worldly way and others for similar reasons. It is hard to find people who love their neighbors sincerely and for Christ's sake as they ought to love. For most are bound together by worldly affairs. Paul loved not this way, but for Christ's sake. Therefore, even when he wasn't loved in the way that he loved, he didn't stop loving them because he had planted the strong root of his affections. In our present sinful state, we find that almost anything produces friendship but this kind of love. . . . But love for Christ's sake is firm. It can't be broken or conquered. Nothing can tear it apart: not lies, dangers, death, or anything like this. Although those who truly love us suffer ten thousand things, they dig deep and will never stop loving us. Those who love to be loved will end their love when they encounter anything painful. But those who are bound by it will never stop.

And the Lord make you to increase and abound in love one toward another, and toward all men, even as we do toward you.
—1 Thessalonians 3:12

"Love for Christ's sake is firm. It can't be broken or conquered. Nothing can tear it apart."

Appropriate Knowledge
Irenaeus

Woe unto them that are wise in their own eyes, and prudent in their own sight!
—Isaiah 5:21

Keep your knowledge in its proper place. Do not be ignorant of the things that are really good or seek to rise above God Himself, for He cannot be surpassed. Neither seek after anyone above the Creator, for you will not discover anyone greater than God because your Maker cannot be contained within limits. Although you may try to measure the universe, pass through all His creation and consider it in all its depth and height and length, you still wouldn't be able to think of anyone above the Father Himself. For you wouldn't be able to outthink Him, but, by trying to think beyond your capacity, you would prove your foolishness. And if you continued to follow such a course, you would fall into utter madness while considering yourself superior to your Creator and imagining that you can overcome His supreme authority.

Faith By Hearing

Clement of Alexandria

"Lord, who hath believed our report?" Isaiah says. For "faith cometh by hearing, and hearing by the word of God," says the apostle Paul. "How then shall they call on Him in whom they have not believed? And how shall they believe on Him whom they have not heard? And how shall they hear without a preacher? And how shall they preach except they be sent?" As it is written, "How beautiful are the feet of those that publish glad tidings of good things!" See how the author brings about faith by hearing and how the apostle's preaching brings one up to the Son of God. . . . Therefore, playing ball depends not only on one throwing the ball skillfully, but also on one catching it easily. Teaching is reliable when the hearers' faith, a sort of natural art, contributes to the process of learning. . . . For even the very best instruction isn't any good without a receptive learner. Even preaching is no good when the hearers lack a teachable spirit. So faith is the voluntary expectation and anticipation of things already comprehended.

So then faith cometh by hearing, and hearing by the word of God.
—*Romans 10:17*

> "Even the very best instruction isn't any good when the hearers lack a teachable spirit."

Distracted Prayer

Cyprian

When we pray, beloved, we should be alert and earnest with our whole heart, intent on our prayers. Let all worldly thoughts pass away. Don't let the soul think about anything but the object of its prayer. . . . Don't allow God's enemy to approach your heart at that time. For frequently he sneaks up on us and . . . he calls our prayers away from God so that we have one thing on our heart and another in our voice. The soul and mind, not the sound of the voice, should be intent on praying to the Lord. How can you be distracted and be carried away by foolish and profane thoughts when you are praying to the Lord! . . . How can you ask God to hear you when you don't hear yourself? Do you want God to remember what you ask when you don't even remember your requests? . . . Such carelessness offends the majesty of God. You may appear watchful, but your heart is asleep. Instead, your heart should be watchful even when your eyes are closed in prayer. In the Song of Songs, the personified church says, "I sleep, yet my heart waketh." The apostle Paul also anxiously and carefully warns us, "Continue in prayer, and watch in the same." He teaches us that those who God sees are watchful in prayer will receive what they ask from Him.

> "Your heart should be watchful even when your eyes are closed in prayer."

God, Our Help

Jerome

Where do we find the power of free choice in this passage? Isn't the whole situation (that Jacob ventured to go to his son Joseph and entrust himself to a nation that didn't know the Lord), due to the help of the God of his fathers? For the people were released from Egypt by a strong hand and an outstretched arm. This wasn't the hand of Moses and Aaron, but of God, who set them free by signs and wonders and by destroying the firstborn of Egypt. As a result, those who were at first persistent in keeping the people eagerly urged them to leave at last. Solomon says, "Trust in the Lord with all thine heart, and lean not upon thine own understanding: in all thy ways acknowledge Him, and He shall direct thy paths." Understand what He says: we must not trust in our wisdom, but in the Lord alone. For He directs a person's steps. We are also called to show Him our ways, to reveal our plans to Him. For they aren't made straight by our own work, but by His assistance and mercy. It is written, "Make my way right before Thy face." Then what is right to You will also seem also right to me. Solomon says the same thing: "Commit thy works unto the Lord, and thy thoughts shall be established." Therefore, thoughts are carried out when we commit everything we do to the Lord our Helper, resting our works on the firm and solid rock, and attributing everything to Him.

And he said, I am God, the God of thy father: fear not to go down into Egypt; for I will there make of thee a great nation: I will go down with thee into Egypt; and I will also surely bring thee up again: and Joseph shall put his hand upon thine eyes.
—*Genesis 46:3-4*

> "We must not trust in our wisdom, but in the Lord alone."

Our Whole Strength

Clement of Rome

This is a faithful saying, and these things I will that thou affirm constantly, that they which have believed in God might be careful to maintain good works. These things are good and profitable unto men.

—Titus 3:8

What shall we do then, brethren? Shall we become lazy in doing good and stop practicing love? God forbid that we should follow any such course! But rather, let us hurry with all energy and readiness of mind to perform every good work. For the Creator and Lord of all Himself rejoices in His works. By His infinitely great power, He established the heavens, and by His incomprehensible wisdom He adorned them. He also divided the earth from the water which surrounds it and fixed it upon the immovable foundation of His own will. The animals of the earth He also commanded by His own Word into existence. So likewise, when He had formed the sea and the living creatures which are in it, He enclosed them within their proper bounds by His own power. Above all, with His holy and undefiled hands, He formed man, the most excellent of His creatures and truly great through the understanding given him—the express likeness of His own image. For thus says God, "Let us make man in Our image and after Our likeness. So God made man; male and female He created them." Having thus finished all these things, He approved them and blessed them and said, "Increase and multiply." We see then how all righteous men have been adorned with good works and how the Lord Himself, adorning Himself with His works, rejoiced. Having therefore such an example, let us without delay assent to His will and let us work the work of righteousness with our whole strength.

Anger and Prayer
Tertullian

So that we may not be as far from the ears of God as from His principles, remembering His principles paves a way for our prayers to heaven. The greatest of these principles is that we don't go up to God's altar before settling any conflicts or offenses we have with our neighbors. For how can you approach the peace of God without peace—the release from debts while you keep them against others? How will those who are angry appease their Father, when, from the beginning, "all anger" is forbidden? For even Joseph, when dismissing his brothers to get their father, said, "And be not angry in the way." He warned us that when, set in "the way" of prayer (for elsewhere our discipline is called "the way"), we must not go to "the Father" with anger. After that, the Lord, "amplifying the Law," openly adds anger to the prohibition of murder. He doesn't even permit it to be vented by an evil word. As the apostle Paul urges, if we ever must be angry, we must not maintain our anger past sunset. But how rash it is to pass a day without prayer while you refuse to make amends with your neighbor or to lose your prayer by remaining angry.

Be not hasty in thy spirit to be angry: for anger resteth in the bosom of fools.
—*Ecclesiastes 7:9*

> "Remembering His principles paves a way for our prayers to heaven."

Passing On the Faith

Irenaeus

Jesus Christ the same yesterday, and today, and for ever.
—*Hebrews 13:8*

The church, although scattered throughout the whole world, yet, as if occupying one house, having received . . . this faith in Jesus, carefully preserves it. She believes these points of doctrine just as if she had one soul and one heart, and she proclaims them, teaches them, and hands them down with perfect harmony as if she possessed only one mouth. For although the languages of the world differ, the significance of the faith is one and the same. For the churches which have been planted in Germany do not believe or hand down anything different, nor do those in Spain, nor those in France, nor those in the East, nor those in Egypt, nor those in Libya, nor those which have been established in the central regions of the world. But like the sun, that creature of God, which is one and the same throughout the whole world, so also the preaching of the truth shines everywhere and enlightens all who are willing to come to a knowledge of the truth. Neither will any of the leaders in the churches, however highly gifted they may be in eloquence, teach doctrines different from these (for no one is greater than the Master). Nor, on the other hand, will one who lacks power of expression inflict injury on the tradition. For the faith is always one and the same. One who is able to speak about it at great length does not add to it; neither does one who can only say a little diminish it.

Firm Faith

Jerome

"According to your faith, be it done unto you," God says. I definitely don't like the sound of those words. If it is done to me according to my faith, I will be destroyed. . . . For the enemy often comes and sows tares in the Lord's harvest. Nothing is better than a pure heart that believes the mystery of God. However, it is hard to find undoubted faith in God.

And the apostles said unto the Lord, Increase our faith.
—Luke 17:5

Let me clarify what I mean. Suppose I stood to pray. I couldn't pray if I didn't believe. But if I really believed, I would cleanse my heart and beat my chest. The tears would stream down my cheeks, my body would shudder, my face grow pale. I would lie at my Lord's feet, weep over them, and wipe them with my hair. I would cling to the cross and not let go until I received mercy. But, as it is, in my prayers I am often either walking between shops, calculating my own interests, or being carried away by evil thoughts. My mind becomes occupied with things that when they are merely mentioned make me blush.

> "If I really believed, I would cling to the cross and not let go until I received mercy."

Where is our faith? Should we assume that Jonah prayed like this? Or the three youths? Or Daniel in the lion's den? Or the robber on the cross? . . . Instead, let all people examine their own hearts. They will find how rare it is to find a soul so faithful that it doesn't do anything out of love for glory or because of people's petty gossip.

Spiritual Delights

Leo I

For bodily exercise profiteth little: but godliness is profitable unto all things, having promise of the life that now is, and of that which is to come.

—1 Timothy 4:8

Dearly beloved, relying on the armor of God, let us enter actively and fearlessly into the contest of faith. Then, in our struggle to fast, we won't rest satisfied, thinking that mere abstinence from food is desirable. For it isn't enough to lose body weight if our soul isn't developed as well. When the outer person is somewhat controlled, let the inner person be somewhat refreshed. And when we deny bodily excess to our flesh, let our minds be invigorated by spiritual delights. Let Christians severely scrutinize themselves and search deep in their hearts. No anger should cling there, no wrong desire should be harbored. Let purity drive weakness far away. Let the light of truth drive away the shadows of deception. Let the swelling of pride subside. Let wrath yield to reason. Let the darts of cruelty be shattered and the chidings of the tongue be bridled. Let thoughts of revenge fall through and pain be wiped out. Let "every plant which the heavenly Father hath not planted be removed by the roots." For only when every foreign bud is uprooted from the field of wheat will the seeds of righteousness be well nourished in us.

> "When we deny bodily excess to our flesh, let our minds be invigorated by spiritual delights."

Conquering Fear
Fear

Augustine

We aren't discouraged by punishment for our sins. It is meant to train us in self-discipline, so that, as we press on in holiness, we can overcome our fear of death. If those who aren't afraid ("because of the faith which worketh by love") are hardly noticed, then there wouldn't be much glory in martyrdom. And the Lord couldn't say, "Greater love hath no man than this, that he lay down his life for his friends." John, in his epistle, expresses it in these words: "As He laid down His life for us, so ought we to lay down our lives for the brethren." Therefore, it would be useless to praise those who face death for righteousness' sake if death wasn't really a severe trial. But those who overcome the fear of death by their faith, will receive great glory and fair compensation for their faith. No one should be surprised, therefore, that death is a punishment for previous sins. Neither should it surprise us that the faithful die after their sins are forgiven to exercise the fearlessness of righteousness by conquering their fear of death.

Behold, God is my salvation; I will trust, and not be afraid: for the LORD JEHOVAH is my strength and my song; he also is become my salvation.
—*Isaiah 12:2*

> "The faithful die after their sins are forgiven to exercise the fearlessness of righteousness."

The Worship of God

Lactantius

And when he had taken the book, the four beasts and four and twenty elders fell down before the Lamb . . . And they sung a new song.
—Revelation 5:8–9a

What is the most righteous way of worshiping God? For no one should think that God desires victims, incense, or valuable gifts. Since He doesn't experience hunger, thirst, cold, or a desire for earthly things, the things presented in temples to earthly gods aren't useful to Him. Just as physical offerings are necessary for physical beings, so spiritual sacrifices are necessary for a spiritual being. Since all the world is under God's power, He doesn't need the things He gave people to use. Since He dwells in the entire world, He doesn't need a temple. Since the eyes and mind can't comprehend Him, He doesn't need an image. Since He kindled the light of the sun and stars for our sake, He doesn't need earthly lights. So then, what does God require from us? Pure and holy worship of our minds. For those things that are made by hand or outside of people are senseless, frail, and displeasing. But true sacrifice isn't from the purse but from the heart. It is offered not by the hands, but by the mind. . . . What's the purpose of incense, clothes, silver, gold, or precious stones if the worshiper doesn't have a pure mind?

> "What does God require from us? Pure and holy worship of our minds."

Stand Firm
Cyprian

Fear of and faith in God should prepare you for everything—the loss of your property, the constant pain of agonizing disorders, the deadly pain of separation from wife, children, or dying dear ones. Don't let these things cause you to sin, but battle them. Don't let them weaken or break your faith, but show your strength in the struggle. All the injuries inflicted by present troubles are considered worthless in light of sure future blessings. Unless the battle comes first, there can't be victory. The crown is given to the victor. For the helmsman is recognized in a storm. In warfare, the quality of a soldier is demonstrated without danger; such behavior is merely an extravagant display, for struggle in adversity is the test of the truth. The tree that is deeply rooted isn't moved by gusts of wind. When the ship made of solid timbers is beaten by the waves, it isn't shattered. On the threshing floor, the strong and robust grains disregard the winds, while the empty chaff is carried away by the blasts against it.

He is like a man which built an house, and digged deep, and laid the foundation on a rock: and when the flood arose, the stream beat vehemently upon that house, and could not shake it: for it was founded upon a rock.
—*Luke 6:48*

> "Struggle in adversity is the test of the truth."

257

Glory to God
Augustine

Better it is to be of an humble spirit with the lowly, than to divide the spoil with the proud.
—*Proverbs 16:19*

When we desire to be respected and loved by others, seeking only to experience a false joy, we lead a distastefully showy, miserable life. Then it is revealed that we don't love You and don't sincerely fear You. You resist the proud, but give grace to the humble. You thunder against the world's greedy pursuits, and "the foundations of the hills" tremble. But some people find it necessary to be loved and honored by others. The enemy of true happiness presses hard against us. He scatters his traps of "well done, well done" everywhere. He hopes that while we eagerly collect these praises, we will be caught suddenly. We will detach our joy from Your truth and fasten it to human deception. We will take pleasure in being loved and respected, not for Your sake, but in place of You. As a result, we will become like the enemy. He will own those who, not in harmony of love but in the fellowship of punishment, seek to serve him and to honor his dark, cold throne. He will own them by imitating You in perverse and distorted ways. But we, O Lord, we are Your "little flock. " Own us, stretch Your wings over us, and let us escape under them. Be our glory. Let us be loved for Your sake and have Your word feared in us.

> "The enemy of true happiness presses hard against us. He scatters his traps of 'well done, well done' everywhere."

Greatest Miracles

Gregory of Nyssa

John, the Son of Thunder, . . . said at the end of his Gospel, "There are also many other things which Jesus did, the which if they should be written every one, I suppose that even the world itself could not contain the books that should be written." Certainly he doesn't mean the miracles of healing, for his narrative records them all, even though it doesn't mention the names of everyone who was healed. When he tells us the dead were raised, the blind received sight, the deaf heard, the lame walked, and that He healed all kinds of sickness and disease, John records every miracle in general terms. But in his profound wisdom, he may mean this: we must not learn the majesty of the Son of God only by the miracles He did in the flesh. For these are small compared to the greatness of His other work. But look up to heaven! Behold its glories! Transfer your thought to the wide compass of the earth, and the watery depths! Embrace with your mind the whole world, and when you have realized His extraordinary nature, learn that these are the true works of Him who came down for you in the flesh. John said, "if each were written" and the nature, manner, origin, and extent of each work was given, the world itself couldn't contain the fullness of Christ's teaching.

Great is our Lord, and of great power: his understanding is infinite.
—*Psalm 147:5*

> "We must not learn the majesty of the Son of God only by the miracles He did in the flesh."

Insults and Abuse
Chrysostom

When a ship is in danger of sinking, the sailors don't know what they throw out of the boat—whether they lay hands on their own or other people's property. They throw overboard all the ship's contents without discriminating between what is precious and what is not. But when the storm has ended, they consider all they have thrown out and shed tears. The aren't aware of the calm due to their losing what they threw overboard. It is the same when passion blows hard and storms rise up. People fling out their words without knowing how to be orderly and appropriate. But when the passion has stopped, they remember what kind of words they spoke. They consider the loss and don't feel the quietness. They remember their words that have disgraced them. They suffer the severest loss, not of money, but of a self-controlled and gentle character. . . . Let this console you when you suffer from insults. Are you insulted? God is also insulted. Are you verbally abused? God was also abused verbally. Are you treated with scorn? Why, so was our Master. He shares these things with us, but not the unfavorable things. For He never insulted someone else unjustly: God forbid! He never verbally abused anyone, never did a wrong. . . . For to endure insults is God's part. To be abusive is the part of the devil.

> "To endure insults is God's part. To merely be abusive is the part of the devil."

Master Creator
Eusebius

People who use the word "chance" think in haphazard and illogical ways. They are unable to understand the causes of things. Due to their feeble understanding, they imagine that the things they can't find a reason for are caused without reason. Unquestionably, some of these things possess wonderful natural properties that are very difficult to understand completely. For example, the nature of hot springs. No one can easily explain the cause of such a powerful fire. It is definitely surprising that, although surrounded on all sides by cold water, the spring loses none of its native heat. . . . Providence ordains that these two directly opposite natures, heat and cold, should proceed from the same source. Such gifts, which God has given to us for comfort and enjoyment, are numberless. Another such gift is the marvelous course of rivers. They flow night and day with unceasing motion and present a type of ever-flowing, never-ceasing life. Equally wonderful is the regular sequence of day and night. May all this prove that nothing exists without reason and intelligence, and that reason itself and providence are from God.

Of old hast thou laid the foundation of the earth: and the heavens are the work of thy hands.

—*Psalm 102:25*

"**Nothing exists without reason and intelligence, and reason itself and providence are from God.**"

Forgiving Trespasses
Augustine

For if ye forgive men their trespasses, your heavenly Father will also forgive you.
—Matthew 6:14

The greatest gift you can give is to genuinely forgive sin committed against you. It is a comparatively small thing to wish someone well or to do good to someone who hasn't hurt you. But it is much greater to love and wish your enemy well. When you have the opportunity, do good to those who want to make you suffer and do you harm. For in doing this you obey God's command: "Love your enemies, do good to them that hate you, and pray for them that persecute you." This is a frame of mind that only the children of God can reach. All believers should strive after it, by prayer earnestly struggling with themselves to attain this standard. However, such a high degree of goodness can hardly be met by all the people who pray, "Forgive us our debts, as we forgive our debtors." In view of all this, those who don't yet love their enemies can fulfill this command when they forgive someone from the heart who has sinned against them.

> "Do good to those who want you to suffer and do you harm."

Trouble Ahead

Commodianus

By thinking that you are safe, even though you fluctuate between Christianity and the world, you go on your way stripped of self-control and broken down by luxury. You are looking forward to so many things in vain. Why do you seek evil things? For you will account for everything you do when you die. Consider this, foolish one. Once you didn't exist, but now you live. You don't know where you have come from, how you are sustained. You avoid the kind and excellent God of your life and your Governor, who wants you to live. You rely on yourself and turn your back to God. You drown yourself in darkness, when you think you are living in the light. Why do you run into the synagogue of the Pharisees to find mercy from the One whom you deny and then go out again to seek healthy things? You hope to live between Christianity and the world, and consequently you will die. Because punishments will be awarded, you ask, "Who is He who has redeemed from death, that we may believe in Him?" Ah! It won't be what you think. For those who live well will benefit after death. You, however, will be taken away to an evil place on the day you die. While those who believe in Christ will be led into a good place and will experience God's kindness, you who are double-minded will receive punishment of your soul, and your torment will provoke you to cry out against your Christian brother.

I call heaven and earth to record this day against you, that I have set before you life and death, blessing and cursing: therefore choose life, that both thou and thy seed may live.

—Deuteronomy 30:19

Making Requests
Augustine

Oh how great is thy goodness, which thou hast laid up for them that fear thee; which thou hast wrought for them that trust in thee before the sons of men!

—*Psalm 31:19*

> "You know what you want, but He knows what is good for you."

Do you think, beloved, that God doesn't know what you need? He knows. And He knows what we want. When He taught His disciples to pray, He warned them not to use many words. He said, "Use not many words; for your Father knoweth what things ye have need of before ye ask Him." . . . So then, seeing that our Father already knows what we need, how and why do we ask? Why seek? Why knock? Why weary ourselves in asking, seeking, and knocking, to instruct the One who knows already? But in another place, the Lord says, we "ought always to pray, and not to faint." If we ought always to pray, how can He say, "Use not many words"? How can I always pray if I must finish so quickly? Here You tell me to finish quickly; there "always to pray and not to faint." What does this mean? In order that you may understand this, "ask, seek, knock." For the door is closed, not to shut you out, but to exercise you. Therefore, we should urge you and ourselves to pray. For we have no other hope amid the many evils of this world than to knock in prayer and to believe firmly in our hearts that the Father won't give us what He knows isn't beneficial for us. For you know what you want, but He knows what is good for you.

The Grape Cluster

Ambrose

Our Lord has not only called Himself a Vine, He was also given by a prophet the title of a Grape-cluster, just as Moses sent spies to the Valley of the Cluster. What is that valley? The humility of the Incarnation and the fruitfulness of the Passion Week. Indeed, I think He is called the Cluster because the Jews were brought out of Egypt from the Vine—fruit grown there for the world's good. No one truly can understand the Cluster as an indication of God's people. Or, if anyone who understands it this way, he leaves no choice but to believe that the Cluster sprang from the Vine. . . . Now, if there is no doubt that the Son of God is called the Vine in respect of His Incarnation, you can see our Lord's hidden truth in saying, "The Father is greater than I." For after establishing this premise, He immediately continued: "I am the true Vine, and My Father is the Husbandman." As a result, you can know that the Father is greater because He prepares and cares for our Lord's flesh, as farmers prepare and care for their vines. Furthermore, our Lord's flesh was able to grow with age and be wounded through suffering. Therefore, the whole human race could rest under the shadow of the cross's outstretched limbs, guarded from the pestilent heat of the world's pleasures.

I am the vine, ye are the branches: He that abideth in me, and I in him, the same bringeth forth much fruit: for without me ye can do nothing.

—John 15:5

Chaff
Augustine

Be not deceived: evil communications corrupt good manners.

—*1 Corinthians 15:33*

We mustn't be shocked by anyone's conversion, whether they come from within or from outside the church. For "the goodness of God leadeth him to repentance," and "visits their transgressions with the rod, and their inquiry with stripes." If they will "love their own soul, pleasing God," then He does not utterly take from them His loving-kindness. The good person "that shall endure unto the end, the same shall be saved," but, the bad; whether from within or without, who persevere in their wickedness to the end won't be saved. . . . Therefore, the Lord warns us well that we shouldn't associate with foolish people who pretend to walk under Christ's name. These kinds of people can be found both within and without. . . .

The apostle Paul said of the vessels in God's house, "If a man therefore purge himself from these, he shall be a vessel unto honor, sanctified, and meet for the Master's use, and prepared unto every good work." And He shows us a little how we should purge ourselves: "Let every one that nameth the name of Christ depart from iniquity." Then, in the last day, we won't hear with the chaff that has already been driven from the threshing floor, or still needs to be separated, "Depart from me, ye that work iniquity."

> "We shouldn't associate with foolish people who pretend to walk under Christ's name."

Jesus' Goodness

Gregory Nazianzen

My trials are merely a fraction of the spitting and blows Christ endured. We face these dangers for Him and with His help. Even taken altogether, these dangers don't deserve the crown of thorns which robbed our Conqueror of His crown. Yet for His sake I am crowned for a hard life. I don't consider these trials even worth . . . the gall or vinegar alone. But by these we were cured of the bitter taste of life. My struggles aren't worthy of the gentleness He showed in His passion. Was He betrayed with a kiss? He corrects us with a kiss, but doesn't strike us. Was He arrested suddenly? He definitely reproves them, but follows willingly. And if through zeal you cut off the ear of Malchus with a sword, He will be angry and will heal it. And if one of us runs away in a linen sheet, He will defend that person. If you ask for the fire of Sodom to come down on His captors, He won't pour it out. And if He sees a thief hanging on the cross for his crime, He will bring him into Paradise through His goodness. Let all who love people be loving in their actions, as Christ was in His sufferings.

Nothing could be worse than refusing to forgive our neighbor of even the smallest wrongs when God died for us.

And they departed from the presence of the council, rejoicing that they were counted worthy to suffer shame for his name.

—Acts 5:41

> "Nothing could be worse than refusing to forgive our neighbor of even the smallest wrongs when God died for us."

God's Providence

John of Damascus

Providence is the will of God that provides suitably for every living thing. But if Providence is God's will, then it stands to reason that everything that happens through Providence must be the best, most fair, and most excellent. For the same person must create and provide for what exists. It is unreasonable that the Creator and Provider of what exists should be separate persons. Then they would both be deficient—the one in creating, the other in providing. God, therefore, is both Creator and Provider. His creative, preserving, and providing power is simply His good will. For the Lord did whatever He pleased in heaven and in earth and no one resisted His will. And He willed that all things should be and they were. He wills the universe to be framed and it is framed. Everything that He wills comes to pass. One can easily see that God provides, and provides excellently. For God alone is good and wise by nature. Since He is good, then, He provides. For those who don't provide aren't good. Even humans and animals provide for their own offspring according to their nature and not their reason. Those who don't provide are blamed. But again, since He is wise, He takes the best care over what exists.

> "**One can easily see that God provides, and provides excellently.**"

Cleansed from Sin

Lactantius

Don't think you have a license to sin because offenses are removed by generosity. For sins are done away with if you give liberally to God because you have sinned. But if you sin by relying on your generosity, your sins are not done away with. God especially desires that we be cleansed from our sins. Therefore, He commands us to repent. To repent is to profess and affirm that one won't sin anymore. Therefore, those who are unaware and incautiously glide into sin are pardoned, but those who sin willfully have no pardon. Don't think that those who are purified from the stain of sin can fail to give liberally because they have no faults to blot out. In truth, they are all the more bound to exercise justice when they have been justified. In addition, people cannot be without sin as long as they are burdened with the infirmity of the flesh, which is subject to the dominion of sin in three ways—in deeds, in words, and thoughts.

Then the people rejoiced, for that they offered willingly, because with perfect heart they offered willingly to the LORD: and David the king also rejoiced with great joy.
—1 Chronicles 29:9

> "To repent is to profess and affirm that one won't sin anymore."

Christians, Beware

Cyprian

My people hath been lost sheep: their shepherds have caused them to go astray, they have turned them away on the mountains: they have gone from mountain to hill, they have forgotten their resting place.

—Jeremiah 50:6

The Lord cries out, "Hearken not unto the words of the false prophets, for the visions of their own hearts deceive them. They speak, but not out of the mouth of the Lord. They say to them that despise the word of the Lord, Ye shall have peace." Those who don't have peace themselves are offering peace. Those who have departed from the church are promising to bring backsliders back into the church. There is one God, and Christ is one. There is one church and one chair founded upon the rock by the word of the Lord. Except for the one altar and the one priesthood, another altar can't be established nor a new priesthood made. Whoever gathers from a different source scatters. . . . Run far away from the contagiousness of such people. Flee from their words and avoid them like a cancer or a plague. The Lord warns you, "They are blind leaders of the blind. But if the blind lead the blind, they shall both fall into the ditch." . . . Beloved, don't let anyone turn from the ways of the Lord. Christians, don't let anyone snatch you from the Gospel of Christ. Don't let anyone take the church's children away from the church. But let those who want to perish, perish alone.

> "Whoever gathers from a different source scatters. Run far away from the contagiousness of such people."

True Athlete

John Cassian

Would you like to hear what a true athlete of Christ said who competes according to the rules and laws of the contest? He said, "I so run, not as uncertainly; I so fight, not as one that beateth the air: but I chastise my body and bring it into subjection, lest by any means when I have preached to others I myself should be a castaway." Notice how he made the main part of the struggle depend on himself, that is, upon his flesh, as if it depended on a sure foundation. Then Paul placed the result of the battle simply in the discipline of his flesh and the submission of his body. "I then so run not as uncertainly." He doesn't run aimlessly because he is looking to the heavenly Jerusalem. He has set a goal and is directed swiftly toward it without any swerving. He doesn't run aimlessly, because, "forgetting those things which are behind, he reaches forth to those that are before, pressing towards the mark for the prize of the high calling of God in Christ Jesus." He always directs his mental gaze there and runs towards it with all speed of heart. Then, he proclaims with confidence, "I have fought a good fight, I have finished my course, I have kept the faith."

And every man that striveth for the mastery is temperate in all things. Now they do it to obtain a corruptible crown; but we an incorruptible.

—1 Corinthians 9:25

> "Paul placed the result of the battle simply in the discipline of his flesh and the submission of his body."

Your Portion
Ambrose

My flesh and my heart faileth: but God is the strength of my heart, and my portion for ever.
—Psalm 73:26

Not everyone can say, "The Lord is my portion." The covetous person can't, for covetousness comes close and says, "You are my portion. I have you under my authority. You have served me. You have sold yourself to me with that gold; by that possession you have submitted yourself to me." The indulgent person also can't say, "Christ is my portion." For luxury comes and says, "You are my portion. I made you mine in that banquet. I caught you in the net of that feast. I hold you by the bond of your gluttony. Don't you know that your table was more valuable to you than your life?" . . . Traitors can't say, "Christ is my portion." For the wickedness of their sin rushes on them and says, "They are deceiving you, Lord Jesus, because they are mine." . . . How many masters does one have who has forsaken the One! But we must not forsake Him. Who would forsake the One they follow if they were bound by chains of love? These chains set free and don't bind. And those who are bound in these chains boast: "Paul the bond servant of Jesus Christ, and Timothy." It is more glorious for us to be bound by Him than to be set free and liberated from others.

> "Who would forsake the One they follow if they were bound by chains of love?"

Greatness
Origen

Observe whether or not change occurs in those who listen honestly to the principles of our faith, harmonized with our inborn understanding. For much instruction on perverted things has the same effect—it has implanted minds with the belief that images are gods and that things made of gold, silver, ivory, and stone deserve worship. Yet common sense tells us that God is not a piece of corruptible matter. Neither is He honored when people try to form Him from dead matter or make some image or symbol of His appearance. Therefore, we say that images are not gods and such creations are not to be compared with the Creator. They are small in contrast to God. He is over all, and He created, upholds, and governs the universe. When the rational soul recognizes its relationship (to the Divine), it at once rejects what it once considered to be gods and resumes its natural love for its Creator. Because of its affection toward Him, the soul receives Him.

Ye shall make you no idols nor graven image, neither rear you up a standing image, neither shall ye set up any image of stone in your land, to bow down unto it: for I am the LORD your God.

—Leviticus 26:1

The Devil's League
Chrysostom

Let us not be desirous of vain glory, provoking one another, envying one another.
—Galatians 5:26

"Envying is even worse than fighting, since those who fight end their hatred when the cause of the war ends."

Why do you bring war into your thoughts? Why do you fill your soul with trouble? Why work up a storm? Why turn things upside down? How will you be able, in this state of mind, to ask forgiveness of sins? For if Christ won't forgive those who won't forgive the things done against them, what forgiveness should He give people who want to hurt those that haven't hurt them? For this is a proof of the worst wickedness. People like this are fighting against the church with the devil. Incidentally, they are even worse than he. For one can guard against the devil, but these kind of people conceal themselves under the mask of friendliness. Secretly they kindle the pile, throwing themselves first into the furnace. They are sick with a disease unworthy of pity but deserving ridicule. . . . What, then, is the remedy? We must all join in prayer and lift up a united voice on their behalf as we would for the demon-possessed. For indeed, these people are even more wretched because their madness is their own choice. This disease needs much prayer and pleading. Even if those who don't love their neighbors give out all their money and have the glory of martyrdom they won't benefit. . . . For envying is even worse than fighting, since those who fight end their hatred when the cause of the war ends. But those who hold grudges would never become our friends.

Our Father

Gregory of Nyssa

It was impossible that Our lives, which were alienated from God, could return to the high and heavenly place through our own power. As a result, the Apostle Paul says He who didn't know any sin became sin for us. He freed us from the curse by taking our curse on Himself as His own. Having taken on this curse, He had "slain" in Himself "the enmity" that came between us and God through sin (in fact, sin was "the enmity"). Having become what we were, He again united humanity to God through Himself. Through purity, He brought our new selves, created after God's image, into a close relationship with the Father of our nature. All of God's fulness physically dwelt in Him. He drew everything that shares in His body and is similar to Him into the same grace. And He proclaims good news . . . to everyone who became a disciple of the Word up until today. The good news is that people are no longer condemned or cast out of the kingdom of God. But they are children again and returned to the position God assigned to them. . . . "For behold," He says, "I and the children whom God hath given Me." For our sakes He took part in flesh and blood and saved us. He brought us back to the place from which we strayed, becoming mere flesh and blood by sin. And so He from whom we were formerly alienated through our revolt has become our Father and our God.

For if, when we were enemies, we were reconciled to God by the death of his Son, much more, being reconciled, we shall be saved by his life.

—Romans 5:10

> "God freed us from the curse by taking our curse on Himself as His own."

Able to Endure
Origen

But he that lacketh these things is blind, and cannot see afar off, and hath forgotten that he was purged from his old sins.
—2 Peter 1:9

"Under every temptation, we have the power to endure if we properly use the strength granted to us."

Under every temptation, we have the power to endure if we properly use the strength granted to us. But it is not the same thing to have the power to conquer and to actually be victorious. The apostle Paul showed us this in very cautious language. He said, "God will make a way to escape, that you may be able to bear it"—not necessarily that you will actually bear it. For many don't endure temptation, but are overcome by it. Now God doesn't enable us to endure temptation (otherwise there wouldn't appear to be a struggle), but gives us the power to endure. This power is given to enable us to conquer. It may be used (according to our capacity for free will) either in a diligent manner and give us victory or in a lazy manner and bring us defeat. For if a power was given to us that would always bring victory and never allow defeat, why would people struggle if they couldn't be overcome? What honor is there in a victory when the power to resist successfully is taken away? But if the possibility of conquering is given to us all equally, and if it is in our own power to use this possibility (i.e., either diligently or slothfully), then the defeated will be judged fairly and the victor will be praised deservedly.

God and Man
Gregory of Nyssa

The Word was with God in the beginning, and the Man was subject to the pain of death. The human nature wasn't eternal, and the divine nature wasn't mortal. All His other attributes are considered in the same way. For it wasn't the human nature that raised up Lazarus, nor was it the power that can't suffer who wept for him while he lay in the grave. The tears came from the Man, but the life came from the true Life. It wasn't the human nature that fed the thousands, nor was it all powerful strength that hurried to the fig tree. Who was weary from the journey, and who made the world exist by His word? What is the brightness of the glory, and what was pierced with the nails? What body was beaten during Passion Week, and what body is externally glorified? This much is clear: that the blows belong to the servant who was the Lord, and honor belongs to the Lord who was a servant. As a result, Christ's natures are unified and their respective attributes belong to both natures. Just as the Lord received the scars of the servant, the servant is glorified with the honor of the Lord. For this is why the cross is called the cross of the Lord of glory, and why every tongue confesses that Jesus Christ is Lord, to the glory of God the Father.

Who, being in the form of God, thought it not robbery to be equal with God: But made himself of no reputation, and took upon him the form of a servant, and was made in the likeness of men.

—*Philippians 2:6-7*

Truth and Lies
Augustine

For I rejoiced greatly, when the brethren came and testified of the truth that is in thee, even as thou walkest in the truth.

—3 John 1:3

When people live according to humanity's ideas and not according to God, they are like the devil. Even an angel lives not according to an angel but according to God if he abides in the truth and speaks God's truth and not his own lie. The apostle Paul says, "If the truth of God hath more abounded through my lie." He distinguishes between "my lie" and "God's truth." Therefore, when people live according to the truth, they live according to their God and not their own ideas. The One who was also God said, "I am the truth." So when people live according to themselves— that is, according to humanity and not according to God—they are conforming to a lie. . . . For we were created to be righteous so that we wouldn't live according to ourselves, but according to our Creator. In other words, we were made to do God's will and not our own. To not live as we were made to live is to live a lie. . . . Therefore, all sin is a lie. All sin is committed by our desire for a good life and our fear of pain. But the things we do for a good life are lies that make us even more miserable than ever before.

> "When people live according to themselves—they are conforming to a lie."

Pray Continually
Cyprian

Let us who are in Christ—who are always in the light—not stop praying even at night. The widow Anna never stopped praying and watching, but persevered in pleasing God. As it is written in the Gospel of Luke, "She departed not from the temple, serving with fastings and prayers night and day." . . . Beloved, who are always in the light of the Lord, consider night the day. Believe that we always walk in the light, and don't be hindered by the darkness we have escaped from. Don't fail to pray in the night hours. . . . You who are newly created and newborn by the Spirit through God's mercy, imitate what we will be someday. Since in the kingdom of heaven we will only have day without night, keep watch at the night as you would in daylight. Since we are going to pray and give thanks to God forever, let us not stop praying and giving thanks in this life also.

Evening, and morning, and at noon, will I pray, and cry aloud: and he shall hear my voice.

—Psalm 55:17

True Wisdom
Gregory Nazianzen

But the wisdom that is from above is first pure, then peaceable, gentle, and easy to be intreated, full of mercy and good fruits, without partiality, and without hypocrisy.
—James 3:17

The greatest wisdom is a praiseworthy life kept pure or being purified for God, the Holy One. He demands that we be purified as His only sacrifice—that is, He demands a repentant heart, a sacrifice of praise, and a new creation in Christ. . . . Supreme wisdom is despising wisdom that consists of language, figures of speech, deception, and unnecessary embellishments. For I would rather speak five words in church with my mind than ten thousand words with my tongue. For the meaningless voice of a trumpet doesn't rouse soldiers to spiritual combat. However, I will praise true wisdom and welcome it. By it, the lowly have won fame and the despised have gained the highest honors. By it, a crew of fishermen took the whole world in the mesh of the gospel-net. Through it, they overcame polished words and cut short useless wisdom. I don't consider the person who is clever in words to be wise, nor one who has a quick tongue but an unstable and undisciplined soul, . . . but those who only speak a little about righteousness but exemplify it in life are wise. Such people prove the trustworthiness of their language by their lives.

> "Those who only speak a little about righteousness but exemplify it in life are wise."

A Short Struggle

Sulpitius Severus

We must run from sin to righteousness. In the same way, those who practice righteousness must beware lest they open themselves up to sin. For it is written that "righteousness shall not profit the righteous on the day on which he has gone astray." We stand up for this then. We who have escaped from sin must work hard not to lose the rewards. The enemy is ready to strike those who are stripped of the shield of faith. Therefore, we must not throw aside our shield; otherwise, our side will be exposed to the attack. We must not put away our sword; otherwise, the enemy will begin to lose all his fear. We know that if the enemy sees us fully armed, he will retreat. We aren't unaware that it is hard and difficult to fight daily against the flesh and the world. But if we think about eternity and consider the kingdom of heaven which the Lord will give even us sinners, I ask us, how can we suffer enough to deserve such things? Besides, our struggle in this world is short. For although death doesn't catch up to us quickly, old age inevitably comes.

Wherefore take unto you the whole armour of God, that ye may be able to withstand in the evil day, and having done all, to stand.

—Ephesians 6:13

> "We know that if the enemy sees us fully armed, he will retreat."

Saved by Grace
Chrysostom

Giving thanks unto the Father, which hath made us meet to be partakers of the inheritance of the saints in light.
—Colossians 1:12

Grace, although it is grace, saves the willing. But it won't save those who don't want it, who turn away from it, fight against it, and oppose it. . . . Be thankful that we are saved by the gift of God, since we can't save ourselves by works. Don't give thanks only with your words also, but through your works and actions. For genuine thanksgiving is shown when we do those things that glorify God and run from those things we have been freed from. If we are honored after insulting the King, instead of being punished, and then go and insult Him again, we deserve the most horrible punishment for our ingratitude. This punishment would be much worse than after the first insult. For our ungratefulness is seen much more when we insult Him after we have been given honor and attention. So then, flee from those things we have been freed from. Don't give thanks only with your mouths, lest it be said of us, "This people honoreth Me with their lips, but with their heart is far from Me."

> "Don't give thanks only with your words also, but through your works and actions."

Our Response
Jerome

The Son of God was made the Son of Man for our salvation. Nine months He waited for His birth in the womb. . . . He who encloses the world in His fist was contained in the narrow walls of a manger. And I'm not even talking about the thirty years when He lived in obscurity, satisfied with His parents' poverty. When He was whipped, He remained calm. When He was crucified, He prayed for His crucifiers. "What shall I render unto the Lord for all His benefits towards me? I will take the cup of salvation and call upon the name of the Lord. Precious in the sight of the Lord is the death of His saints." The only fitting response we can make toward Him is to give blood for blood. Because we are redeemed by the blood of Christ, we should gladly desire to lay down our lives for our Redeemer. What saints have ever won their crowns without competing first? For righteous Abel was murdered, and Abraham was in danger of losing his wife. I don't need to elaborate. Find out others for yourself. You will find that all holy people have suffered persecution. . . . Which is best—to fight for a short time, to carry stakes for the stockade, to bear arms, and to faint under heavy battles in order to rejoice as victors forever, or to become slaves forever because we can't endure for a single hour?

Blessed is the man that endureth temptation: for when he is tried, he shall receive the crown of life, which the Lord hath promised to them that love him.

—James 1:12

> "Because we are redeemed by the blood of Christ, we should gladly lay down our lives for our Redeemer."

Coming Reward
Lactantius

As righteousness tendeth to life: so he that pursueth evil pursueth it to his own death.
—*Proverbs 11:19*

Let those who are hungry come and be fed with heavenly food that will satisfy continual hunger. Let those who are thirsty come and with a full mouth drink the water of salvation from an everflowing fountain. By this divine food and drink the blind shall see, the deaf hear, and the dumb speak; the lame will walk, the foolish will be wise, the sick will be strong, and the dead will come to life again. The supreme and honest Judge will raise to life and to eternal light whoever has trampled on the corruptions of the earth by their righteousness. Let no one trust in riches, in badges of authority, or even in royal power. These things don't make a man immortal. For those who disregard the discipline of maturing by seeking present things throw themselves face first to the ground and will be punished as deserters from their Lord, Commander, and Father. Therefore, let us strain toward righteousness. It alone, as an inseparable companion, will lead us to God. "While a spirit rules these limbs," let us serve God with unwearied service. Let us keep our posts and watches. Let us boldly fight against the enemy, knowing that we have victory and will triumph. Then we will obtain the reward of courage which the Lord has promised.

> "Let us strain toward righteousness. It alone, as an inseparable companion, will lead us to God."

Beyond Death

Gregory Nazianzen

Strengthen yourself beforehand with the seal. Secure yourself for the future with it, the best and strongest aids. Sign both your body and soul with it, as ancient Israel guarded itself with the blood of the firstborn lamb that night. Then what can happen to you? And what do you achieve? Listen to the Proverbs: "If thou sittest, he says, thou shalt be without fear; and if thou sleepest, thy sleep shall be sweet." Listen to David giving good news: "Thou shalt not be afraid for the terror by night, for mischance or noonday demon." While you live, this will contribute greatly to your sense of safety. For a branded sheep isn't snared easily, but the unmarked ones are easy prey for thieves. But at your death the seal will be a shroud that is more precious than gold. . . . No, if everything abandons you or is violently taken away from you (money, possessions, thrones, nobility, and every earthly thing), you can still lay down your life in safety. For you haven't lost any of the helps God gave you for your salvation.

Now he which stablisheth us with you in Christ, and hath anointed us, is God; Who hath also sealed us, and given the earnest of the Spirit in our hearts.
—*2 Corinthians 1:21-22*

> "At your death the seal will be a shroud that is more precious than gold."

Avoid Pride
Chrysostom

He that is void of wisdom despiseth his neighbour: but a man of understanding holdeth his peace.
—*Proverbs 11:12*

Even if we rise to the pinnacle of holiness, we should consider ourselves least of all. For pride can throw down from heaven those who aren't careful to avoid it. But a mind of humility can raise someone who thinks rationally high above the abyss of sin. For it was humility that placed the tax collector before the Pharisee. Humility of mind, however, and the acknowledgment of his sins brought the robber into Paradise before the apostles. For pride and arrogance are even worse than the devil's supernatural power. Now, even if people gain too much confidence by confessing their own sins and consider their good qualities while humbling their own souls, they will win great crowns. . . . If pride combined with righteousness drags someone down by the weight of its own wickedness, won't those who combine pride with sinfulness experience an even deeper hell? I don't say these things so that we may become careless with righteousness, but so that we may avoid pride. I don't mean that we should sin, but that we should be sensible. For humility of mind is foundational for the love of wisdom.

> "Pride and arrogance are even worse than the devil's supernatural power."

God is Good

Ambrose

Isn't God good? Consider how He fed thousands of the people in the wilderness with bread from heaven. He prevented famine and the people didn't even need to work for it. They enjoyed rest for forty years, their clothing didn't grow old, and their shoes didn't wear out. Isn't He good? He brought earth up to heaven, so that, just as the stars reflect His glory in the sky like a mirror, the choirs of apostles, martyrs, and priests shine like glorious stars and give light throughout the world. So then, He is not only good, but is more. He is a Good Shepherd . . . to His sheep, "for the good shepherd layeth down his life for his sheep." . . . It is to my advantage to believe that God is good, for "It is a good thing to trust in the Lord." It is good to confess that He is Lord, for it is written: "Give thanks unto the Lord, for He is good."

O taste and see that the LORD is good: blessed is the man that trusteth in him.
—*Psalm 34:8*

Effective Prayer
Tertullian

Pray without ceasing.
—*1 Thessalonians 5:17*

Prayer alone prevails over God. But Christ has willed that it doesn't operate for evil. He gave it all its virtue when used for good. And so it knows only . . . how to transform the weak, restore the sick, purge the possessed, open prison bars, and loosen the bonds of the innocent. Likewise, it washes away faults, repels temptations, extinguishes persecutions, consoles the faint-spirited, cheers the down-trodden, escorts travelers, calms waves, frightens robbers, nourishes the poor, governs the rich, raises the fallen, rescues the falling, confirms the standing. Prayer is the wall of faith. It arms us and hurls missiles against the enemy who watches us on all sides. So we never walk unarmed. By day, we are aware of our post—by night, of our vigil. Under the armor of prayer, we guard the banner of our General. We wait in prayer for the angel's trumpet. . . . What more do we need then, but the duty of prayer? Even the Lord Himself prayed, to whom be honor and virtue for ages and ages!

> "Under the armor
> of prayer, we
> guard the banner
> of our General."

Straight Paths
Origen

The way of the Lord is made straight in two ways. First, through contemplation: when your thoughts are cleared of falsehood by truth. And then through conduct: when we contemplate what to do and act accordingly. The statement, "Make straight the way of the Lord," can be compared with the proverb, "Depart not, either to the right hand or to the left." For those who deviate in either direction have given up on keeping their paths straight. They no longer deserve God's attention, since they have strayed from the straight journey. For "the Lord is righteous, and loves righteousness, and His face beholds straightness." The one whom the Lord notices and who benefits as a result says, "The light of Thy countenance was shown upon us, O Lord." Therefore, let us stand in sound contemplation and conduct. As Jeremiah exhorts, let us search for the ancient ways of the Lord. Let us find the good way and walk in it . . . For it is a good way that leads the good person to the good Father. These are the people who bring good things from the good treasure of their hearts. They are the good and faithful servants.

And thine ears shall hear a word behind thee, saying, This is the way, walk ye in it, when ye turn to the right hand, and when ye turn to the left.

—Isaiah 30:21

> "It is a good way that leads the good person to the good Father."

Heirs of God
Clement of Alexandria

I could provide examples of ten thousand Scripture verses of which not "one tittle shall pass away" without being fulfilled, for the Holy Spirit has spoken these things from the mouth of the Lord. He says, "Do not any longer, my son, despise the chastening of the Lord, nor faint when thou art rebuked of Him." O His surpassing love for us! The Lord gently admonishes His children, not as a Teacher speaking to his students, not as a Master to his servants, nor as God to men, but as a Father to His children. Therefore, Moses confesses that "he was filled with quaking and terror" while he listened to God speak about the Word. Aren't you afraid when you hear the voice of the Divine Word? Aren't you distressed? Don't you fear and hurry to learn of Him—that is, of salvation—dreading wrath, loving grace, eagerly striving after the hope set before us so that you might escape the judgment threatened against you? Come, come, my young people! If you don't become like little children and aren't born again, as the Scripture says, you will not receive the truly existing Father, neither will you ever enter into the kingdom of heaven. For how is a stranger permitted to enter? Well, as I take it, when people are enrolled and made citizens and receive God as their Father, they will be occupied with the Father's concerns. They will then be considered worthy to be made His heirs and will share the kingdom of the Father with His own dear Son.

Discernment Needed

Athanasius

The Lord said that "there shall arise false Christs and false prophets, so that they shall deceive many." And the devil has come, speaking by these people and saying, "I am Christ, and the truth is with me." He has made them all liars like himself. It's strange that, while all heresies are at odds with one another, they are united together by lies. They have the same father who has sown seeds of falsehood in them all. But faithful Christians and true disciples of the Gospel continually stand firm and secure away from these deceits. For they have the grace to discern spiritual things and have built their faith upon a rock. The ignorant, however, aren't thoroughly grounded in knowledge. They only consider the words they hear but don't perceive their meaning. Immediately they are drawn away by their tricks. As a result, it is important to pray for discernment. Then everyone can know whom to reject and whom to receive as friends of the faith.

Beloved, believe not every spirit, but try the spirits whether they are of God: because many false prophets are gone out into the world.
—1 John 4:1

> "It's strange that, while all heresies are at odds with one another, they are united together by lies."

The Promise after Death

Cyprian

And they departed from the presence of the council, rejoicing that they were counted worthy to suffer shame for his name.

—Acts 5:41

The Lord desired that we rejoice and leap for joy in persecutions. When persecutions occur, then the crowns of faith are given, then the soldiers of God are tested, then heaven is opened to martyrs. For we haven't enrolled for war in order to think only about peace and withdraw from battle. But in this very warfare of persecution, the Lord walked first. He is the Teacher of humility, endurance, and suffering. What He tells us to do, He did first. And what He urges us to suffer, He suffered first for us. Beloved, observe that He alone bore all the Father's judgment and will come Himself to judge.

He has already declared His future judgment and recognition. He has foretold and testified that He will confess before His Father those who confess Him and will deny those who deny Him. If we could escape death, we might reasonably fear death. But since it is necessary for a mortal man to die, we should embrace the occasion as coming from God's promise to reward us in the end with eternal life. We shouldn't fear being slain, since we are sure that we will be crowned when we are slain.

> "He has foretold and testified that He will confess before His Father those who confess Him and will deny those who deny Him."

God Provides

Leo I

Foolish people too often dare to complain against their Creator, not only when they lack something, but also when they have plenty. When something isn't given to them, they complain. And when they have certain things in abundance, they are ungrateful. . . . Let us rejoice in whatever gifts He gives. Those who have used great possessions well should also use small ones well. For plenty and scarcity may be equally good for us. Even in spiritual progress we won't be discouraged by small results if our minds aren't dry and barren. For what the earth doesn't give must spring from the soil of our heart. Those who don't stop giving will always be supplied with the means to give. We must use what each year gives us in godly works. Difficult seasons must not hinder our Christian generosity. For the Lord knows how to replenish the widow's jars, which her holy hospitality emptied. He knows how to turn water into wine. He knows how to satisfy 5,000 hungry persons with a few loaves. And the One we feed through His poor people can multiply what He takes of what He gave us.

The liberal soul shall be made fat: and he that watereth shall be watered also himself.
—Proverbs 11:25

> "Those who don't stop giving will always be supplied with the means to give."

No Excuses
Chrysostom

And now also the axe is laid unto the root of the trees: therefore every tree which bringeth not forth good fruit is hewn down, and cast into the fire.

—Matthew 3:10

"All Christians can serve their neighbors if they do their part."

Nothing is more frigid than a Christian who doesn't care about other peoples' salvation. You can't plead poverty, for the woman who cast down the two mites will accuse you. Also Peter said, "Silver and gold have I none." And Paul was so poor that he was often hungry and lacked necessary food. You can't plead lowness of birth, for they were also people of common birth to common parents. You can't claim that you lack education, for they were also "unlearned men." Even if you are a slave or a runaway slave, you can do your part. Although Onesimus was a runaway slave, notice what Paul calls him and how he elevates him with great honor: "that he may communicate with me "in my bonds," he says. You can't plead illness, for Timothy was often ill. Paul says to him, "Use a little wine for thy stomach's sake, and thine often infirmities." All Christians can serve their neighbors if they do their part. Don't you see the unfruitful trees? Do you see how strong they are, how beautiful, how large, smooth, and tall? But if we had a garden, we should much rather have pomegranates or fruitful olive trees than these. Although the others delight our eyes, they benefit us very little. Such are those who only consider their own interests. No, these people are only fit to be burned, whereas the other trees are useful both for building and for saving those within.

Perfection Will Come

Origen

Regarding "things which are the objects of perception," Paul calls them "things seen." However, he calls the objects of understanding "things unseen." He knows that visible things which are "seen" are "temporal," but that things "not seen," which we can know by our minds, are "eternal." Paul wants to think continually about these eternal things. Because of his earnest longing for them, he considers all sufferings as "light" and as "nothing." During the season of suffering and trouble, he wasn't ever weighed down by them, but, by his contemplation of divine things, he believed every disaster was light. . . . Therefore, after the troubles and struggles we suffer here, we hope to reach the highest heavens. We pleasantly receive Jesus' teaching as the fountains of water that spring us up to eternal life. We are being filled with the rivers of knowledge and will be united with those waters above the heavens that praise His name. Those of us who praise Him won't be swayed by the movement of heaven but will always concentrate on the invisible things of God. We won't understand these things through His creation anymore but as Jesus' disciple said, we will see them "then face to face," for, "When that which is perfect is come, then that which is in part will be done away."

Set your affection on things above, not on things on the earth.

—Colossians 3:2

Truth Himself
Gregory of Nyssa

While they promise them liberty, they themselves are the servants of corruption: for of whom a man is overcome, of the same is he brought in bondage.

—2 Peter 2:19

The Divine Word doesn't want us to be slaves of anything; our nature has been changed for the better. He has taken everything that was ours with the agreement that He will give what is His to us in return. Just as He took disease, death, condemnation, and sin, He also took our slavery. He doesn't keep what He took, but purged our nature of such evil. Our defects are being swallowed up and done away with in His stainless nature. Therefore, there won't be disease, condemnation, sin, or death, in the life that we hope for. And slavery will also vanish. The Truth Himself testifies of this. He says to His disciples, "I call you no more servants, but friends." . . . If "the servant knoweth not what his lord doeth," and if Christ owns all the Father's things, then let those who are reeling with alcohol become sober at last. Let them now, as never before, look up at the truth and see that He who owns all the Father's things is Lord of all and isn't a slave.

Holy
Meditation
Augustine

"Watch, therefore, and pray that you enter not into temptation." Such prayers warn you that you need the Lord's help. You shouldn't rely on yourself to live well. Don't pray for the riches and honors of this world, or for any worthless possession. But pray that you won't enter into temptation. You wouldn't ask for this in prayer if you could accomplish it for yourself. . . . In fact, when you begin to exercise this wisdom, you will have a reason to give thanks. "For what have you which you have not received? But if you have received it, beware that you boast not as if you had not received it," that is, as if you could have had it by your own power. When you have received the gift, ask the One who began giving it to you that it may be perfected. "Work out your own salvation with fear and trembling: for it is God that worketh in you, both to will and to do, of His good pleasure," for "the will is prepared by God," and "the steps of a good man are ordered by the Lord, and He delighteth in his way." Holy meditation on these things will preserve you. Your wisdom will become holiness. That is, by God's gift you will be good and will be grateful for the grace of Christ.

O LORD, I know that the way of man is not in himself: it is not in man that walketh to direct his steps.

—Jeremiah 10:23

> "You need the Lord's help. You shouldn't rely on yourself to live well."

Finding Truth

Irenaeus

A sound mind that avoids danger and is devoted to piety and truth will meditate eagerly on those things God has made understandable. People with sound minds will acquaint themselves with and come easily to understand this knowledge by daily study. These things can be seen plainly. They are clearly and unambiguously expressed in the sacred Scriptures. . . . Therefore, since the entire Scriptures, the prophets, and the Gospels can be clearly, unambiguously, and harmoniously understood by everyone (although not all believe them), and since they proclaim that one God, to the exclusion of all others, formed all things by His word, whether visible or invisible, heavenly or earthly, in the water or under the earth, . . . those who blind their eyes to such clear evidence and who won't accept the truth of the message are fools. They blind themselves and by their obscure interpretations of the parables imagine that they have found a God of their own.

Heart and Lips
Hilary of Poitiers

Our confession must not contain lazy or deliberately vague words. There must not be any space between our heart and lips, lest what should be the confession of true reverence become a mask for evil. The Word must be near us and within us. There must not be any delay between the heart and the lips. We must have a faith of conviction as well as of words. . . . The Apostle Paul explains the prophet's words: "That is the word of faith, which we preach; because if thou shalt confess with thy mouth Jesus as Lord, and shalt believe in thy heart that God hath raised Him up from the dead, thou shalt be saved." True devotion consists in rejecting doubt, and in righteousness from believing, and salvation from confessing. Don't dally with ambiguities. Don't babble vainly. Don't debate God's powers in any way or try to limit His strength. Stop searching over and over again for the causes of unsearchable mysteries. . . . Faith lies in simplicity, righteousness in faith, and true godliness in confession. For God doesn't call us to the blessed life through tiring investigations. He doesn't tempt us with rhetoric. The way to eternity is plain and easy: believe that God raised Jesus from the dead and confess that He is the Lord. . . . Jesus Christ died so that we could live in Him.

That if thou shalt confess with thy mouth the Lord Jesus, and shalt believe in thine heart that God hath raised him from the dead, thou shalt be saved. For with the heart man believeth unto righteousness; and with the mouth confession is made unto salvation.
—Romans 10:9-10

> "We must have a faith of conviction as well as of words."

The Tamer
Augustine

For our conversation is in heaven; from whence also we look for the Saviour, the Lord Jesus Christ: Who shall change our vile body, that it may be fashioned like unto his glorious body, according to the working whereby he is able even to subdue all things unto himself.
—*Philippians 3:20-21*

Our hope is in Him. Let us submit ourselves to Him and beg for His mercy. Let us place our hope in Him and, until we are tamed, that is, perfected thoroughly, let us endure our Tamer. For our Tamer often uses His whip. If you use a whip to tame your animal, shouldn't God do the same to tame His beasts and make us His children? You tame your horse. But what do you give your horse when it carries you gently, bears your discipline, obeys your commands, and becomes your faithful, useful beast? How do you repay it, when you won't so much as bury it when it dies, but will throw it to birds of prey? God, however, reserves an inheritance for you when you are tamed. And this inheritance is God Himself. Though you may be dead for a little while, He will raise you to life again. He will restore your body to you, down to every hair. He will place you with the angels forever, where you won't need His taming hand anymore. You will only need His abundant mercy. For God will then be "all in all." Unhappiness won't drive us to exhaustion, but happiness alone will feed us.

> "God reserves an inheritance for you when you are tamed."

Rise Above
Basil

The Lord doesn't send suffering to the servants of God without a purpose. It tests the genuineness of our love for God the Creator. Just as athletes win crowns struggling in the arena, Christians are perfected by the trial of their temptations if they patiently and gratefully accept what God sends them. Everything is ordained by the Lord's love. We must not be distressed by anything that happens to us even if it affects our present weaknesses. For although we don't know why everything that happens to us is sent by God as a blessing, we should be convinced that everything that happens to us is for our good. Every trial either provides a reward for our patience or keeps our soul from lingering too long in this life and being filled with the world's wickedness. If the Christian's hope was limited to this life, dying prematurely would be a bitter thing. But if those who love God know that the separating of the soul from these bodily restraints begins our real life, why do we grieve like those who have no hope? Be comforted, then, and don't fall under your troubles. Show that you are superior to them and can rise above them.

And we know that all things work together for good to them that love God, to them who are the called according to his purpose.
—*Romans 8:28*

> "We should be convinced that everything that happens to us is for our good."

Faith's Foundation

Eusebius

For thou hast been a strength to the poor, a strength to the needy in his distress, a refuge from the storm, a shadow from the heat, when the blast of the terrible ones is as a storm against the wall.
—Isaiah 25:4

How can someone doubt God's presence and help who has experienced various dangers and has been saved from them by His simple nod, who has passed through the sea that the Savior calmed and that supplied a solid road for the people? I believe that finding miracles like these performed and perfected at God's command is the foundation of faith and the basis for confidence. Therefore, even in the midst of trials there is no reason to turn from our faith. But we have an unshaken hope in God. When this habit of confidence is firmly rooted in the soul, God Himself will dwell in our deepest thoughts. His power can't be overcome. Therefore the soul in which He dwells won't be overcome by dangers surrounding it. We see this truth demonstrated in God's own victory. While He intended to bless humanity, He was severely insulted by malicious, ungodly people. However, He suffered through His passion unharmed and gained a mighty victory over sin and an everlasting crown of triumph. Therefore He accomplished His providential purpose, loved the righteous, and destroyed the cruelty of the unrighteous.

"Even in the midst of trials there is no reason to turn from our faith. But we have an unshaken hope in God."

Without Limits
Cyprian

All our power is from God. From God, I say. From Him we have life, from Him we have strength. By the power originated in and received from Him we know the signs of things to come while we are still in this world. Let fear keep you innocent; then the Lord, who has mercifully flooded our hearts with grace, will dwell in your grateful mind. And our assurance won't give way to a carelessness that would allow the old enemy to creep up on us again.

But if you keep the way of innocence and righteousness, if you walk with a firm and steady step, if you depend on God with all your strength and all your heart, and simply *are* what you have begun to be, then freedom and power will be given to you proportionate to His grace. For, unlike earthly benefits, these heavenly gifts dispensed by God are not regulated or restrained. The Spirit flows freely and isn't restrained by any limits. It isn't held back by any barriers but flows continually and liberally. Let our hearts be thirsty and ready to receive.

Who, when he came, and had seen the grace of God, was glad, and exhorted them all, that with purpose of heart they would cleave unto the Lord.
—Acts 11:23

> "Let our hearts be thirsty and ready to receive."

Testing Faith
Tertullian

He that overcometh shall not be hurt of the second death.
—*Revelation 2:11b*

Do we test the quality of the faith by the person, or the person by the faith? No one is wise, no one is faithful, no one excels in dignity but the Christian. And no one is a Christian unless he perseveres to the end. You know other people from outside appearance. You think as you see. You see only as far as your eyes can look. But Scripture says, "the eyes of the Lord are lofty." "Man looketh at the outward appearance, but God looketh at the heart." "The Lord beholdeth and knoweth them that are His;" "the plant which my heavenly Father hath not planted, He rooteth up;" "the first shall be last;" and "He carries His fan in His hand to purge His threshing floor." Let the chaff of a fickle faith fly off at every blast of temptation. Then that heap of corn for the Lord's granary will be all the purer. Didn't certain disciples turn back from the Lord when they were offended? Yet the rest didn't think they must turn away from following Him. Because they knew He was the Word of Life and had come from God, they continued in His company to the very end.

> "Let the chaff of a fickle faith fly off at every blast of temptation."

Rocky Roads
John Cassian

Clearly, we are the ones who roughen up the right, smooth paths of the Lord with the nasty, hard stones of our desires. We are the ones who most foolishly forsake the royal road that was stony from the apostles' and prophets' flint, but tread down the footsteps of all the saints and of the Lord Himself. We are the ones who seek pathless, thorny places, blinded by the allurements of present delights. We tear our way through dark paths, with torn legs and our ripped wedding garments, because they are overgrown with the briars of sin. We are not only pierced by sharp thorns but also crippled by the bites of deadly serpents and scorpions lurking there. For "there are thorns and thistles in wrong ways, but he that feareth the Lord shall keep himself from them." The Lord speaks of such people through the prophet Jeremiah saying, "My people have forgotten, sacrificing in vain, and stumbling in their ways, in ancient paths, to walk in them in a way not trodden." . . . But those who truly give up this world, take up Christ's yoke, learn from Him, and daily endure wrong (for Christ is "meek and lowly of heart") will never be troubled by temptations. "All things will work together for good to him." For the prophet Obadiah says that God's words are "good to him that walketh uprightly," and, "For the ways of the Lord are right, and the just shall walk in them; but the transgressors shall fall in them."

Who is wise, and he shall understand these things? prudent, and he shall know them? for the ways of the LORD are right, and the just shall walk in them: but the transgressors shall fall therein.
—*Hosea 14:9*

> "We are the ones who roughen up the right, smooth paths of the Lord with the nasty, hard stones of our desires."

Good and Faithful
Aphrahat

Now faith is the substance of things hoped for, the evidence of things not seen.

—*Hebrews 11:1*

Beloved, let us draw near to faith, since its powers are so great. For faith raised Enoch up to heaven. . . . It caused the barren to bear children. It delivered people from the sword. It raised us from the pit. It enriched the poor. It released the captives. It delivered the persecuted. It brought down fire. It divided the sea. It split the rock and gave water for the thirsty to drink. It satisfied the hungry. It raised the dead and brought them up from Sheol. It stilled the storm. It healed the sick. It conquered armies. It overthrew walls. It stopped the mouths of lions and quenched the flames of fire. It humiliated the proud and brought the humble honor . . . When you have read and learned about the works of faith, you can be like the tilled land the good seed fell on. For it produced fruit of thirty-, sixty-, and a hundred-fold. Then, when you come to your Lord, He will call you a good servant, thoughtful and faithful. On account of His faith that abounds in you, you will enter the kingdom of your Lord.

> "Beloved, let us draw near to faith, since its powers are so great."

The Disease of Pride

Augustine

Pride is the source of all sins. If doctors merely cure symptoms, but not causes, they seem to heal their patients for a while. But as long as the causes remain in the body, the diseases will repeat themselves. For example, consider an illness in the body that produces scaly skin or sores, a high fever, and intense pain. Certain remedies are applied to curb dry skin and to relieve the sores' heat. When the remedies are applied, they work and the person is healed. But because the fluid wasn't expelled from the body, it will come back again as ulcers. Recognizing this, the doctor eliminates the illness and removes the cause so there won't be any more sores. So what causes sin? Pride. Cure pride and there won't be any more sin. Consequently, the Son of God came down and was humiliated to cure pride, the cause of all sin. Why are you proud? God humbled Himself for you. Perhaps you would be ashamed to imitate a lowly person, but at any rate, imitate the lowly God. The Son of God came as a man and was made low. . . . So recognize that you are human yourself. Humility is to know yourself . . . And Christ said, "I came not to do my own will, but the will of Him that sent me." This is the glory of humility. Where pride does its own will, humility does the will of God.

Take my yoke upon you, and learn of me; for I am meek and lowly in heart: and ye shall find rest unto your souls.
—Matthew 11:29

> "The Son of God came down and was humiliated to cure pride, the cause of all sin."

Victorious Return
Cyprian

For our light affliction, which is but for a moment, worketh for us a far more exceeding and eternal weight of glory.
—*2 Corinthians 4:17*

The Apostle Paul says: "The sufferings of this present time are not worthy to be compared with the coming glory which shall be revealed in us." Who wouldn't work with all his might to attain to such a glory, to become the friend of God, to rejoice with Christ, and to receive rewards from God after earthly tortures and punishments? It is glorious for soldiers of this world to return home after defeating the enemy. But it is much more glorious to return to Paradise triumphant over the devil. How excellent to bring victorious trophies back to the place whence Adam was driven out as a sinner when you have cast down the one who cast him down. How much better it is to offer to God the most acceptable gift—an uncorrupted faith, an unyielding strength of mind, and an evident devotion; to accompany Him when He takes revenge against His enemies; to stand at His side when He sits to judge; to become coheir of Christ; to be made equal to the angels; and with the patriarchs, apostles, and prophets; to rejoice, having obtained the heavenly kingdom! What persecution can conquer us, what tortures can overcome us with these thoughts in mind? The brave and loyal mind, established on such thoughts, endures. When it is strengthened by the sure and solid faith of things to come, the soul cannot be moved.

Danger in the Mind

Tertullian

Our actions originate with our will. Unless some sins are due to chance, necessity, or ignorance, all sin is willful. Since our will is the origin of our actions, isn't it also accountable as the first to take part in sin? The Lord demonstrates this by adding a superstructure to the Law and prohibiting sins of the will as well as other sins. Doesn't He define an adulterer as not only the man who had actually invaded another's marriage bond, but also the one who violates a woman by his lustful gaze? As a result, it is dangerous for the mind to dwell on what is forbidden, to perform, and to plan out sin rashly. Even without carrying out our sinful desires, what we will is considered done. Therefore, it will be punished as an action. It is utterly in vain to say, "I willed, but yet I did not." Rather, you should carry it out because you willed it. Otherwise, don't will it at all if you won't carry it out. By your mind's confession, you condemn yourself. For if you eagerly desired a good thing, you would have been anxious to carry it out. Similarly, even if you do not carry out something evil, you should not have eagerly desired it. Wherever you take your stand, you are bound by guilt if you have willed evil and haven't carried out good.

But every man is tempted, when he is drawn away of his own lust, and enticed.

—James 1:14

> "You are bound by guilt if you have willed evil and haven't carried out good."

God's Beauty
Hilary of Poitiers

The heavens declare the glory of God; and the firmament sheweth his handywork.
—*Psalm 19:1*

While the faithful soul was lost and confused by its own feebleness, it caught a glimpse of God's magnitude in the prophet's voice. He said, "By the greatness of His works and the beauty of the things that He hath made the Creator of worlds is rightly discerned." The Creator of great things is supreme in greatness. Of every beautiful thing He is superior in beauty. Since His handiwork is beyond our thoughts, and the Maker is greater than thought itself, heaven, air, earth, and sea are beautiful. In fact, the whole universe is beautiful. And the Greeks agree. Because of its beautiful order, they call it *kosmos* (that is, order). Our minds can estimate this beauty of the universe by natural instinct. We also see this instinct in certain birds and animals whose voices we can't understand, but whose language is clear to each other. Since all speech expresses thought, a meaning apparent to them lies in these voices. So must not the Lord of this universal beauty also be recognized as the most beautiful among all the beauty that surrounds Him? For although the splendor of God's eternal glory exhausts our mind's best powers, we can't help but see that He is beautiful. We must truthfully confess that God is most beautiful. For even though His beauty is incomprehensible, it forces itself on our perception.

United Prayer
Cyprian

The Lord says to the church that if only two or three gather together and pray in agreement according to His commands, they will receive what they ask from God's sovereign power. "Wheresoever two or three are gathered together in My name, I am with them," He says. That is, He is with the simple and peaceable, with those who fear God and keep His commandments. Although only two or three, God will treat them in the same way that He treated the three youths in the fiery furnace. Because they lived for God unconditionally and in unity, He gave them life with the breath of dew in the midst of the surrounding flames. In the same way, He was present with the two apostles shut up in prison, because they were devoted and of one mind. Having loosened the bolts of the dungeon, He placed them in the marketplace to declare the Word they had faithfully preached. Therefore, when He says in His commandments, "Where two or three are gathered together in my name, I am with them," He rebukes the faithless for their disagreements and entrusts peace to the faithful by His Word. He shows that He is with two or three who pray with one mind, rather than with a large number who differ. More can be obtained by the unified prayer of a few than by the disunited supplication of many.

These all continued with one accord in prayer and supplication, with the women, and Mary the mother of Jesus, and with his brethren.

—Acts 1:14

> "More can be obtained by the unified prayer of a few than by the disunited supplication of many."

Keep Running
Chrysostom

Not as though I had already attained, either were already perfect: but I follow after, if that I may apprehend that for which also I am apprehended of Christ Jesus.
—*Philippians 3:12*

I am only intent on "one thing," says Paul, "in stretching forward to the things which are before." But included in this "one thing," he says, is "forgetting the things which are behind, and stretching forward to the things which are before, I press on toward the goal unto the prize of the high calling of God in Christ Jesus." Forgetting the past things made him reach forward to the things ahead. So then, any who think they have accomplished it all and need no further perfecting can stop running. They have reached their goal. But those who think they are still far from the goal will never stop running. You should think like the latter, even if you perform ten thousand good deeds. For if Paul thought thus, after ten thousand deaths and so many dangers, how much more should we? . . . We should act like him, forget our successes, and throw them behind us. For runners don't think about how many laps they have finished, but how many are left. We, too, should think not about how we are advanced in holiness, but about how much farther we have to go. For how do we profit from what we have when we don't add what we lack? In addition, Paul didn't say, "I don't think about," but "I don't even remember." For we become eager when we diligently work toward what is left, when we forget everything else.

> "Runners don't think about how many laps they have finished, but how many are left."

Standing at Your Post
Clement of Alexandria

The cure for self-conceit (like every sickness) is threefold: discovering the cause, finding a method for its removal, and training the soul to make correct decisions. Just like a dysfunctional eye, the soul darkened by false doctrines cannot discern the light of truth but overlooks what is right in front of it.

And just as mischievous boys lock out their teacher, false teachers shut out the teachings from their church, regarding them with suspicion. In fact, they stitch together a mass of lies and fabrications in order to appear as though they are acting reasonably by not admitting the Scriptures. So then, they are not pious since they are not pleased with the commands of the Holy Spirit. They are deprived of the counsel of God and the traditions of Christ and are bitter like the wild almond. Their doctrine (except for evident truths they could not discard or conceal) begins with themselves.

Therefore, as the soldier in war must not leave the post assigned to him by the commander, we must not desert the post assigned by the Word. It guides us in knowledge and life. Most, however, haven't even asked if there is One we should follow, who this One is, or how to deal with lies. But the believer should live according to what the Word says in order to follow God.

We have also a more sure word of prophecy; whereunto ye do well that ye take heed, as unto a light that shineth in a dark place, until the day dawn, and the day star arise in your hearts.

—2 Peter 1:19

Overcame Faults
Jerome

But to do good and to communicate forget not: for with such sacrifices God is well pleased.
—Hebrews 13:16

The world's philosophers drive out an old passion by instilling a new one. They hammer out one nail by hammering in another. The seven princes of Persia acted towards King Ahasuerus on this principle. They overcame his regret for losing Queen Vashti by persuading him to love other maidens. However, where they cured one fault by another fault and one sin by another sin, we must overcome our faults by learning to love their opposite virtues. "Depart from evil," says the psalmist, "and do good; seek peace and pursue it." For if we don't hate evil, we can't love good. More than this, we must do good if we want to depart from evil. We must seek peace if we want to avoid war. It isn't enough merely to seek peace, we must pursue it with all our energy when we have found it and it runs from us. For "it passeth all understanding," and God dwells in peace.

> "We must overcome our faults by learning to love their opposite virtues."

God's Rewards
Lactantius

Since good and evil things are set before us, we should remember that it is much better to offset short-term evils by eternal things than to endure eternal evils for short-term and perishable things. For in a contest, in this life, an enemy is set before you. You must work hard first so that you can enjoy rest afterwards, you must suffer hunger and thirst, you must endure heat and cold, you must rest on the ground, and must watch and experience dangers, so that your children, house, and property will be preserved and you can enjoy all the blessings of peace and victory. But, if you choose present ease over hard work, you do yourself the greatest harm: the enemy will surprise you and find you not resisting. Your lands will be devastated, your house plundered, your wife and children become prey, and you will be slain or taken prisoner. To prevent these things from happening, you must abandon present benefits for a greater and more lasting advantage. God has provided an opponent for us so that we may acquire virtue. Therefore, present gratification must be laid aside, lest the enemy overpower us. In short, we must patiently submit to everything that is unpleasant and painful, all the more because God, our Commander, has appointed us eternal rewards for our efforts. Since in this earthly warfare people expend so much effort trying to acquire things that will perish in the same way they were acquired, surely we shouldn't refuse any work that will bring a reward that can never be lost.

If any man's work abide which he hath built thereupon, he shall receive a reward.

—1 Corinthians 3:14

315

God's Justice
Clement of Alexandria

He is the Rock, his work is perfect: for all his ways are judgment: a God of truth and without iniquity, just and right is he.
—Deuteronomy 32:4

There are two kinds of fear. One is accompanied with reverence, such as citizens show toward good rulers, as we show God and as right-minded children show their fathers. "For an unbroken horse turns out unmanageable, and a son who is allowed to take his own way turns out reckless." The other species of fear is accompanied by hatred that slaves feel toward hard masters and the Hebrews felt, who made God a master, not a Father. And as far as piety is concerned, voluntary and spontaneous actions differ a lot, if not entirely, from forced ones. "For He," it is said, "is merciful; He will heal their sins, and not destroy them, fully turn away His anger, and not kindle all His wrath." See how the Instructor's justice, which deals in rebukes, and God's goodness, which deals in compassion, are shown. David—that is, the Spirit through him—embracing both fears, sings of God Himself: "Justice and judgment are the preparation of His throne: mercy and truth shall go before Thy face." He says that it is by the same power both to judge and to do good. For there is power over both, and judgment separates that justice from its opposite. And He who is truly God is just and good, who is Himself all.

Stand Tall
Chrysostom

How can we receive grace? By doing what pleases God and obeying Him in everything. In great households, the servants who disregard their own interests and zealously and promptly promote their masters' interests are favored. They serve not out of compulsion but from their own affection and good character. They order everything well, don't occupy themselves with private concerns, and don't care for their own interest. But they consider their master's concerns their own when they are in full view and when they are engaged in the house. . . . If the world's favored servants prefer their master's interests to their own, and, in so doing, actually elevate their own interest, such devotion should also characterize servants of God. He wills this Himself. Despise each concern and cling to the kingdom of heaven. Dwell there, not here. Stand tall there, not here. If you stand tall, even the demons will fear you. If your dependence is on worldly wealth, however, they will scorn you along with other people. . . . If you despise riches, you will be radiant in the house of the King.

Wherefore we receiving a kingdom which cannot be moved, let us have grace, whereby we may serve God acceptably with reverence and godly fear.
—*Hebrews 12:28*

"In great households, the servants who disregard their own interests and zealously and promptly promote their masters' interests are favored."

Holy Scriptures
John of Damascus

But his delight is in the law of the LORD; and in his law doth he meditate day and night. And he shall be like a tree planted by the rivers of water, that bringeth forth his fruit in his season; his leaf also shall not wither; and whatsoever he doeth shall prosper.

—Psalm 1:2-3

To search the Scriptures is an excellent and profitable work for souls. Just as a tree is planted by streams of waters, the soul watered by divine Scripture is enriched and gives fruit (that is, righteous belief) in its season. It is adorned with evergreen branches—actions pleasing to God. Through the Holy Scriptures, we are trained to think rightly and to act in a manner pleasing to God. For in these words we are encouraged toward every virtue and dissuaded from every evil. If we love learning, we will be learned in many things. For by carefulness, hard work, and the grace of the giving God, everything is accomplished. All who ask receive, those who seek find, and to those who knock it shall be opened.

Therefore, let us knock at the beautiful garden of Scripture. It is fragrant, sweet, and blooming with various sounds of spiritual and divinely inspired birds. They sing all around our ears, capture our hearts, comfort the mourners, pacify the angry, and fill us with everlasting joy. Scripture sets our mind on the gold, gleaming, brilliant back of the divine dove. Its bright wings rise to the Only-begotten Son who is the Heir of the spiritual vineyard's Farmer. The divine dove brings us through Him to the Father of Lights.

> "To search the Scriptures is an excellent and profitable work for souls."

Jealousy's Fire
Cyprian

What a gnawing worm of the soul, what a plague of our thoughts, what a rust of our heart it is to be jealous of someone's strength or happiness. That is, to hate one's deserved profit or divine benefits, to turn others' advantages into your harm, to be tormented by the prosperity of famous men, to make other people's glory your own penalty, and, as it were, to execute yourself or to bring tormentors to your thoughts and feelings, that they might tear up your stomach and strike the secret places of the heart with hatred. To such a person no food is joyous, no drink can be cheerful. They are always sighing, groaning, and grieving. Since the envious never put off envy, the crazed heart is torn violently day and night. Other diseases have their limit, and the wrong done is confined by the completion of the crime. . . . Jealousy has no limit; it is an evil that continually endures and a sin without end. The lies of jealousy burn hotter in proportion to the increasing success of the person envied.

Therefore, as I live, saith the Lord GOD, I will even do according to thine anger, and according to thine envy which thou hast used out of thy hatred against them; and I will make myself known among them, when I have judged thee.
—*Ezekiel 35:11*

> "Jealousy has no limit; it is an evil that continually endures and a sin without end."

I Am

Chrysostom

Isn't He right in turning from us and punishing us, when He gives Himself up for us entirely and yet we resist Him? Surely, it is plain to everyone. For whether you desire to adorn yourself, "Let it, He saith, be with My ornaments"; or to equip yourself, "with My arms"; or to clothe yourself, "with My raiment"; or to feed yourself, "at My table"; or to travel, "on My way"; or to inherit, "My inheritance"; or to enter a country, "the city of which I am Builder and Maker"; or to build a house "amongst My tabernacles." . . . What can equal this generosity: that, "I am Father, I am Brother, I am Bridegroom, I am dwelling place, I am food, I am raiment, I am Root, I am foundation, all whatsoever thou willest, I am"?—and "Be thou in need of nothing, I will be even a servant, for I came to minister, not to be ministered to; I am Friend, member, Head, Brother, sister, and mother; I am all; only cling closely to Me. I was poor for you, and a wanderer for you, on the cross for you, in the tomb for you; above I intercede for you to the Father, on earth I have come for your sake as an Ambassador from My Father. You are all things to Me, brother, joint heir, friend, and member." What more could you ask for?

Fleshly Burden
Augustine

We should pray not only not to be led into evil but also to be delivered from the evil we have already been led into. When this happens, we won't need to fear temptation or anything else. But as long as we live in our fleshly state, which the serpent led us into, we can't hope for such deliverance. We should hope, however, that it will take place in the future. This is the unseen hope that the apostle Paul spoke about: "But hope which is seen is not hope." Nevertheless, the faithful servants of God shouldn't neglect the wisdom given to us in this life. We should avoid the things the Lord says to avoid with the greatest caution. We should seek after the things the Lord says to seek after with the strongest love. For after we set aside the remaining burden of our flesh in death, we will be perfected. Every part of us will be perfected into the purity we have strained every nerve to obtain.

Who shall change our vile body, that it may be fashioned like unto his glorious body, according to the working whereby he is able even to subdue all things unto himself.
—*Philippians 3:21*

> "After we set aside the remaining burden of our flesh in death, we will be perfected."

God Empowers
Eusebius

O that there were such an heart in them, that they would fear me, and keep all my commandments always, that it might be well with them, and with their children for ever!
—Deuteronomy 5:29

Our perception is obscured when we receive with anger and impatience commands that were given to bless us. . . . For obedience to God is rewarded by imperishable and everlasting life. Those who know Him can aim for this and shape their lives to be examples for others, a continual standard of righteousness to imitate. Therefore, doctrine was entrusted to wise people. The truths they communicated could then be kept carefully and with pure consciences by their households. Then true, steadfast obedience to God's commands could be established and produce boldness in the face of death. Such boldness comes from a pure faith and genuine holiness before God. Those who are armed like this can withstand the world's storms. . . . They boldly overcome the greatest terrors and are considered worthy of a crown of glory. People like this don't accept praise but know full well that God gave them the power to endure and to fulfill His commands zealously. Such people will always be remembered and will receive everlasting honor.

"Those who know Him can shape their lives to be examples for others, a continual standard of righteousness to imitate."

Restore My Soul

Augustine

How can I find rest in You? Who will send You into my heart to strengthen it, so that I may forget my sorrows, and embrace You, my only good? What are You to me? Have compassion on me, so that I may speak. What am I to You that You demand my love and, unless I give it, are angry and threaten me with great sorrows? Then is it a light sorrow to not love You? Have mercy on me! O Lord my God, compassionately show me what You are to me. "Say unto my soul, I am thy salvation." Say this so I can hear You . . . When I hear, may I run and cling to You. Don't hide Your face from me. Let me die, because only if I die can I see Your face. My soul is constricted. Expand it so that You can enter in. It is in ruins; restore it. It will offend Your eyes. I confess and know this, but who will cleanse it? To whom can I cry out but to You? Cleanse me from my secret sins, O Lord, and keep Your servant from the secret sins of others. . . . You are the truth and I don't fight against Your judgment. I won't deceive myself, for fear that my iniquity would lie against itself. Therefore, I don't fight against Your judgment. For "if Thou, Lord, shouldest mark iniquities, O Lord, who shall stand?"

But your iniquities have separated between you and your God, and your sins have hid his face from you, that he will not hear.
—Isaiah 59:2

> "My soul is constricted. Expand it so that You can enter in."

Evil Temptations
Dionysius of Alexandria

The Lord knoweth how to deliver the godly out of temptations, and to reserve the unjust unto the day of judgment to be punished.
—2 Peter 2:9

After saying, "In the world ye shall have tribulation," Christ added, "But be of good cheer, I have overcome the world." He taught the disciples to pray that they wouldn't fall into temptation. He said, "And lead us not into temptation," which means, "Do not let us fall into temptation." To show that this implied not that they wouldn't be tempted but that they would be saved from evil, He added, "But deliver us from evil." Perhaps you will say, "What difference is there between being tempted, and falling or entering into temptation?" Well, if a person is overcome by evil (and he will be overcome unless he struggles against it, and unless God protects him with His shield), that person has entered into temptation and has been taken captive to it. But if one resists and endures, one is tempted but hasn't entered into temptation or fallen under it. Therefore, the wicked one draws us into evil temptations when he tempts us. But God tests us as one untempted by evil. For God, it is said, "cannot be tempted of evil." The devil, therefore, drives us on by violence, drawing us to destruction. But God leads us by the hand, training us for our salvation.

> "The devil drives us on by violence, drawing us to destruction. But God leads us by the hand, training us for our salvation."

Blessed Repentance
Tertullian

The task of calculating the abundant good of repentance should be expressed with great eloquence. However, in proportion to our narrow abilities let us emphasize one point—that what God commands is good and best. I believe one who disputes the "good" of a divine command is bold and arrogant. For it is not the fact that it is good which binds us to obey, but the fact that God has commanded it. The Majesty of Divine power has the superior right to demand obedience. The authority of Him who commands has priority over His servants. "Is it good to repent, or not?" Why do you question this? God commands. He doesn't merely command, but also appeals to us. He invites us to obey by offering a reward—salvation. By His promise, "I live," He desires that we trust Him. Oh, we are blessed, for whose sake God promises salvation! But we are most miserable if we don't believe the Lord even when He promises! Therefore, what God so highly commends, what He even promises, we are bound to approach and to regard with the utmost seriousness. Then, by permanently living in faith in God's solemn pledge of divine grace, we will be able to persevere and receive its fruit.

For I have no pleasure in the death of him that dieth, saith the Lord GOD: wherefore turn yourselves, and live ye.
—*Ezekiel 18:32*

> "We are most miserable if we don't believe the Lord even when He promises!"

Temporal Riches

Athanasius

For riches are not for ever: and doth the crown endure to every generation?
—*Proverbs 27:24*

We must not faint, thinking that this period of time is long, or that we are doing something great. "For the sufferings of this present time are not worthy to be compared with the glory which shall be revealed to us." As we look at the world, we must not think that we have given up anything important, for the earth is very small compared to heaven. Even if by chance we ruled over the entire earth and gave it all up, it wouldn't be worthy of the kingdom of heaven. . . . For someone who ruled over the entire earth and gave it up, would have given up very little but received a hundred times as much. . . . Moreover, even if we don't give things up for righteousness' sake, when we die we will leave them behind—often (as Solomon said) to those we do not want to have them. Why then wouldn't we give them up for righteousness' sake in order to inherit a kingdom? Don't let the desire to possess things take hold of you. For what do we gain by acquiring things we cannot take with us? Why not get the things we can take with us instead—namely wisdom, justice, self-control, courage, understanding, love, kindness to the poor, faith in Christ, freedom from wrath, and hospitality? If we possess these things, they will prepare a welcome for us in the land of the humble.

> "Don't let the desire to possess things take hold of you. For what do we gain by acquiring things we cannot take with us?"

Bits and Spurs
Origen

Unless a horse continually feels the spur of his rider and has his mouth irritated by a bit, he becomes stubborn. A boy also, unless constantly disciplined, will grow up to be an arrogant youth, ready to fall recklessly into wickedness. Consequently, God abandons and neglects those He considers unworthy of punishment. "For whom the Lord loveth He chasteneth, and scourgeth every son whom He receiveth." We must believe that those who have been punished and disciplined have been given the status and affection of His children. As a result, while enduring trials and tribulations, they can say, "Who shall separate us from the love of God which is in Christ Jesus? Shall tribulation, or anguish, or famine, or nakedness, or peril, or sword?" For by these things one's commitment is demonstrated and displayed. The firmness of one's perseverance is made known, not so much to God, who knows all things before they happen, but to rational and heavenly angels . . . as assistants to and servants of God.

For whom the LORD loveth he correcteth; even as a father the son in whom he delighteth.

—*Proverbs 3:12*

Recovering in Battle

Augustine

The sting of death is sin; and the strength of sin is the law. But thanks be to God, which giveth us the victory through our Lord Jesus Christ.

—1 Corinthians 15:56-57

What is the full and perfect liberty found in the Lord Jesus? He said, "If the Son shall make you free, then shall ye be free indeed." And when will we have full and perfect liberty? When hostility ends and death, our last enemy, is destroyed. "For this corruptible must put on incorruption, and this mortal must put on immortality. And when this mortal shall have put on immortality, then shall be brought to pass the saying that is written: 'Death is swallowed up in victory.' O death, where is thy struggle?" . . . Now we will never die but live in Him who died for us and rose again. . . . As those who are wounded, we should be praying for a physician. We must be carried into the inn to be healed. For He who pitied the man left half alive on the road by robbers, promises salvation. . . . He healed the man's wounds. He placed him on his animal. He took him to the inn. He placed him in the innkeeper's care. Who was the innkeeper? Perhaps it was Paul, the one who said, "We are ambassadors for Christ." He gave also two coins to pay for healing the man's wounds. Perhaps these are the two commandments on which the Law and the prophets all hang. Therefore, beloved, the church is the traveler's inn where the wounded are healed. But above the church is the life and liberty we inherit.

> "The church is the traveler's inn where the wounded are healed."

The Body and Soul

Tertullian

Every soul has its nature in Adam until it is born again in Christ. It is unclean without this regeneration. Because the soul is unclean, it is actively sinful. And because it is connected to the body, it fills with its own shame. Yes, the flesh is sinful, and we are forbidden to conform to it. . . . However, the flesh is not disgraced on its own account. For on its own it doesn't think or feel anything that would recommend or demand sin. How could it? The flesh is only an instrument. It doesn't serve like an employee or familiar friend—living and human beings—but rather like a vessel or something of that kind. It is body, not soul. Now a cup may minister to a thirsty man, but if the thirsty man won't put the cup to his mouth, it will not serve him. Therefore a person's distinguishing feature isn't his earthly body. Neither is the flesh the human person and a personal quality. Instead, it functions for the soul, although it is united with the soul as a slave or instrument for duties of life. How absurd to attribute sin to something that doesn't have any good actions or character of its own! . . . The flesh is quite a different substance and different condition from the soul in form and function.

And the very God of peace sanctify you wholly; and I pray God your whole spirit and soul and body be preserved blameless unto the coming of our Lord Jesus Christ.

—1 Thessalonians 5:23

> "Every soul has its nature in Adam until it is born again in Christ."

Give Thanks
Athanasius

In every thing give thanks: for this is the will of God in Christ Jesus concerning you.

—1 Thessalonians 5:18

Knowing that the Lord loves thankful people, His faithful servants never stop praising Him. They always give thanks to the Lord. Whether they are in times of ease or of suffering, they offer praise to God with thanksgiving. . . . Therefore, Job, who had more courage than anyone, thought of these things when he prospered. But when he suffered, he patiently endured the pain and gave thanks. David also sang praises during times of pain and sorrow. He said, "I will bless the Lord at all times." And Paul, in all of his epistles, never stopped thanking God. In times of ease he didn't falter, and he gloried in times of suffering. For Paul knew that "tribulation worketh patience, and patience experience, and experience hope, and that hope maketh not ashamed." As followers of such men, we must not let any season pass without thanksgiving. . . . For the Apostle Paul, who gave thanks always, urges us to draw near to God in the same way. He said, "Let your requests, with thanksgiving, be made known unto God." Desiring that we would always continue doing this, he says, "At all times give thanks; pray without ceasing." For he knew that believers are strong while they give thanks. And, while rejoicing, they pass over the enemy's walls. These people are like the saints who said, "Through Thee will we pierce through our enemies, and by my God I will leap over a wall."

> "We must not let any season pass without thanksgiving."

Perseverance
Cyprian

Let us stay alert and hold fast to Christ's patience, by which we can reach God. This patience, abundant and diverse, is not restrained by narrow limits, nor confined by straight boundaries. But the virtue of patience is demonstrated widely. Even though its fertility and liberality come from a single source, . . . patience both recommends us to God and preserves our relationship with Him. It relieves anger, bridles the tongue, governs the mind, guards peace, rules discipline, and breaks the force of lust. It represses the violence of pride, extinguishes the fire of hostility, checks the power of the rich, and soothes the needs of the poor. Patience protects the blessed integrity of virgins and the careful purity of widows, and those united under a single affection in marriage. It makes men humble in prosperity, brave in adversity, and gentle towards wrongs and disrespect. It teaches us to pardon quickly those who wrong us, and, if we do wrong, to beg earnestly for forgiveness. It resists temptations, suffers persecutions, perfects passions and martyrdoms. Patience firmly strengthens the foundations of our faith and elevates our increasing hope. It directs our actions so that we hold fast to the way of Christ while walking by His patience. While we imitate our Father's patience, we persevere as sons of God.

Howbeit for this cause I obtained mercy, that in me first Jesus Christ might shew forth all longsuffering, for a pattern to them which should hereafter believe on him to life everlasting.

—1 Timothy 1:16

> "While we imitate our Father's patience, we persevere as sons of God."

Answered Prayers
Chrysostom

Pray without ceasing.
—*1 Thessalonians 5:17*

Those things we don't have the strength to perform on our own, we can accomplish easily through persevering prayer. For we have the duty to pray without ceasing. Those in pain and those spared from pain must pray. So must those in danger and those in prosperity. For those who have ease and wealth must pray that these things may never change. Those in pain and danger must pray that some favorable change will come to them, and so that they may move into a comfortable, calm state.

Are you in a calm time? Then beg God that your calm may continue. Has a storm risen up against you? Earnestly beg God to make the crashing wave pass, and to calm the storm. Have you been heard? Then be heartily thankful. Have you not been heard? Then persevere in order to be heard. For if God ever delays giving an answer, it isn't because of hatred and hostility. It is because of His desire to keep you with Him forever by postponing an answer, just as affectionate fathers do.

> "Have you been heard? Then be heartily thankful. Have you not been heard? Persevere in order to be heard."

Greater Grace
Ambrose

Paul teaches "What will ye? Shall I come to you with a rod, or in love and a spirit of meekness?" . . . What He means by the rod is shown by his speech against fornication, his denunciation of incest, his criticism of pride (because those who should be mourning were puffed up), and lastly, his sentence on the guilty to be . . . delivered to the enemy who would destroy their flesh and not their souls. The Lord didn't give Satan power over Job's holy soul, but allowed him to attack Job's body. Similarly, sinners are delivered to Satan to destroy the flesh. Although the serpent can lick the dust of their flesh, he can't hurt their souls. So then, our flesh must die to lusts. It must be captive to and subdued by, and not war against, the law of our mind. Instead, it must die as a slave to a good service. Take Paul, for example. He beat his body to make it submit, so that his preaching would become more worthy. . . . For the flesh dies when the Spirit swallows its wisdom. Then it no longer has a taste for the things of the flesh, but for the things of the Spirit. I want to see my flesh weakening. I don't want to be dragged into captivity to the law of sin. I don't want to live in the flesh, but in the faith of Christ! So there is greater grace in the body's pain than in its health.

But I keep under my body, and bring it into subjection: lest that by any means, when I have preached to others, I myself should be a castaway.
—1 Corinthians 9:27

> "Our flesh must be captive to and subdued by, and not war against, the law of our mind."

Test of Will

Jerome

For in that he him-self hath suffered being tempted, he is able to succour them that are tempted.
—Hebrews 2:18

The Apostle James, knowing that the baptized can be tempted and fall by their own free choice, says: "Blessed is the man that endureth temptation: for when he hath been approved, he shall receive the crown of life, which the Lord promised to them that love him." So that we won't think we are tempted by God, . . . he adds: "Let no man say when he is tempted, I am tempted of God: for God cannot be tempted with evil, and He Himself tempteth no man. But each man is tempted when he is drawn away by his own lust and enticed. Then the lust, when it hath con-ceived, beareth sin: and the sin, when it is full-grown, bringeth forth death." God created us with free will, and we aren't forced into righteous-ness or wickedness. If we were forced, there wouldn't be a crown. But God perfects us in good works. For we don't reach perfection because of our will or because we run towards it, but because God pities us and helps us to reach the goal.

> "We don't reach perfection because of our will or because we run towards it, but because God pities us and helps us to reach the goal."

Persecution's Purpose

Tertullian

As persecutions increasingly threaten us, we must ask all the more earnestly how faith should respond to them. . . . Nothing happens outside of God's will. Persecution is especially worthy of God and required for the approving or the rejecting of His professing servants. What is the point of persecution? What is its result other than . . . the Lord sifting His people? Persecution . . . is just the judgment of the Lord. And the judging belongs to God alone. It is the fan that cleans the Lord's threshing floor, the church. It sifts the mixed heap of believers and separates the grain of martyrs from the chaff of deniers. . . . The one great thing in persecution is the promotion of God's glory, as He tests and throws away, lays on and takes off. What glorifies God will surely come to pass by His will. When is trust in God stronger than when there is a greater fear of Him and when persecution breaks out? Then faith is both more zealous in preparation and better disciplined in fasts and meetings, prayers and humility, in brotherly kindness and love, in holiness and restraint. There is no room for anything but fear and hope.

Whose fan is in his hand, and he will throughly purge his floor, and gather his wheat into the garner; but he will burn up the chaff with unquenchable fire.

—Matthew 3:12

Loving Your Neighbor
Augustine

*And this command-
ment have we from
him, That he who
loveth God love his
brother also.
—1 John 4:21*

Since you should not even love yourself for your own sake, but for God who is most worthy of your love, others have no right to be angry at you if you love them for God's sake. For this is the law of love, laid down by Divine authority: "Thou shalt love thy neighbor as thyself," and "Thou shalt love God with all thy heart, and with all thy soul, and with all thy mind." So, you must offer all your thoughts, your whole life, and your whole intelligence to Him who gives you everything. When He says, "With all thy heart, and with all thy soul, and with all thy mind," He means that no part of our life should be unoccupied, allowing room for other wishes. But anything else that appears to be worthy of love must be directed into the same channel through which the whole current of our affections flows. Therefore those who love their neighbors should urge them to love God with their whole heart, soul, and mind. For by loving their neighbors as themselves, they turn the whole current of their love for others into the channel of the love of God.

> "Since you should not even love yourself for your own sake, but for God who is most worthy of your love, . . ."

Children
of Martyrs
Basil

Is the trial heavy, beloved? Let us endure the toil. No one who avoids the blows and the dust of battle wins a crown. Are the devil's mockeries and the attack of the enemy insignificant? These trials are troublesome because they serve the Lord. They are despised because God has combined wickedness with weakness in them. But let us beware of crying out too loud over a little pain and, as a result, being condemned. Only one thing is worth heartache: losing oneself for momentary credit (if you can really say making ourselves a public disgrace is to your credit).

Blessed are ye, when men shall revile you, and persecute you, and shall say all manner of evil against you falsely, for my sake.
—Matthew 5:11

Then you have deprived yourself of the everlasting reward given to the righteous. You are children of those who confess Christ. You are children of martyrs. You have resisted sin to the point of shedding blood. Therefore, use the examples of those near and dear to you to make you brave for religion's sake. None of us have been torn by lashes from the whip. None of us have suffered from confiscation of our houses. We haven't been driven into exile. We haven't suffered imprisonment. What great suffering have we undergone? Unless perhaps the fact that we haven't suffered anything and aren't considered worthy of Christ's sufferings is in itself a source of pain?

> "Use the examples of those near and dear to you to make you brave for religion's sake."

Have Patience
Hermas

Know ye not that ye are the temple of God, and that the Spirit of God dwelleth in you?
—1 Corinthians 3:16

If you are patient, the Holy Spirit that dwells in you will be pure. He will not be darkened by any evil spirit, He will rejoice and be glad; and with the vessel in which He dwells, He will serve God in gladness, having great peace within Himself. But if any outburst of anger takes place, the Holy Spirit seeks to depart because He does not have a pure place. For the Lord dwells in patience, but the devil in anger. The two spirits, then, when living in the same place, are in conflict with each other and are troublesome to the person in whom they dwell. For if an extremely small piece of wormwood is put into a jar of honey, isn't the honey entirely destroyed? And doesn't the extremely small piece of wormwood take away the sweetness of the honey entirely so that it no longer pleases its owner, but has become bitter and lost its use? But if the wormwood isn't put into the honey, then the honey remains sweet and is useful to its owner. You see, then, that patience is sweeter than honey. It is useful to God, and the Lord dwells in it. But anger is bitter and useless. If anger is mixed with patience, then the patience is polluted, and its prayer becomes useless to God.

> "Patience is sweeter than honey. It is useful to God, and the Lord dwells in it."

Holding on Despite

Lactantius

People see that those who are tortured remain patient while the executioners grow weary. As a result, they realize that the agreement of so many and the steadfastness of those dying must have meaning. They see that patience alone could not handle these tortures without God's help. For robbers and strong men can't endure such abuse. They yell out and groan because they are overcome by pain. They haven't had patience ingrained in them. But in our case, boys and delicate women (not to mention men) overpower their torturers in silence. Even fire won't make them groan. . . . Notice that even the weak, fragile, and aged endure physical torture and burning. They don't endure because they have to, for they are allowed to escape if they want. But they endure torture and death of their own free will because they have put their trust in God.

For we which live are alway delivered unto death for Jesus' sake, that the life also of Jesus might be made manifest in our mortal flesh.
—2 Corinthians 4:11

Possessions and Sacrifice

Augustine

The fishermen of Galilee found pleasure not only in leaving their ships and nets at the Lord's command, but also in declaring that they had left everything and followed Him. Those who reject not only everything they have but everything they hoped to possess truly give up everything. What they may have desired is only seen by God. What they actually possessed is seen by human eyes. In addition, when we love unimportant, earthly things, somehow we are more firmly married to what we have than to what we want to have. Why did the man who asked the Lord about eternal life go away sorrowful when he heard that he must sell everything and give it to the poor in order to be saved? For it is one thing to avoid gaining what we want, but it is another thing to give away that which has become a part of us. The former action is like declining food, the latter is like cutting off an arm. How great and wonderful is the joy of Christian generosity we obtain when, in obedience to the Gospel of Christ, we cheerfully sacrifice what that rich man grieved over and refused to give up.

> "Those who reject not only everything they have but everything they hoped to possess truly give up everything."

Pleasure's Dangers

Gregory of Nyssa

It is perfectly clear that no one can come near God's purity who hasn't become pure first. Therefore, we must place between us and sensual pleasures a high, strong wall of separation. Then as we approach God, our heart's purity won't be soiled again. . . . Pleasure is all the same, as we learn from the experts. For just as water separates into various streams from a single fountain, pleasure spreads itself over the pleasure-lover through the various avenues of the senses. And the person who succumbs to pleasure through any sensation has been wounded by that sensation. This corresponds with Christ's teaching that "he who has satisfied the lust of the eyes has received the mischief already in his heart." For I take it that, in this particular example, our Lord was speaking about any of the senses. So we can add to His saying, "He who has heard to lust after"; "He who has touched to lust after"; "He who has lowered any faculty within himself to the service of pleasure has sinned in his heart." To prevent this, we want to use self-control in our lives. We must never let our minds dwell on anything where pleasure has hid its bait. . . . In everything we do, we must choose the useful amount and leave the rest untouched that would merely indulge the senses.

He that loveth pleasure shall be a poor man: he that loveth wine and oil shall not be rich.

—*Proverbs 21:17*

> "We want to use self-control in our lives. We must never let our minds dwell on anything where pleasure has hid its bait."

Guard Your Mouth

Ambrose

Whoso keepeth his mouth and his tongue keepeth his soul from troubles.
—Proverbs 21:23

Let there be a door on your mouth so that it can be shut when necessary. Let it be closed carefully so that no one can rouse your voice to anger and make you pay back abuse with abuse. You have heard it read, "Be ye angry and sin not." Therefore, although we are angry (as a result of our nature, not our will), we must not utter one evil word with our mouths, lest we fall into sin.

But our words should be . . . humble and moderate so that our tongues are enslaved to our minds. Hold your tongue in check with a tight rein. Restrain it and call it back to moderation. Test the words it utters by scales of justice so that if your meaning is serious, your speech has substance and your words have gravity. Those who abide by this will be patient, gentle, and modest by guarding their mouths, restraining their tongues, thinking before they speak, and weighing their words. Such people question whether or not to say something or give an answer and ponder whether it is an appropriate time for their remark. . . . We should act like this for fear that our words, which should give beauty to our inner lives, would plainly show that we have evil morals.

> "Hold your tongue in check with a tight rein. Restrain it and call it back to moderation."

Heavenly Thoughts

Gregory I

I wonder much why the words of earthly people agitate you when you have fixed your hearts on heaven. For when the friends who came to console him broke out into rebuke, Job said, "For behold my witness is in heaven, and He that knows me is on high." Those who have the witness of their lives in heaven shouldn't be afraid of human judgments. Paul, a leader of good men, also said, "Our glory is this, the testimony of our conscience." And again he says, "Let every man prove his own work, and so shall he have glory in himself, and not in another." For if we rejoice in praises and are broken down by ridicule, we don't draw our glory from ourselves, but from the mouths of others. Indeed, the foolish virgins didn't take any oil in their vessels, but the wise ones took oil in their vessels along with their lamps. Now our lamps are good works. It is written, "Let your light shine before men, that they may see your good works and glorify your Father which is in heaven." And we take oil in our vessels along with our lamps when we don't seek glory for our good works from our neighbors' praise, but preserve it in the testimony of our conscience.

I say the truth in Christ, I lie not, my conscience also bearing me witness in the Holy Ghost.
—Romans 9:1

> "Those who have the witness of their lives in heaven shouldn't be afraid of human judgments."

The Great Instructor
Clement of Alexandria

Admonition is the judgment of loving care and produces understanding. The Instructor demonstrates such admonitions when He says in the Gospel, "How often would I have gathered thy children, as a bird gathers her young ones under her wings, and ye would not!" And again, the Scripture admonishes, saying, "And they committed adultery with stock and stone and burned incense to Baal." It is a very great proof of His love that, although He knew well the shamelessness of the people that had kicked and run away, He nevertheless exhorts them to repentance and says by Ezekiel, "Son of man, thou dwellest in the midst of scorpions; nevertheless, speak to them, if peradventure they will hear." Further, He says to Moses, "Go and tell Pharaoh to send My people forth; but I know that he will not send them forth." He shows both things: His Divinity by His foreknowledge of what would take place, and His love by providing an opportunity for the soul to choose repentance. Caring for people, He also admonishes by Isaiah when He says, "This people honor Me with their lips, but their heart is far from Me." What follows is reproving judgment: "In vain do they worship Me, teaching for doctrines the commandments of men." Here His loving care shows their sin and salvation side by side.

Cling to Love
Testaments of the Twelve Patriarchs

Hatred is evil, because it always tolerates lying or speaking against the truth; it makes small things great, considers darkness to be light. It calls sweet things bitter, and teaches slander, war, violence, and evil. It fills the heart with devilish poison. I say these things from experience, my children, so that you will run from hatred and cling to the love of the Lord. Righteousness casts out hatred and humility destroys hatred. For those that are righteous and humble are ashamed to do wrong. They aren't rebuked by someone else, but by their own heart, because the Lord sees their motives. They don't speak against anyone, because their fear of the Most High overcomes hatred. Because they fear offending the Lord, they won't do anything wrong to anyone, even by their thoughts. . . . For true, godly repentance destroys unbelief, drives away the darkness, enlightens the eyes, gives knowledge to the soul, and guides the mind to salvation. Those things which it hadn't learned from people, it knows through repentance.

Whosoever hateth his brother is a murderer: and ye know that no murderer hath eternal life abiding in him.

—1 John 3:15

> **"Run from hatred and cling to the love of the Lord."**

Changed by God
Rufinus

Could I doubt that He who made me from the dust of the earth can make me, a guilty person, innocent? Could I doubt that He who made me see when I was blind, or hear when I was deaf, or walk when lame, can recover my lost innocence for me? Look at nature's testimony—to kill a man isn't always criminal, but to kill maliciously and not by law is criminal. Then it isn't the deed in such cases that condemns me (sometimes it is done rightly), but the mind's evil intentions. If my mind is corrected, which was considered criminal and caused sin, then why couldn't I be made innocent when I once was criminal? . . . For crime doesn't consist in the deed but in the will. Just as an evil will, prompted by an evil demon, has exposed me to sin and death, the will changed to good and prompted by the good God has restored me to innocence and life. It is the same with all other crimes. As a result, we can't find any contradiction between our faith and natural reason. For forgiveness of sins isn't given to deeds that can't be changed once they're done, but to the mind, which can change from bad to good.

> "Crime doesn't consist in the deed but in the will."

Building Blocks
Origen

If we confess Christ, we will become like Peter. We will be considered blessed as he was. Flesh and blood haven't revealed to us that Jesus is the Christ and the Son of the living God, but the Father in heaven has, so that we can be citizens of heaven. This revelation carries to heaven those who unveil their hearts and receive "the spirit of the wisdom and revelation" of God. And if we say like Peter, "Thou art the Christ, the Son of the living God," not because flesh and blood revealed it to us, but because our heavenly Father's light has shone in our hearts, we become a rock, or a Peter. . . . Christ is the spiritual Rock from whom His people drank and every disciple of Christ is a rock. Every word of the church and its government is built upon every such rock. For the church is built by God through each of the perfect ones who provide blessing through their words, deeds, and thoughts.

For with the heart man believeth unto righteousness; and with the mouth confession is made unto salvation.

—Romans 10:10

DECEMBER 13

Seek and Find
Augustine

Buy the truth, and sell it not; also wisdom, and instruction, and understanding.
—*Proverbs 23:23*

Perfection in this life, Paul tells us, is to forget the things behind us and to reach forward and press on toward the things ahead of us. Those who seek until they reach the goal have the most secure direction. For the right goal starts from faith. True faith is, in some way, the starting point of knowledge. But true knowledge won't be perfected until after this life when we will see Christ face-to-face. Therefore, know that seeking the truth is safer than presuming that unknown things can be known. So seek as if you will find, and, as a result, find as if you were about to seek. For "when a man hath done, then he beginneth." . . . Try to understand this. Pray for help from the One we want to understand. And, as much as He allows, religiously and anxiously seek to explain what you have come to understand to others.

> "Seek as if you will find, and, as a result, find as if you were about to seek."

Follow the Leader
Athanasius

Beloved, how should we regard the loving-kindness of our Savior? We should cry out and praise His goodness with power and with trumpets! Not only should we appear like Him, but should follow Christ's example for heavenly conversation. We should carry on what He began. In suffering, we shouldn't threaten. When we are verbally abused, we shouldn't berate in return. Instead, we should bless those that curse us and commit ourselves to God in everything. For He judges righteously. Those who do this adapt themselves to the Gospel. They will have a part with Christ, and, as imitators of apostolic conversation, He considers them worthy of praise. They will receive the praise Paul gave to the Corinthians when he said, "I praise you that in everything ye are mindful of me." Afterwards, because some people perverted Paul's words according to their own lusts, . . . he proceeded to say, "And as I have delivered to you traditions, hold them fast." Of course that means that we shouldn't think things other than what the Teacher has delivered.

Bless them that curse you, and pray for them which despitefully use you.
—*Luke 6:28*

> "We should bless those that curse us and commit ourselves to God in everything."

Harmony of Creation

Irenaeus

Now ye are the body of Christ, and members in particular.
—1 Corinthians 12:27

All things originate from one God. Since created things are various and numerous, they are well fitted and adapted to the whole creation. However, when viewed individually, they are mutually opposite and inharmonious like the sound of the lyre, which consists of many and opposite notes but gives rise to one unbroken melody through the intervals that separate each one from the others. The lover of truth, therefore, should not be deceived by the interval between the notes or imagine that one was due to one artist and author and another to someone else. He should not think that one person fitted the treble, another the bass, and yet another the tenor strings. But he should hold that one person formed the whole, so as to prove the soundness, goodness, and skill exhibited in the whole work. Those, too, who listen to the melody ought to praise and exalt the artist, to admire the tension of some notes, to attend to the softness of others, to catch the sound of others between both these extremes, and to consider the special character of others. Then they can inquire at what each one aims and what is the cause of the variety, never failing to apply our rule, neither giving up the one artist, nor casting off faith in the one God who formed all things, nor blaspheming our Creator.

Two Blessings
Augustine

There are two kinds of blessings: temporal and eternal. Temporal blessings are health, honor, friends, wealth, children, a home, a wife, and other things from our journey in life. But we reside in the hotel of life as travelers moving on, not as owners intending to remain. For eternal blessings are eternal life, the body and soul's incorruption and immortality, the allegiance of angels, the heavenly city, unfailing glory and the Father—the former without death, the latter without an enemy. These blessings make us desire them with eagerness and ask for them with perseverance. We don't ask with lengthy words, but with groans. A longing desire is always praying even though the tongue is silent. For if you ever long for these things, you are praying. When does prayer sleep? When desire grows cold. So then, let us beg for these eternal blessings with eager desire. Let us seek these good things with entire earnestness. Let us ask for them with assurance. . . . Beloved, ask also for temporal blessings, but in moderation. Be sure that if we do receive them, He who knows what is beneficial for us gives them to us. You have asked. Hasn't He given you what you asked for? Trust your Father. He would give it to you if it was beneficial for you.

For here have we no continuing city, but we seek one to come.
—Hebrews 13:14

> "Let us beg for eternal blessings with eager desire. Let us seek for these good things with entire earnestness."

Restrain Anger
Ambrose

Stand in awe, and sin not: commune with your own heart upon your bed, and be still.
—Psalm 4:4

An old saying says to make ourselves habitually consistent. Then our lives can be like pictures, preserving the same representation they first received. How can one be consistent who is inflamed by anger one minute and the next blazes up with fierce resentment? Or what about one whose face burns at first, but, in an instant, is changed to paleness—varying and changing its color every minute? It is natural for one to be angry because generally there is good reason. However, it is our duty to restrain anger. We must not be carried away by fury like a lion, unable to settle down. We must not spread tales or make family quarrels worse, for it is written, "A wrathful man diggeth up sin." One who is double-minded won't be consistent. Those who can't restrain themselves when they're angry can't be consistent. David says it well, "Be ye angry and sin not." He doesn't condemn his anger, but indulges his natural tendency. One can't prevent these tendencies but can moderate them. Therefore, even though we are angry, we must only admit that our emotion is natural and must not sin.

> "It is natural for one to be angry because generally there is good reason. However, it is our duty to restrain anger."

Older Christians

Gregory of Nyssa

God has placed older believers as a lighthouse for those of us who live around them. Many of them were youths in their prime, but have grown gray by their consistent practice of self-control and restraint. . . . The only love they tasted was that of wisdom. This isn't because their natural instincts were different from everyone else's, for all "flesh lusteth against the Spirit." But they listened to those who said self-control "is a tree of life to them that lay hold upon her." They sailed across the swelling storms of life, as though on a boat, and anchored themselves in the haven of God's will. After such a fortunate voyage they are enviable as they rest their souls in sunny, cloudless calm. They now ride safely, anchored by a good hope and far out of reach of the storm's tumult. And for others who follow, they radiate the splendor of their lives like fires on a high watchtower. Indeed, we have a signal to guide us safely over the ocean of temptations. Why ask the too curious question whether or not such people have fallen? Why despair as if the achievement was beyond your reach? Look at the one who has succeeded and boldly launch out on your voyage with confidence that it will be prosperous. Sail on under the breeze of the Holy Spirit with Christ your Pilot and with oars of good cheer.

The hoary head is a crown of glory, if it be found in the way of righteousness.

—Proverbs 16:31

> "God has placed older believers as a lighthouse for those of us who live around them."

In Their Shoes
Lactantius

Bear ye one another's burdens, and so fulfil the law of Christ.
—*Galatians 6:2*

Compassion is closely connected to harmlessness. For although the latter doesn't hurt anyone, the former works good. The latter begins justice, the former completes it. . . . God has given us the affection of compassion so that we can protect lives by helping one another. If we are created by one God, descended from one man, and, therefore, are thus connected by the law of kinship, we should love everyone. As a result, we are bound not only to abstain from hurting others, but even not to take revenge when we are hurt. Then we will be completely harmless. Regarding this, God commands us always to pray for our enemies. We should be animals fitted for companionship and society so that we will protect ourselves by giving and receiving assistance. For our frailty is prone to many accidents and inconveniences. Expect that what you see happening to someone else may also happen to you. You will be stirred to help someone if you shall assume the mind of those who, being placed in danger, beg for your help.

A Kind Teacher
Athanasius

If some students can't learn through more difficult subjects, a kind, caring teacher will come down to their level and teach them by simpler means. Christ, the Word of God, did this. Paul said, "For seeing that in the wisdom of God the world through its wisdom knew not God, it was God's good pleasure through the foolishness of the word preached to save them that believe." Christ saw that people wouldn't think about God. Instead, with downcast eyes, they sought the knowledge of God in nature and in the sensory world. They imagined that mortal humans and demons were their gods. Therefore, the loving Savior of all, the Word of God, took on a body and walked among people like a human being. He met the mental capacity of all people halfway. That is to say, those who think God is physical can see the truth and recognize the Father through the Lord's physical works. Therefore, the people were drawn to Christ through whatever objects they fixed their minds on and learned the truth from all angles.

But of him are ye in Christ Jesus, who of God is made unto us wisdom, and righteousness, and sanctification, and redemption.

1 Corinthians 1:30

> "The loving Savior of all, the Word of God, took on a body and walked among people like a human being."

Loving Neighbors
Pseudo-Clement

Seeing ye have purified your souls in obeying the truth through the Spirit unto unfeigned love of the brethren, see that ye love one another with a pure heart fervently.

—1 Peter 1:22

Those who fight with nature for the sake of what is reasonable are righteous. For example, it is natural for people to love those who love them. But the righteous also try to love their enemies and to bless those who defame them. They even pray for their enemies and are compassionate toward those who do wrong to them. Therefore they refrain from doing wrong and bless those who curse them, pardon those who strike them, and submit to those who persecute them. They salute those who do not salute them, share things they have with those who don't have, and persuade those that are angry with them. They pacify their enemies, warn the disobedient, instruct the unbelieving, and comfort the mourners. In distress, they endure being ungratefully treated and don't become angry. Having devoted themselves to love their neighbors as themselves, they aren't afraid of poverty, but become poor by sharing their possessions with those who have none. They don't exclude sinners. As they want to be praised, blessed, and honored, and to have all their sins forgiven, so they do the same to their neighbors. They love others like themselves. In summary, what they wish for themselves, they wish for their neighbors. For this is the law of God and of the prophets. This is the doctrine of truth.

Shelter
Chrysostom

The things that make up countless evils are these: being a slave to the appetite, doing anything for vainglory, being a slave to the madness of riches, and, most powerful of all, desiring more. . . . How can we have victory over the enemy? By running to God for shelter the way Christ taught us. We must not be depressed in times of famine but believe that God can feed us without a word. We must not tempt Him who gives good gifts with the good things we receive from Him. But we should be content with heavenly glory, disregard human things, and always despise excess. For nothing makes us fall under the devil's power as surely as longing for more and loving covetousness. We can see this even now. For even now some say, "All these things will we give thee, if thou wilt fall down and worship." They are human by nature, but have become the devil's instruments. . . . For as much as God has blessed you, follow Christ's example and imitate His victory.

The name of the LORD is a strong tower: the righteous runneth into it, and is safe.
—*Proverbs 18:10*

> "How can we have victory over the enemy? By running to God for shelter."

Patience, Patience

Tertullian

Better is the end of a thing than the beginning thereof: and the patient in spirit is better than the proud in spirit.

—*Ecclesiastes 7:8*

The evil one's operation, hurling various irritations at our spirit, is broad and wide. The trifling ones you can despise because they are little. You might yield to the very great ones because they are overpowering. When the injury is smaller, there is no need for impatience. But when the injury is greater, the injury's remedy—patience—is more necessary. Therefore, let us strive to endure the evil one's afflictions so that the lack of emotions seen in our composure may mock the passion of the enemy. . . . The reward of that duty is great—namely, happiness. For the Lord has called the patient happy. He says, "Blessed are the poor in spirit, for theirs is the kingdom of heaven." I guarantee this, that none is "poor in spirit" except the humble. Well, who is humble except the patient? For no one can humble himself or bear humiliation without patience. "Blessed," He says, "are the weepers and mourners." Who is tolerant of such unhappiness without patience? But consolation and laughter are promised to such people. . . . He says, "Rejoice and exult, as often as they shall curse and persecute you; for very great is your reward in heaven." Of course, He isn't making a promise to joy, for no one will "exult" in misfortunes unless he first learns to despise it. No one will despise misfortunes unless he has learned to practice patience.

> "No one can humble himself or bear humiliation without patience."

Drawing Near
Origen

We, whose spiritual eyes have been opened by the Word, Jesus Christ, and who see the difference between light and darkness, prefer to take our stand "in the light." We won't have anything at all to do with darkness. In addition, the true Light, endowed with life, knows who to reveal His full splendor to and to whom His light. For He doesn't just display His brilliance due to the weakness in the recipient's eyes. And whose eyes are affected and injured if we must speak of them at all? Those who are ignorant of God and whose passions prevent them from seeing the truth. Christians, however, aren't blinded by the words of those who opposed worshiping God. But let those who know they are blinded by following crowds who are in error and groups that keep festivals to demons, draw near to the Word, Jesus Christ. He can give the gift of sight. Like the poor and blind whom . . . Jesus healed because they said to Him, "Son of David, have mercy upon me," those who draw near to Him will also receive mercy and recover their eyesight, created fresh and beautiful by the Word of God.

Then spake Jesus again unto them, saying, I am the light of the world: he that followeth me shall not walk in darkness, but shall have the light of life.
—*John 8:12*

> "The true Light, endowed with life, knows who to reveal His full splendor to, and to whom His light."

359

Power of Jesus' Birth

Leo I

For the grace of God that bringeth salvation hath appeared to all men, Teaching us that, denying ungodliness and worldly lusts, we should live soberly, righteously, and godly, in this present world.
—Titus 2:11-12

O Our dearly beloved Savior was born today. Let us be glad! For there isn't a proper place for sadness when we celebrate the birthday of the Life. For this Life destroys our fear of death and brings us the joy of promised eternity. Everyone can share in this happiness. There is the same amount of joy for everyone. For our Lord destroys sin and death and finds everyone guilty, but has come to free us all. Let saints rejoice at their nearness to victory. Let sinners be glad that they are invited to be pardoned. . . . Let us, then, dearly beloved, give thanks to God the Father, through His Son, in the Holy Spirit. Because of "His great mercy, wherewith He has loved us," He had pity on us. And "when we were dead in sins, has quickened us together in Christ," so that we can be new creations in Him. So then, let us put off the old self with its deeds and, sharing in Christ's birth, let us defy fleshly works. Christians, acknowledge your dignity. As you become a partner in God's nature, refuse to return to the old, wicked behavior. Remember the Head and the body which you are members of. Remember that you were rescued from the power of darkness and brought out into God's light and kingdom.

> "This life destroys our fear of death and brings us the joy of promised eternity."

Worthy to Compete

John Cassian

As long as athletes of Christ are in the body, they never lack victory in contests. But in proportion to their growth by triumphant successes, more severe struggles confront them. For when the flesh is restrained and conquered, swarms of foes and masses of enemies are egged on by such triumphs and rise up against the victorious soldier of Christ! They fear that such soldiers of Christ might relax their efforts in the ease of peace and forget about the glorious struggles of their contests. They fear that, through the idleness caused by immunity from danger, soldiers could relax and be cheated of their prizes and rewards. So if we want to rise to these stages of triumph with ever-growing righteousness, we should enlist into battle in the same way. We should begin by saying with Paul, "I so fight, not as one that beateth the air, but I chastise my body and bring it into subjection." Then when this conflict is ended, we could say with him once more, "We wrestle not against flesh and blood, but against principalities, against powers, against world-rulers of this darkness, against spiritual wickedness in heavenly places." Otherwise, we can't possibly battle against these enemies. We don't deserve to compete spiritually if we are conquered even in fleshly contests and beaten in our struggle with our stomachs. We will deserve to hear the apostle's words of blame, "Temptation does not overtake you, except what is common to man."

But I keep under my body, and bring it into subjection: lest that by any means, when I have preached to others, I myself should be a castaway.

—1 Corinthians 9:27

Infinite Care
Chrysostom

But God forbid that I should glory, save in the cross of our Lord Jesus Christ, by whom the world is crucified unto me, and I unto the world.
—Galatians 6:14

Truly the symbol of the cross is considered despicable according to the world and among people. But in heaven and among the faithful, it is the highest glory. Poverty, too, is seen as despicable, but we boast in it. It is cheapened by the public and they laugh at it, but we are elated by it. In the same way, we boast in the cross. Paul doesn't say, "I boast not," or "I will not boast," but "Far be it from me that I should." It is as though he hates it, considers it absurd, and asks for God to help him avoid it.

But what is boasting in the cross? Boasting in the fact that Christ took on the form of a slave for my sake and suffered for me when I was the slave, the enemy, the unfeeling one. He loved me so much that He gave Himself over to a curse for me. What can compare to this? If servants only receive praise from their masters, who they are bound to kin by nature, and are elated by it, how much more must we boast when our Master, God Himself, isn't ashamed of the cross Christ endured for us. Therefore, we must not be ashamed of His unspeakable tenderness. He wasn't ashamed of being crucified for you—will you be ashamed to confess His infinite care for you?

> "He loved me so much that He gave Himself over to a curse for me. What can compare to this?"

Faith and Love

Augustine

Three things are found in faith. Those who work out their faith through love must hope for what God promises. Hope, therefore, is the partner of faith. For hope is necessary as long as we don't see what we believe, or else, by not seeing we would fail. Not seeing makes us sad, but the hope of seeing comforts us. . . . Love is also the partner of faith. We long, glow with desire for it, and hunger and thirst for it. So together there is faith, hope, and love. . . . Take away faith and all you believe in evaporates; take away love and all that you do evaporates. For the purpose of faith is to believe; of love, to do. For if you believe without love, you don't diligently perform good works. Or, if you do, you do so as a slave out of fear of punishment instead of as a child out of love of righteousness. Therefore, faith purifies the heart and is worked out by love.

Even so faith, if it hath not works, is dead, being alone.
—James 2:17

"Take away love and all that you do evaporates."

Now Is the Time

Gregory Nazianzen

For this shall every one that is godly pray unto thee in a time when thou mayest be found: surely in the floods of great waters they shall not come nigh unto him.

—Psalm 32:6

It would be absurd to grasp for money but throw away your health, or to cleanse your body lavishly but neglect cleansing your soul. It is ridiculous to seek for freedom from earthly slavery but not care about heavenly freedom, or to zealously do good to others without wanting to do good to yourself. It is foolish to eagerly try to dress and live extravagantly, but never consider how you yourself could become precious. If you could buy goodness, you wouldn't spare any money. But when mercy is offered freely at your feet, you despise it for its cheapness. Every moment is fitting to cleanse yourself, because you may die at any moment. With Paul, I shout to you with his loud voice, "Behold, now is the accepted time; behold, now is the day of salvation." *Now* doesn't point to a specific time, but is every present moment. Also, "Awake, thou that sleepest, and Christ shall give thee light." He will dispel the darkness of sin. For as Isaiah says, it is terrifying to receive hope at night, but profitable to receive it in the morning.

> "If you could buy goodness, you wouldn't spare any money. But when mercy is offered freely at your feet, you despise it for its cheapness."

Continue On
Cyprian

I urge you by our common faith, by my true and simple love for you. Hold fast to your glory with courage, perseverance, and strength, having overcome the enemy. We are still in the world. We are still placed in the battlefield. We fight daily for our lives. Take care in order to profit from these battles and to finish what you have begun to be. It is a small thing to attain something, but it is more important to keep what you have attained. Faith and saving birth makes alive, not by being received, but by being preserved. It isn't actually the attainment, but the perfecting, that keeps a man for God. The Lord taught this when He said, "Behold, thou art made whole; sin no more, lest a worse thing come unto thee." Imagine Him as saying this to one who confesses Him, "Lo, thou art made a confessor; sin no more, lest a worse thing come unto thee." Solomon, Saul, and many others were able to keep the grace given to them as long as they walked in the Lord's ways. But when they abandoned the Lord, grace also abandoned them.

Your iniquities have turned away these things, and your sins have withholden good things from you.
—Jeremiah 5:25

> "Faith and saving birth makes alive, not by being received, but by being preserved."

Spiritual Battle
Clement of Alexandria

O that there were such an heart in them, that they would fear me, and keep all my commandments always, that it might be well with them, and with their children for ever!
—Deuteronomy 5:29

> "This is the true athlete—one who is crowned for having victory over all passions in the great stadium, the world."

This is the true athlete—one who is crowned for having victory over all passions in the great stadium, the world. For He who directs the contest is the Almighty God, and He who awards the prize is the Only-begotten Son of God. Angels and demons are spectators. And the contest, containing all the different exercises, is "not against flesh and blood," but against the spiritual powers of unregulated passions that work through the flesh. Those who master these struggles and overthrow the tempter, win eternal life. The spectators are called to come to the contest, and the athletes contend in the stadium. The one who has obeyed the trainer's directions wins the day. For the rewards God offers to everyone are equal, and He is indisputable. His judgment is always right. Those who have strength receive mercy, and those who have exercised willpower are mighty. Also, we have received intelligence so that we might understand what we are doing. The command, "Know thyself" means to know what we are born for. We are born to obey the commandments, if we are willing to be saved. . . . The athlete who has obeyed the trainer's directions wins the day. Man's duty, then, is obedience to God. One who readily receives and keeps the commandments, considering them appropriately, is faithful.

More about the Early Church Fathers

Ambrose (c. 339–397). Ambrose was the first Latin church father born into a Christian family. He devoted himself to studying the law and was rewarded by being appointed governor of the northern section of Italy in 370. Four years later, the people of Milan appointed him as bishop of their city. Ambrose faced down emperors while teaching the truths of Jesus on a weekly basis to the people. He did much to advance congregational singing, was instrumental in bringing a young Augustine to Jesus, and composed an influential book on Christian ethics—*On the Duties of the Church's Servants.* Other key writings of Ambrose include *On the Holy Spirit, On the Incarnation,* and *On the Faith.*
Selections are found on January 22, 31; February 2, 11; March 27; April 23; May 1, 18; June 5; July 23; August 21; September 21, 28; October 13; November 28; December 7, 17.

Aphrahat (early fourth century). The author of *Demonstrations,* a series of works in Syriac detailing fundamental aspects of the Christian faith, was unknown for two centuries following their translation. Today, scholars have determined that the author was Aphrahat, known as the "Persian Sage." Almost nothing is known of Aphrahat's life, except that he was a Christian theologian and possibly a bishop. Medieval tradition made him head of a monastery in Mar Mathai, near the city of Nineveh. *A selection is found on November 1.*

Athanasius (c. 295–373). Born in Alexandria, Egypt, Athanasius received a primarily Christian education. In 328, he was selected to be bishop of Alexandria, where he began a crusade against the Arian belief that the Son was a created being. Athanasius countered this heretical belief by insisting that if that was the case, Christ could not save people from their sins. His writings and teachings caused him to be exiled five times by four different rulers, but his home church accepted him with open arms each time he returned. His most important works include *The Three Orations Against the Arians, On the Incarnation,* and *The Life of Antony,* which promoted monasticism for future generations.
Selections are found on January 25; February 3; March 9, 21, 28; April 1; May 10; June 16; August 7, 17, 29; October 17; November 21, 25; December 14, 20.

Augustine (354–430). Augustine is considered by many to be the most important church father, and is likely the most widely known due to his *Confessions*, a personal account of his conversion to Christianity. He was born in North Africa to a pagan father and a Christian mother. As a young adult, he was a follower of Greek pagan teachings. But he was moved by sermons of Ambrose, and he was later prompted by a voice to read Romans 13:13–14, which brought him to a saving faith. Augustine then adopted a very simple lifestyle, selling all his possessions and devoting his gifts to Jesus. He was appointed presbyter to the church in Hippo in 391 and made bishop four years later. Augustine became the spiritual leader of the Western church and his teachings can be found in his numerous treatises, sermons, and *The City of God*, written in response to the sack of Rome in 410.

Selections are found on January 7, 17, 27; February 5, 9, 14, 20; March 6, 10, 15, 22; April 2, 20, 25, 30; May 2, 6, 9, 25, 29; June 1, 6, 20, 25, 27; July 7, 10, 18, 21, 25; August 2, 5, 22; September 11, 14, 18, 20, 22; October 4, 23, 26; November 2, 16, 18, 23; December 1, 5, 13, 16, 28.

Basil (c. 330–379). Born into the family that included Gregory of Nyssa, Basil received an excellent rhetorical education and later became a powerful influence on the church in Caesarea in Cappadocia. At school, he became good friends with Gregory Nazianzen and later taught rhetoric in Athens. Influenced by his sister Macrina, he became a monk and started a monastery at his family residence. Later in life Basil became a presbyter and finally the bishop in the church of Caesarea. Despite the persecution of Emperor Valens, he remained steadfastly loyal to his Lord. His greatest works include the *Hexaemeron*, a series of lectures on the beginning chapters of Genesis, and a treatise entitled *On the Holy Spirit*.

Selections are found on January 6; February 18, 29; March 1; April 15, 27; June 19; July 19; August 23; October 27; December 2.

Clement of Rome (30–100). A bishop of the Roman church, St. Clement wrote what is considered the oldest Christian work outside of the New Testament. In his letter to the Corinthians (c. 96), known as *1 Clement*, Clement encouraged the Christians to restore to their position elders who had been replaced by younger members of the congregation. Little is known about the details of Clement's life, although he is viewed as the successor to the apostle Peter—either immediately or after two others. The anonymous sermon known as *2 Clement* has sometimes been attributed to Clement of Rome, but scholars do not believe that he was its author, so in this book excerpts from it are labeled as "anonymous."

Selections from 1 Clement *and* 2 Clement *are found on January 18; February 7; March 7; April 3, 16; May 12, 17; June 3, 24; July 28; August 4, 16, 25; September 6; October 16; November 8, 11; December 9, 21.*

Clement of Alexandria (c. 155–c. 220). Clement was a philosopher and became a Christian through his studies. Little is known of his early life except that he traveled in Greece, Italy, and Syria in quest of learning. Seeking the best teachers in the world, he came to Alexandria where he studied under Pantaenus and received vast amounts of Scriptural knowledge. In 190, Clement succeeded Pantaenus as head of the developing school of Alexandria and taught there until 202. His writings focused on Christian morality *(The Exhortation)*, drawing pagans to the Christian faith *(The Instructor)*, and the creation of a Christian philosophy based on faith in Jesus *(Miscellanies)*.
Selections are found on January 5, 20, 26; March 18; June 29; August 28; September 3; December 31.

Commodianus (third century). Little is known about Commodianus. Scholars have placed him variously in the third and fifth centuries and in different parts of the empire. In his latin poem known as *Instructions,* he defends the Christian faith against pagan gods such as Saturn, Jupiter, and Hercules and addresses moral precepts to Christians of all stations.
A selection is found on September 19.

Constitutions of the Holy Apostles (third—fourth centuries). This eight-book compilation in Greek was made by an unknown author who drew upon earlier Syrian documents and the writings of Hippolytus of Rome (c. 170–c. 236).
A selection is found on May 20.

Cyprian (c. 200–258). Little is known about the early years of Cyprian except that he was educated for the purpose of becoming a rhetorician. After spending time with Caecilius, a presbyter in the church in Carthage, he professed faith in Jesus in 246. From there, he devoted himself to studying the Scriptures and was made bishop of Carthage two years later. During the persecution by Decius in 250–251, Cyprian hid in a place near the city and led the church from there. He later imposed strict conditions for those who had "lapsed" (denied Christ under threats of death) to reenter the church. Circumstances later moved him to greater leniency. Cyprian also played a role in a controversy over the validity of baptism by heretics with Stephen, bishop of Rome, that ended when Stephen died in 257. The next year, Cyprian was exiled and beheaded. His works are primarily concerned with the administration of the church.
Selections are found on January 21; February 1, 13, 16; March 29; April 6, 8, 28; May 13, 15, 28; June 10; July 12, 24, 27; August 8; September 4, 13, 26; October 5, 18, 29; November 3, 6, 14, 26; December 30.

Dionysius of Alexandria (200–c. 264). Dionysius may have come from a wealthy family; in any event he was clearly well educated. Eusebius says that he studied under Origen and became head of the Alexandrian catechetical school. Dionysius assumed the role of bishop of Alexandria in 246 but found his reign to be tumultuous. The persecution of Emperor Decian and a number of controversies within church walls caused him much anguish. None of his writings survive intact; however, Athanasius and Eusebius have large fragments included in their works.
Selections are found on March 4, 31; July 13; November 19.

Cyril of Jerusalem (c. 310–386). Nothing is known about the early years of Cyril. He was ordained as a presbyter at Jerusalem by 343. Around 348, Cyril was appointed bishop of Jerusalem, a position which he held despite attacks by leaders of other sects and three separate exiles. His most important contribution to Christian literature is his *Catechetical Lectures* for people desiring to join the church. His messages focused on the importance of Jesus' death and resurrection as the cornerstone of the Christian faith.
Selections are found on February 17; March 17; July 1; August 10.

Ephraim Syrus (died 373). Ephraim (also spelled "Ephrem" or "Ephraem") was born in the city of Nisibis during the reign of Constantine to Christian parents. After his city was ceded to the Persians in 363, he moved to Edessa, where he lived his remaining years as a teacher and a defender of the Christian faith. Ephraim's hymns and versified homilies (in Syriac) establish his reputation as the greatest early Christian poet. He also wrote commentaries on biblical books.
A selection is found on June 12.

Eusebius of Caesarea (c. 260–c. 340). Eusebius is commonly known as the "father of church history." Little is known of his early life, but it is assumed he was born in Syria and received an education in both secular and Christian philosophy. Eusebius later became an assistant to his teacher Pamphilus in Caesarea, admiring him so much he called himself Eusebius Pamphili. After the persecution of Diocletian in 303–313, Eusebius was elected bishop of Caesarea, which he held until 325 when his rebuke of Bishop Alexander over Arius (leader of a sect) led to his excommunication. He was restored later that year at the Council of Nicea, where he presented a creed that was accepted by the assembled bishops, but afterward he resumed his opposition to the opponents of Arianism. His writings cover various aspects of the Christian faith, the most notable being his *Church History*.
Selections are found on August 26; September 17; October 28; November 17.

Gregory I (540–604). Gregory was born into a godly family of considerable influence in Rome. After the death of his father, he proceeded to set up seven monasteries, of one of which he became abbot. Gregory wasn't allowed to stay for long; the pope called him to be one of the seven deacons of Rome and subsequently sent him to Constantinople to be a representative at the imperial court. In 590, after the death of the pope, he was called to take his place. Gregory called himself "servant of the servants of God," a title every pope has used since. His most important writings are the *Pastoral Rule,* a handbook for bishops; numerous teachings, letters, dialogues; and the *Exposition of Job.*
Selections are found on February 10; June 28; August 31; December 8.

Gregory Nazianzen (c. 330–389). Gregory grew up in a wealthy and religious Christian household. His father was bishop of Nazianzus, and his mother helped rear him in the knowledge of the Lord. Gregory studied in most of the major centers of learning in the eastern part of the empire before being baptized in 358 and undertaking to live a monastic life. His father forced him to accept ordination as a presbyter in 361, but ten years later his friend Basil's attempt to force him to accept ordination as bishop failed. He finally agreed to accept responsibility for the orthodox church in Constantinople in 379, where he served for two years before resigning under fire from various opponents. His poetry, letters, and orations establish his reputation as a writer, orator, and theologian with few peers in the early centuries of Christian history. Along with Basil of Caesarea and Gregory of Nyssa (the other two "Cappadocian fathers"), he played an important role in the shaping of orthodox Trinitarian and Christological doctrine.
Selections are found on January 16; May 11, 23; June 21; July 20, 26; September 23; October 6, 11; December 29.

Gregory of Nyssa (330–c. 395). Gregory was born in the city of Caesarea near the middle of the fourth century. He was given a comprehensive education by his brother Basil and his sister Macrina. His first profession of the Christian faith came from a vision in which the martyrs of the church appeared to him, chided him for his indifference to the faith, and beat him with rods. Gregory became a rhetorician but in 371 was forced by his brother to become bishop of Nyssa, where he remained until removed in 376. His most important contribution to the Christian faith is the twelve-book *Against Eunomius* (an Arian), in addition to his treatises on such doctrines as the Trinity, the Resurrection, and Jesus' baptism.
Selections are found on January 2; March 26; April 4, 9, 19; May 19; July 5, 29; August 13; September 15; October 1, 3, 22; December 6, 18.

Hermas (first or second century). This is the name used by the author of the *Shepherd of Hermas*, a writing used by some early Christians alongside the books of the New Testament. In modern times Hermas has been treated as one of the Apostolic Fathers. One ancient document identifies Hermas as the brother of Pius, a bishop of Rome who died around 154, but at least some portions of the *Shepherd* seem to have been written around six decades earlier. The *Shepherd* consists of five *Visions*, twelve *Mandates* or *Commandments*, and ten *Similitudes*. Its central theme is the problem of repentance.
Selections are found on January 9; March 14; April 11; May 27; December 3.

Hilary of Poitiers (c. 315–367). Hilary of Poitiers is best known for his stands against the Arian sect in his two treatises, *On the Trinity* and *On the Synods*. His early years were devoted to the study of pagan philosophy and rhetoric before he was converted to the Christian faith. Around 350, he was appointed as bishop of Poitiers despite having a wife. His six years as bishop were spent refuting the Arians and upholding the teachings of Athanasius. Under the emperor Constantius he was banished to Phrygia in Asia Minor, where he composed his treatises. Hilary returned to Poitiers and spent the rest of his life defending the Christian faith from heretical teachings.
Selections are found on January 19; June 17; July 4; August 1; October 25; November 5.

Ignatius of Antioch (died c. 120). Ignatius was bishop of Antioch. He was arrested under the emperor Trajan and sent to Rome for trial. Along the way, he wrote seven letters to various churches in which he expressed his desire to suffer martyrdom for Christ. In these letters he also argued that each congregation should have one particular leader (the bishop) in order to ensure unity in doctrine and church life. Polycarp, who collected his letters, had no firm information about what happened to him at Rome but assumed that he was in fact martyred. His letters are included in the Apostolic Fathers.
A selection is found on March 5.

Irenaeus (c. 115–c. 202). Irenaeus was born at Smyrna, in Asia Minor, where he learned Johannine theology from bishop Polycarp. He seems to have lived for a time at Rome before settling by 177 in Lyons, where he succeeded Pothinus as bishop of a Greek-speaking Christian community. His major writing, *Against Heresies*, describes and refutes the teachings of Gnostics, who claimed to have secret teachings unknown to most Christians. Irenaeus replies that the four Gospels, especially as interpreted by the bishops who succeeded the apostles in major cities such as

Rome, constitute a valid and public witness to Christ, who, as Paul taught, "sums up all things." Secret traditions and private revelations are to be rejected. His influence on later theologians has gained him recognition as the first great theologian of the postbiblical universal church.
Selections are found on February 23; May 4; June 9; August 9; September 2, 8; October 24; December 15.

Jerome (c. 345–c. 419). Jerome was born at Stridon, near the Adriatic Sea, and acquired an education in Rome due to his wealthy parents. It is believed that he became a Christian after going with a group of friends to visit the tombs of the martyrs (around 366). In 374, Jerome had a vision in which he was rebuked him for following Cicero and not Jesus. That sparked a devotion to the study of the Bible for Jerome. He later met Gregory Nazianzen and became secretary for Pope Damascus, who commissioned him to create the *Vulgate,* a new Latin translation of the Scriptures. After Damascus died he lived a monastic life at Bethlehem, devoting his energies to translating and writing biblical commentaries.
Selections are found on January 14, 30; May 16; June 15, 26; July 15; August 12, 24; September 5, 9; October 9; November 9, 29.

John Cassian (c. 360–c. 432). Little is known about John Cassian's early life. He spent a decade in a monastery in Bethlehem. Cassian and a friend wanted to learn more about the monastic life, so they went to Egypt and received expert teaching from the monks there. John Chrysostom ordained him a deacon in Constantinople, later sending him to Rome with a letter to Pope Innocent I describing the harsh persecutions occurring there. Cassian eventually settled in Marseilles, where he set up two monasteries and wrote his three most influential works: *The Institutes, The Conferences,* and *On the Incarnation against Nestorius.*
Selections are found on February 25, 27; March 20; April 13; June 8; July 9; August 19; September 27; October 31; December 26.

John Chrysostom (c. 347–407). Known as the "Golden Mouth" for the eloquence of his sermons, Chrysostom was born in Antioch and raised by his mother, who at twenty had become a widow. He became a monk and later was appointed deacon (381) and priest (386) in Antioch. His reputation as a preacher increased, and in 398, Chrysostom was appointed, against his will, to be bishop of Constantinople. His sermons led the city through many crises, but his enemies eventually convinced the emperor to exile him on three occasions, and he died in exile. Chrysostom's sermons and commentaries on the Bible have led many to consider him the second greatest church father after Augustine.

Selections are found on January 1, 8, 10, 13, 23, 29; February 15, 19, 22, 24, 28; March 12, 16, 24; April 12, 14, 26; May 14, 21, 24; June 2, 11, 14, 22, 30; July 3, 6, 31; August 20, 27; September 1, 16, 30; October 8, 12, 20; November 7, 12, 15, 27; December 22, 27.

John of Damascus (c. 675–749). John is considered one of the last great fathers of the Greek church. He was born in Damascus to a wealthy family and for a time represented Christians in the court of the caliphs. A few years later he became a monk, living in Jerusalem. John's most famous work is *The Fountain of Knowledge,* a three section treatise against the sects of the fifth and sixth centuries. His teachings and writings became the framework for the Greek Orthodox Church of today.
Selections are found on June 4; September 24; November 13.

Justin Martyr (c. 100–165). Born in Samaria, Justin Martyr studied in the schools of the philosophers, becoming a disciple of Socrates and Plato. He was impressed that Christians did not fear death, and after a conversation with an elderly Christian, he became a Christian. Justin Martyr is known as one of the first Christian apologists (defenders of the faith). His first, *Apology* was addressed to Emperor Pius and explained the falsity of common slurs on Christian morality. His *Dialogue with Trypho,* portrayed a debate between Jewish and Christian ideas. His life was cut short in 165 in Rome when Marcus Aurelius martyred him for his beliefs.
Selections are found on January 12; August 14.

Lactantius (c. 240–c. 320). Lactantius's writings have such a style and grace about them that he has been called the Christian Cicero. It is assumed he was a native of Africa, where he attained prominence as a teacher of rhetoric. Diocletian invited him to live in Nicomedia and teach, but he had such a difficult time there that he focused on composition. He became a Christian late in life and was hired by Emperor Constantine to teach his son Crispus. Lactantius's writings defend the Christian faith and refute prevailing heresies.
Selections are found on January 11; February 21, 26; March 11, 13, 23; April 24; May 30; June 13; July 17, 22; August 11; September 12, 25; October 10; November 10; December 4, 19.
There is debate as to whether Lactantius actually wrote the selection for March 23.

Leo I (died 461). Leo, known as "the Great," was elected bishop of Rome in 440. During a time when the western Roman Empire was crumbling under barbarian assaults, he managed to consolidate the power of the papacy, claiming authority as successor of Peter over churches not in Italy but throughout the west. As a theologian, he was not an original thinker, but his *Tome,* a position paper that he sent to the Council of Chalcedon in 451, summed up church doctrine about Christ in a way that effectively ended debate on that topic in the west. Many of his letters and sermons are extant.

Selections are found on April 29; May 3, 22; August 3; September 10; October 19; December 25.

Melito (second century). Melito was bishop of Sardis in the last third of the second century. His homily *On the Pascha* (i.e., on Easter), discovered and published in 1940, shows that he used a flowery rhetorical style. He is the first writer we know of to refer to the Hebrew Bible as the Old Testament; his theology features Christ as the fulfillment of Old Testament precursors. The Syriac fragments given under Melito's name in the *Ante-Nicene Fathers,* including the *Discourse in the Presence of Antoninus Caesar,* are probably spurious.

A selection is found on March 19.

Minucius Felix (third century?). The writings of Jerome suggest that Minucius Felix was an advocate in Rome before he was converted to the Christian faith. Nothing else is known with certainty about him. His only surviving work is the *Octavius,* an argument between a Christian and a pagan which Minucius Felix mediated.

A selection is found on May 7.

Origen (c. 185–c. 251). Origen was one of the most scholarly and prolific writers of the early church. He was born to Christian parents in Alexandria, a major center of learning. His father was martyred in 201. While still in his twenties he instructed new converts to Christianity while pursuing his studies in philosophy. Disagreements with the bishop of Alexandria eventually forced him to relocate to Caesarea; the bishops of Caesarea and Jerusalem were more appreciative of his contributions. He died as a martyr for the faith but has remained controversial throughout church history, largely because of the way in which fifth-century heretics developed certain ideas which he had set forth in a cautious and tentative way before the development of church doctrine ruled them out. No other Christian before the modern era matched his abilities in linguistic and textual scholarship, which bore fruit in approximately two thousand written works, including many sermons and commentaries on biblical books, in which he derives a spiritual meaning hidden within the literal text of Scripture. He also produced a massive edition of the Old Testament called the *Hexapla* (now extant only in fragments) that compared various Greek translations with the Hebrew text. His other writings include an apology *Against Celsus,* which refutes pagan attacks on Christianity, and *On First*

Principles, a systematic exposition of his own theological views.
Selections are found on January 3, 24, 28; February 4, 8; March 2, 30; April 7, 10; June 7, 18, 23; July 2, 30; August 6; September 29; October 2, 15, 21; November 22; December 12, 24.

Rufinus (c. 345–410). Rufinus was born at Concordia (in Italy) and studied at Rome, where he met Jerome. He subsequently lived for a time in an ascetic community in Italy before moving to Egypt and later to a monastery near Jerusalem. His major literary work was the translation of Greek writings, especially those of Origen, into Latin in a period when the knowledge of the Greek language was declining in the west. His former friend Jerome harshly attacked the quality of his translations, but modern scholars believe that they are essentially reliable. Among his original works, his *Commentary on the Apostles' Creed* is somewhat dependent on the writings of Cyril of Jerusalem.
Selections are found on February 6; December 11.

Sulpitius Severus (c. 363–c. 420). Sulpitius (or Sulpicius) Severus was born in Aquitania to a distinguished family and began the career of a lawyer. After the sudden death of his wife, however, he became an ascetic. His hero, the former soldier turned miracle-working monk and bishop, Martin of Tours, is the subject of his *Life of St. Martin*, a literary masterpiece that became a model for many medieval lives of saints.
Selections are found on March 8; July 16; October 7.

Tertullian (late second–early third century). Tertullian was a native of Carthage in North Africa. His writings imply that he was raised as a pagan and subsequently converted to Christianity and became a presbyter. He was evidently married, since treatises *To His Wife* are included among his writings. He appears to have embraced Montanism (a charismatic and morally rigorous sect of Christianity) by around 205, but it is not known whether he definitively separated from the catholic church at Carthage. His numerous writings constitute the first major body of Christian literature in Latin. In them he defends Christianity against paganism, expounds Christian doctrine over against Gnosticism and other heresies, especially Marcionism, and discuss issues in Christian ethics.
Selections are found on February 12; March 3, 25; April 5, 17, 21; May 8, 21; July 8; August 18; September 7; October 14, 30; November 4, 20, 24, 30; December 23.

Testaments of the Twelve Patriarchs (late second century?). This work claims to present the last words of each of the twelve sons of Jacob. Each son gives moral exhortation based on passages in Genesis or on later Jewish tradition about the patriarchs. These exhortations were obviously not composed by the patriarchs themselves. They may have been composed by a Christian writer sometime around 200, since they contain a number of obviously Christian passages, but many scholars believe that they were written by a Jew in the Maccabean period and later adapted by a Christian editor.

Selections are found on April 18; December 10.

Theodoret (c. 393–c. 460). Theodoret was born in Antioch to a wealthy family and educated by monks. After the death of his parents, he sold all his possessions and entered a monastery. In 423 he was elected bishop of the nearby town of Cyrus. As a theologian, he is notable primarily for his advocacy of a two-natures Christology. His opposition to the powerful bishop Cyril of Alexandria, whose theology Theodoret regarded as implicitly monophysite, led to his exile. He was restored by the Council of Chalcedon in 451, but a century later his writings against Cyril were condemned by another council. His surviving writings include biblical commentaries, *A History of the Monks of Syria* and a church history covering the period from 323 to 428, and around 200 letters.

Selections are found on January 4, 15; April 22; May 5; July 11.

Theonas (late third century). Little is known about Theonas except that he was bishop of Alexandria from 281/2 to around 300. Scholars consider the *Epistle to Lucianus* to be spurious.

A selection is found on August 15.

Theophilus (second century). Theophilus was born near the Tigris and Euphrates Rivers and converted to Christianity as an adult. He became bishop of Antioch late in the second century and completed his only surviving work, the three books *To Autolycus,* sometime after 180. These books defend belief in God as creator and in the resurrection, attack pagan religion, comment on the creation account in Genesis, and present a chronology of the world that is meant to demonstrate the priority of Moses to Homer and the other Greek writers.

A selection is found on May 26.

Vincent of Lérins (died c. 450). Vincent was a monk at Lérins, France during the fifth century. He may have been a soldier before abandoning the secular life. In his work, the *Commonitory,* Vincent seeks to provide ways to distinguish the Christian faith from sects and heresies.

A selection is found on August 30.

Sources

The Early Church Fathers (38-volume set). Hendrickson: Peabody MA, 1994.

Di Berardino, Angelo, ed. *Encyclopedia of the Early Church.* Translated by Adrian Walford. New York: Oxford University Press, 1992.

Douglas, J.D. *Who's Who in Christian History.* Tyndale: Wheaton IL, 1992.

Dowley, Tim. *The History of Christianity.* Lion: Oxford, 1990.

Ferguson, Everett, ed. *Encyclopedia of Early Christianity.* 2d edition. New York: Garland, 1997.

Freedman, David Noel, ed. *Anchor Bible Dictionary.* New York: Doubleday, 1992.

Lane, Tony. *Concise Book of Christian Faith.* Harper and Row: San Francisco CA, 1984.

Sources of the Readings

Readers who wish to explore further the writings paraphrased in this collection will find older, but generally quite reliable, English versions of all of them in the thirty-eight volume set of *The Early Christian Fathers* (repr. Peabody, Mass.: Hendrickson, 1994). The first eleven volumes, titled *The Ante-Nicene Fathers*, contain writings from the period before the Council of Nicea in a.d. 325. *The Nicene and Post-Nicene Fathers, Series One*, devotes eight of its fourteen volumes to selected works of Augustine and six to works of John Chrysostom. The writings of other post-Nicene figures are in the fourteen volumes of *The Nicene and Post-Nicene Fathers, Series Two*. The annotated index prepared for the Hendrickson edition of these works by William DiPuccio and printed as pages 267–375 of *The Ante-Nicene Fathers, vol. 10*, provides the easiest way to locate specific works within these volumes. More recent English versions of many of these works have been published individually and in series such as *The Classics of Western Spirituality* and *Ancient Christian Writers* (both published by Paulist Press) and *The Fathers of the Church* (Catholic University of America Press).

March 3	Tertullian, *On the Flesh of Christ* 5
March 4	Dionysius of Alexandria, *On the Reception of the Lapsed to Repentance* (Exegetical Fragments 7)
March 5	Ignatius, *Epistle to the Ephesians* 14–15
March 6	Augustine, *City of God* 14.13
March 7	Clement of Alexandria, *Instructor* 1.9
March 8	Sulpitius Severus, *Life of St. Martin* 3
March 9	Athanasius, Festal *Letter* 19, §7
March 10	Augustine, *Confessions* 10.8
March 11	Lactantius, *Divine Institutes* 6.12
March 12	John Chrysostom, *Exhortation to Theodore after His Fall* 6
March 13	Lactantius, *Divine Institutes* 6.24
March 14	Shepherd of Hermas, *Commandments* 5.2
March 15	Augustine, *On Grace and Free Will* 33
March 16	John Chrysostom, *Homily 24 on Ephesians*
March 17	Cyril of Jerusalem, *Protocatechesis* 11
March 18	Clement of Alexandria, *Exhortation to the Heathen* 9
March 19	Pseudo-Melito, *Discourse in the Presence of Antoninus Caesar*
March 20	John Cassian, *Institutes* 12.32
March 21	Athanasius, *Festal Letter* 1
March 22	Augustine, *On Christian Doctrine* 1.29
March 23	Lactantius, *Poem on the Passion of the Lord*
March 24	John Chrysostom, *Homily 4 Concerning the Statues*, §§11–12
March 25	Tertullian, *Prescription against Heretics* 9
March 26	Gregory of Nyssa, *On Virginity* 18
March 27	Ambrose, *Of the Holy Spirit* 1.9
March 28	Athanasius, *Life of Antony* 42
March 29	Cyprian, *Epistle* 55, §8
March 30	Origen, *Against Celsus, Preface*
March 31	Eusebius, *Oration of Constantine* 23
April 1	Athanasius, *Life of Antony* 20
April 2	Augustine, *Letter* 130, §18
April 3	1 Clement 49–50
April 4	Gregory of Nyssa, *Against Eunomius* 11.2
April 5	Tertullian, *Chaplet* 14
April 6	Cyprian, *Treatise* 4, §§14–15
April 7	Origen, *First Principles* 3.1.15
April 8	Cyprian, *Treatise* 7, §2
April 9	Gregory of Nyssa, *On Virginity* 9
April 10	Origen, *Commentary on Matthew* 12.27
April 11	Shepherd of Hermas, *Commandments* 9.1
April 12	John Chrysostom, *Homily 30 on Acts*
April 13	John Cassian, *Institutes* 4.35
April 14	John Chrysostom, *Homily 28 on Matthew*, §1

April 15	Basil the Great, *Letter* 233
April 16	2 Clement 8
April 17	Tertullian, *On Patience* 8
April 18	*Testaments of the Twelve Patriarchs,* Benjamin 6
April 19	Gregory of Nyssa, *Against Eunomius* 10.1
April 20	Augustine, *On Forgiveness of Sins and Baptism* 2.6
April 21	Tertullian, *Prescription against Heretics* 11
April 22	Theodoret, *Letter* 14
April 23	Ambrose, *Exposition of the Christian Faith* 5.2
April 24	Lactantius, *Divine Institutes* 6.12
April 25	Augustine, *Homily 1 on 1 John*
April 26	John Chrysostom, *Homily 45 on Acts*
April 27	Basil the Great, *Homily 7 on the Hexaemeron,* §5
April 28	Cyprian, *Epistle* 7, §7
April 29	Leo the Great, *Sermon* 42
April 30	Augustine, *Enchiridion* 81
May 1	Ambrose, *Exposition of the Christian Faith* 2.5.14
May 2	Augustine, *Sermon* 32, §4
May 3	Leo the Great, *Sermon* 88
May 4	Irenaeus, *Against Heresies* 2.28
May 5	Theodoret, *Letter* 134
May 6	Augustine, *Letter* 93, §4
May 7	Minucius Felix, *Octavius* 36
May 8	Tertullian, *On Flight in Persecution*
May 9	Augustine, *Sermon on the Mount* 1.7
May 10	Athanasius, *Festal Letter* 3
May 11	Gregory Nazianzen, *Orations* 40.16
May 12	Clement of Alexandria, *Instructor* 1.8
May 13	Cyprian, *Epistle* 6, §3
May 14	John Chrysostom, *Homily 10 on 1 Timothy*
May 15	Cyprian, *Epistle* 1, §14
May 16	Jerome, *Letter* 52
May 17	2 Clement 15–16
May 18	Ambrose, *Epistle* 63
May 19	Gregory of Nyssa, *Answer to Eunomius' Second Book* (p. 282)
May 20	*Apostolic Constitutions* 2.13
May 21	John Chrysostom, *Homily 45 on Matthew,* §3
May 22	Leo the Great, *Sermon* 12
May 23	Gregory Nazianzen, *Orations* 40.25
May 24	John Chrysostom, *Homily 20 on Romans*
May 25	Augustine, *Homily 7 on 1 John,* §10
May 26	Theophilus, *To Autolycus* 1.5
May 27	Shepherd of Hermas, *Commandments* 7
May 28	Cyprian, *Epistle* 55, §6

May 29	Augustine, *Homily 6 on 1 John*, §3
May 30	Lactantius, *Divine Institutes* 6.21
May 31	Tertullian, *Prescription against Heretics* 4
June 1	Augustine, *City of God* 10.6
June 2	John Chrysostom, *Homily 30 on Hebrews*
June 3	1 Clement 37–38
June 4	John of Damascus, *Exact Exposition of the Orthodox Faith* 1.1
June 5	Ambrose, *Epistle* 63
June 6	Augustine, *On Forgiveness of Sins and Baptism* 2.5
June 7	Origen, *Against Celsus* 1.52
June 8	John Cassian, *Institutes* 8.13
June 9	Irenaeus, *Against Heresies* 3.26
June 10	Cyprian, *Treatise* 4, §4
June 11	John Chrysostom, *Homily 9 on Ephesians*
June 12	Ephraim Syrus, *Homily* 1, §15
June 13	Lactantius, *Divine Institutes* 5.24
June 14	John Chrysostom, *Homily 42 on Acts*
June 15	Jerome, *Letter* 12
June 16	Athanasius, *Life of Antony* 19
June 17	Hilary of Poitiers, *On the Trinity* 1.37
June 18	Origen, *Commentary on Matthew* 6
June 19	Basil the Great, *Homily 7 on the Hexaemeron*
June 20	Augustine, *Confessions* 2.15
June 21	Gregory Nazianzen, Orations 3.7
June 22	John Chrysostom, *To Those Who Had Not Attended the Assembly* 7
June 23	Origen, *First Principles* 3.1
June 24	Clement of Alexandria, *Miscellanies* 2.2
June 25	Augustine, *Enchiridion* 60
June 26	Jerome, *Against Jovinianus* 1.12
June 27	Augustine, *Sermon* 13, §2
June 28	Gregory the Great, *Epistles* 2.48
June 29	Clement of Alexandria, *Who Is the Rich Man That Shall Be Saved?* 21
June 30	John Chrysostom, *Homily 61 on Matthew*, §5
July 1	Cyril of Jerusalem, *Catechetical Lectures* 1.3
July 2	Origen, *Against Celsus* 7.60
July 3	John Chrysostom, *Homily 19 on Matthew*, §12
July 4	Hilary of Poitiers, *On the Trinity* 8.33
July 5	Gregory of Nyssa, *On Virginity* 24
July 6	John Chrysostom, *Homily 23 on John*
July 7	Augustine, *On the Trinity* 14.17
July 8	Tertullian, *Chaplet* 15
July 9	John Cassian, *Institutes* 5.12
July 10	Augustine, *On Forgiveness of Sins and Baptism* 2.27
July 11	Theodoret, *Letter* 78

August 25	Clement of Alexandria, *Miscellanies* 5.1
August 26	Eusebius, *Oration of Constantine* 26
August 27	John Chrysostom, *Homily 59 on Matthew,* §5
August 28	Clement of Alexandria, *Instructor* 1.12
August 29	Athanasius, *Festal Letter* 10, §7
August 30	Vincent of Lérins, *Commonitory* 23.55–56
August 31	Gregory the Great, *Epistles* 9.106
September 1	John Chrysostom, *Homily 60 on Matthew,* §3
September 2	Irenaeus, *Against Heresies* 2.25
September 3	Clement of Alexandria, *Miscellanies* 2.6
September 4	Cyprian, *Treatise* 4, §31
September 5	Jerome, *Against the Pelagians* 3.8
September 6	1 Clement 33
September 7	Tertullian, *On Prayer* 11
September 8	Irenaeus, *Against Heresies* 1.10
September 9	Jerome, *Dialogue against the Luciferians*
September 10	Leo the Great, *Sermon* 39
September 11	Augustine, *On Forgiveness of Sins and Baptism* 2.54
September 12	Lactantius, *Epitome of the Divine Institutes* 58
September 13	Cyprian, *Treatise* 7, §12
September 14	Augustine, *Confessions* 10.36
September 15	Gregory of Nyssa, *Answer to Eunomius' Second Book* (p. 262)
September 16	John Chrysostom, *Homily 39 on Acts*
September 17	Eusebius, *Oration of Constantine* 7–8
September 18	Augustine, *Enchiridion* 73
September 19	Commodianus, *Instructions* 24
September 20	Augustine, *Sermon* 30, §2
September 21	Ambrose, *Exposition of the Christian Faith* 4.12
September 22	Augustine, *On Baptism, Against the Donatists* 4.14
September 23	Gregory Nazianzen, *Orations* 33.14
September 24	John of Damascus, *Exact Exposition of the Orthodox Faith* 2.29
September 25	Lactantius, *Divine Institutes* 6.13
September 26	Cyprian, *Epistle* 39, §5
September 27	John Cassian, *Institutes* 5.17
September 28	Ambrose, *Epistle* 63
September 29	Origen, *Against Celsus* 3.40
September 30	John Chrysostom, *Homily 7 on Romans*
October 1	Gregory of Nyssa, *Against Eunomius* 12.1
October 2	Origen, *First Principles* 3.2
October 3	Gregory of Nyssa, *Against Eunomius* 5.5
October 4	Augustine, *City of God* 14.4
October 5	Cyprian, *Treatise* 4, §36
October 6	Gregory Nazianzen, *Orations* 16.2
October 7	Sulpitius Severus, *Letter* 1, §2

November 21	Athanasius, *Life of Antony* 17
November 22	Origen, *First Principles* 3.1
November 23	Augustine, *Tractate 41 on John*, §13
November 24	Tertullian, *A Treatise on the Soul* 11
November 25	Athanasius, *Festal Letter* 3, §5
November 26	Cyprian, *Treatise* 9, §20
November 27	John Chrysostom, *Homily Concerning Lowliness of Mind* 11
November 28	Ambrose, *Concerning Repentence* 1.13
November 29	Jerome, *Against Jovinianus* 2.3
November 30	Tertullian, *On Flight in Persecution* 1
December 1	Augustine, *On Christian Doctrine* 1.22
December 2	Basil the Great, *Letter* 240
December 3	Shepherd of Hermas, *Commandments* 5.1
December 4	Lactantius, *Divine Institutes* 5.13
December 5	Augustine, *Letter* 31, §5
December 6	Gregory of Nyssa, *On Virginity* 21
December 7	Ambrose, *Duties of the Clergy* 1.3–4
December 8	Gregory the Great, *Epistles* 11.45
December 9	Clement of Alexandria, *Instructor* 1.9
December 10	*Testaments of the Twelve Patriarchs~*, Gad 5
December 11	Rufinus, *Commentary on the Apostles' Creed* 40
December 12	Origen, *Commentary on Matthew* 12.10
December 13	Augustine, *On the Trinity*, 9.1
December 14	Athanasius, *Festal Letter* 2
December 15	Irenaeus, *Against Heresies* 2.25
December 16	Augustine, *Sermon* 30, §7
December 17	Ambrose, *Epistle* 63
December 18	Gregory of Nyssa, *On Virginity* 24
December 19	Lactantius, *Epitome of the Divine Institutes* 65
December 20	Athanasius, *On the Incarnation of the Word* 15
December 21	Pseudo-Clement, *Homily* 12, §32
December 22	John Chrysostom, *Homily 13 on Matthew*, §§5–6
December 23	Tertullian, *Of Patience* 11
December 24	Origen, *Against Celsus* 6.67
December 25	Leo the Great, *Sermon* 21
December 26	John Cassian, *Institutes* 5.19
December 27	John Chrysostom, *Commentary on Galatians* 6:14
December 28	Augustine, *Sermon* 3, §11
December 29	Gregory Nazianzen, *Orations* 40.13
December 30	Cyprian, *Epistle* 6, §2
December 31	Clement of Alexandria, *Miscellanies* 7.3